AND IN THE END

AND IN THE END
THE LAST DAYS OF THE BEATLES

Ken McNab

THOMAS DUNNE BOOKS
NEW YORK

First published in the United States by Thomas Dunne Books,
an imprint of St. Martin's Publishing Group

www.thomasdunnebooks.com

The Library of Congress Cataloging-in-Publication Data
is available upon request.

ISBN 978-1-250-75875-0 (hardcover)
ISBN 978-1-250-75876-7 (ebook)

Our books may be purchased in bulk for promotional, educational,
or business use. Please contact your local bookseller or the
Macmillan Corporate and Premium Sales Department at
1-800-221-7945, extension 5442, or by email at
MacmillanSpecialMarkets@macmillan.com.

Originally published in Great Britain by Polygon, an imprint of
Birlinn Ltd

First U.S. Edition: 2020

10 9 8 7 6 5 4 3 2 1

For the other half of the sky — in memory of
Bridget, Kieran and Brian

All four Beatles climbed the stairs to the roof of the Apple building in Savile Row for their last public performance – played in the teeth of a bitter wind – that served as the climax to Michael Lindsay-Hogg's film documentary *Let It Be.*

All the rainbow colours of the outside world seemed to have been extinguished, replaced by a grim, cheerless darkness. The only sounds came from the heavy footsteps of two men – Mal Evans, the faithful roadie, and Kevin Harrington, the faithful gofer – lugging in guitar cases, amplifiers and drums, the sound of their heels echoing in the stillness. The guitars were positioned in a circle beside three chairs. Already in place stood a Blüthner piano. The drums were then mounted on a high-riser, the black lettering with the familiar dropped 'T' a clue to their owner.

Close by, people worked stealthily, checking camera angles and light meters. Men with headphones tested their audio equipment, checking noise levels. Snaking all over the floor and around the chairs were seemingly endless lengths of cables and wires. On the morning of 2 January, the sound stage at London's Twickenham Film Studios was a hive of muffled activity. The only people missing, though soon to arrive, were the main players from Central Casting: John Lennon, Paul McCartney, George Harrison and Ringo Starr.

It was in these desolate surroundings that The Beatles hoped to get back to where they once belonged - back to the days when their music set in motion a chain reaction that altered western youth culture. A new year. A new hope. For the next couple of weeks at least, the studios would serve as their creative hub.

The premise was simple. The four most famous musicians in the world would be filmed writing and rehearsing new songs for a fly-on-the-wall TV documentary. The pay-off would be their first proper live show since 29 August 1966, at Candlestick Park in San Francisco.

The prime mover, as he had been for the last two years, was McCartney, the Beatle-cheerleader-in-chief. 'The idea was that you'd see The Beatles rehearsing, jamming, getting their act together and then finally performing somewhere in a big end-of-show concert,' he recalled. Driven by a relentless work ethic, his enthusiasm for the group remained as full-on as ever. And so, it appeared, was the love held for them by fans who had been with them every inch of the way. Through early Beatlemania. Through the druggy mystery tour of the Summer of Love. Through the reinvented rock of *The Beatles* (aka theWhite Album).

Proof of their longevity lay in the fact that, as the decade entered its final year,The Beatles still sat imperiously at the top of the album charts on both sides of the Atlantic.The White Album, a four-sided record, had, despite its difficult birth, been hailed as an amalgam of pop, rock, country and soulful blues. But six years of unparalleled and dazzling success, combined with the relentless vagaries of fame, had taken an inevitable toll on relationships within the band.

Memories of the marathon sessions for the album, which was released in November 1968, were still fresh. The price for creating the music had been frayed nerves, angry bust-ups and, in the case of Starr, a week-long walkout.

By the turn of the year, McCartney, more than any of them, worried that the band was on life support, but he was not prepared to be the one to administer the last rites. He remained in denial over the serious disconnect that now existed between each of them. The cure, he was convinced, lay in a back-to-basics approach, the four of them creating great music in the studio and then going back on the road. Or at least playing a one-off gig to prove they could still cut it as a live band. He was even considering a surprise rock'n'roll-style drop-in, drop-out tour of northern dance halls. That was the fantasy he sold, and it was persuasive enough for them all to hook up at Twickenham on the second day of the year to begin sessions for a project tentatively and wistfully dubbed 'Get Back'.

They were, of course, no longer the four callow kids who first stepped onto the world's stage in 1963. Lennon had found Yoko Ono, the Japanese avant-garde artist seven years his senior for whom he broke up his marriage and with whom he dabbled in heroin. Harrison, having discovered a new inner confidence through Indian mysticism, was on a quest for Krishna consciousness. McCartney was enjoying the fame and acclaim that was his heart's desire. And

Starr, whose childhood had been wrecked by illness, simply couldn't believe his luck at such a reversal of fortune.

But the symbiosis that once touched on telepathy had been replaced by lethargy. And now here they were, two days in to a new year, in a freezing studio they didn't know, hemmed in and tapped out and working once again under an autocratic conductor: McCartney.

As she had been during the White Album sessions, Yoko remained umbilically attached to Lennon, an awkward situation which acted like dry tinder. Harrison simply wanted to be somewhere – anywhere – else; Starr had a ringside seat at the long goodbye. It was far too soon after the fractious atmosphere of the White Album to get back to the future, but no one had the courage to say out loud what needed to be said.

Lennon recalled: 'Paul had this idea that we were going to rehearse or . . . see, it all was more like Simon and Garfunkel, like looking for perfection all the time. And so he has these ideas that we'll rehearse and then make the album. And of course we're lazy fuckers and we've been playing for twenty years, for fuck's sake, we're grown men, we're not going to sit around rehearsing. I'm not, anyway. And we couldn't get into it. And we put down a few tracks and nobody was in to it at all.

'It was a dreadful, dreadful feeling in Twickenham Studio, and being filmed all the time. I just wanted them to go away, and we'd be there, eight in the morning. You couldn't make music at eight in the morning or ten or whatever it was, in a strange place with people filming you and coloured lights.'

Lennon's heart may not have been in it right from the start but he, like all of them, had initially appeared to buy in to the 'Get Back' project, the seed for which had been planted after their first appearance before a live audience for two years. That had been at Twickenham, too: they had showcased 'Hey Jude' and Lennon's 'Revolution' before the cameras for *Frost on Sunday*. The clips, broadcast on British TV on 8 September, were directed by Michael Lindsay-Hogg, a talented American filmmaker, whose entry into the band's orbit had come in 1966 when he oversaw the groundbreaking videos for 'Paperback Writer' and 'Rain'.

The 'Hey Jude' video captures McCartney smiling angelically while seated at an upright piano with the band surrounded by roughly a hundred extras who were providing the 'audience'. Looking back at the footage after fifty years, it's hard to disagree with Lennon's post-break-up assessment that he, Harrison and Starr had become McCartney's sidemen.

But at the time all four were surprisingly pleased with the result. Denis O'Dell, head of Apple Films, said: 'The "Hey Jude" promo is possibly more important than most fans realise. The Beatles' unexpected enjoyment at performing for the clip was to be a key factor in the new direction that they were about to take. After shooting, we ran the final edit of the tapes in the recording truck. They were absolutely delighted. Drinking a whisky and Coke with them at four in the morning, we agreed a good night had been had by all. In fact, they had enjoyed it so much they suggested, there and then, that we should make another film. I was elated. That was the start of "Get Back"/*Let It Be*.'

But that was then – and this was now. And Lennon, always the prime mover in The Beatles' power network, had almost no interest in going over old musical ground, with McCartney especially. The creative spark that once bound them was largely gone. He was bored with The Beatles and bored with his musical partner, who no longer stimulated him intellectually the way Yoko now did. They were different people, always had been. But they had always recognised in each other a friendly rivalry that drove the music. Now, though, they were rarely singing from the same song sheet.

Lennon's dread was fuelled by more than just scorn over the music. Apple Corps, the company they had set up in 1967 as a multi-faceted Beatle business, was now haemorrhaging thousands of pounds a week due to a culture of spend, spend, spend that outweighed the money coming in. By the start of 1969, the company's bean counters were warning that they faced bankruptcy unless serious steps were taken to address the losses. It was the ultimate corporate contradiction. The White Album had sold millions of copies while the success of 'Hey Jude' in singles charts across the world had also generated much income. The *Yellow Submarine* album, an ad hoc collection of oldies, new songs and instrumentals was released on 17 January to accompany the release of the film of the same name. Apple Records also included the likes of Mary Hopkin, whose debut single, 'Those Were The Days', had overtaken 'Hey Jude' at the top of the UK lists in late September 1968. But the accountants' inescapable conclusion was that Apple was fast running out of cash.

Even before a note could be sung at Twickenham, there would have to be preconditions. None of the four wanted to repeat the formula of the White Album. Musically, The Beatles had always been about breaking boundaries, but they had been ceding ground to a new wave of groups, such as Led Zeppelin, Fleetwood Mac and the Paul Butterfield Blues Band, while contemporaries such as the Rolling Stones and The Who were widening their artistic boundaries; the Stones had just released *Beggars Banquet*, an acclaimed return to their R&B roots, while The Who had started recording *Tommy*, the first rock opera, in September 1968 (the landmark double album was released in May 1969).

Lennon's solution was to ditch the high-end production values that had been the hallmark of their long-time producer, George Martin. The music would be stripped down, recorded warts-and-all. Martin was relegated to an ad hoc role: Glyn Johns, who had worked with the Stones and Zeppelin on their groundbreaking debut album, jumped at the chance to man the desk.

'It was funny actually,' recalled Johns. 'I got a phone call from someone with a Liverpudlian voice and I thought it was Mick Jagger taking the piss. Anyway, it was Paul McCartney. And you don't turn down Paul McCartney. The idea was something like [Bob Dylan and The Band's] *The Basement Tapes*, to show what they were really like. I'd worked with everyone and their mother by then, so I was quite used to being around people who were famous. But when I got the call, to walk in and be privy to those guys sitting around, doing what they did, and to be invited in, was pretty astonishing. I didn't know them. I was the same as every other punter on the planet, who saw them as these extraordinary icons of marvellousness.

'And although they could hardly be normal people, because of what their success had done to them,' Johns added, 'I was witnessing them being normal to each other. Which no one else had got to see, and which nobody really had a clue about. And so my concept of the record was: how fantastic to have a record of them playing live, sitting around mocking each other, just having a laugh. It was very weird. But George Martin, being the gentleman that he is, he realised that I had been compromised in a way, and he saw fit to put me at ease about the situation. He took me to lunch, and he said, "You're not to worry about a thing." I was feeling really awkward about the whole thing, and he was completely at ease about the situation.'

Johns was unaware that he had just signed a Faustian deal that would haunt him for at least the next twelve months. For the moment, however, his job was to coax the world's greatest band back from the brink. But they were up already against the clock.

Starr had agreed to take a substantial role in a Peter Sellers film, *The Magic Christian*, Terry Southern's anarchic comedy satirising America's obsession with money, TV, guns and sex. Starr was due on set – at, coincidentally, Twickenham – in the first week of February, a timescale that instantly posed a creative challenge for The Beatles. And therein lay the crux of the problem: the Lennon and McCartney songbook currently contained only a couple of jewels and several unpolished stones.

In those first days of January, Lennon unveiled 'Don't Let Me Down', 'Child Of Nature' (exhumed from the initial White Album sessions and later retooled as 'Jealous Guy', a stand-out track on *Imagine*), and 'Sun King'. McCartney, on the other hand, arrived with several promising works in progress that would be given the full band treatment over the next week. These included 'Golden Slumbers/Carry That Weight', 'Oh! Darling', 'Two Of Us', 'Teddy Boy', 'Junk' and 'Let It Be' (a song that Lennon had little affection for) and 'Maxwell's Silver Hammer' (which Lennon simply loathed.)

In the early days, when they worked together, fine-tuning and editing each other's material was never a problem for Lennon and McCartney. Now, though, they rarely wrote together. Which meant the naturally lazy Lennon was constantly trying to play catch-up to McCartney's habitually prodigious output. Now expensively divorced from Cynthia, his obsession with Yoko continued to drive a wedge between him and the others.

He was also in thrall to heroin, a fixation that further alienated him from McCartney, who tended to stick to pot. Indeed, that month, during an interview for Canadian television, Lennon pulled a 'whitey' – junkie jargon for throwing up as he craved his next fix. His lack of new material betrayed the effect that heroin was having on his creativity, notably his lyrics, which had once been his strongest suit.

The fact was that, at the outset of filming for 'Get Back', Lennon and McCartney were ferreting around in their bottom drawers for decent material. That left them having to present snatches of half-finished tunes and half-baked ideas to their colleagues. Ironically, Harrison was armed with some of the best songs he had ever written. Encouraged by the material he delivered for the White Album – 'While My Guitar Gently Weeps' had been hailed as an instant classic – he had found his voice and was already channelling his assertive future self with songs such as 'Something', 'All Things Must Pass', 'Hear Me Lord', 'Let It Down' and 'Isn't It A Pity'. He had also co-written 'Badge' with Eric Clapton for Cream's farewell album and was enjoying a new-found freedom playing with other musicians.

His self-confidence had been boosted by the kind of celebrity endorsement available to only a few. At that time, only Bob Dylan existed on a higher plane of credibility than The Beatles. In November 1968 Harrison had been invited to stay with Dylan and his family in Bearsville, near Woodstock, while Bob worked with The Band, the rootsy Canadian-American group that had garnered worldwide acclaim for the sheer diversity of their musical prowess.

Harrison marvelled at Dylan and The Band's egalitarianism. It was the complete antithesis of his own situation.

Occasionally, during those dark January days at Twickenham, Harrison tried to tempt his bandmates into trying one of his songs. But they rarely took up the offer. 'All Things Must Pass' was given only rudimentary run-throughs and can be heard on bootleg tapes more as ghostly background noise to forced banter. Others, such as 'Something', would be given similarly brusque dismissals before the month was out. It wasn't difficult to see the lyrics to 'All Things Must Pass' as an astute commentary on the band's moribund state.

Over the next few days, Harrison would also roll out 'I Me Mine', the title of which also laid bare his antipathy. 'It was like being back in the winter of discontent . . . straight away it was back to the old routine,' he would later recall. 'We had been together so long that we just pigeon-holed each other.' Something had to give, and it did. On 6 January, four days after the sessions began, Harrison and McCartney squabbled over how to play a guitar part on 'Two Of Us'. Their exchanges were caught on camera. McCartney tried to persuade Harrison – the Beatle he had known the longest – that his own feel for the song was the one that should hold sway. Harrison was tactful: 'I'll play what you want me to play. Or I won't play at all if you don't want me to. Whatever it is that'll please you, I'll do it.'

As he later told *Rolling Stone*: 'My problem was that it would always be very difficult to get in on the act, because Paul was very pushy in that respect. When he succumbed to playing on one of your tunes, he'd always do good. But you'd have to do fifty-nine of Paul's songs before he'd even listen to one of yours.'

The exchange has gone down in Beatles folklore as pointing to Harrison's eventual make-or-break decision on his future with the band, but it would be another three days before matters really came to a head.

Chaotic as the sessions were musically, the most discordant note surrounded McCartney's obsession with either a full-blown tour or a one-off show. McCartney, backed by Lindsay-Hogg, was keen to push the envelope. Discussions included talk of an amphitheatre in North Tunisia with thousands of fans holding torches and making their way to the venue across miles of sand dunes. An alternative was to hold it on board an ocean liner. Apathy, though, stonewalled every suggestion until, one day, McCartney's patience snapped: 'I don't see why any of you, if you're not interested, got yourselves into this,' he told them. 'What's it for? It can't be for the money. Why are you here? I'm here because I want to do a show, but I don't see an awful lot of support. There are only two choices. We're going to do it or we're not going to do it. And I want a decision because I'm not interested in spending my days farting around here while everyone makes up their mind whether they want to do it or not. If everyone wants to do it, great. But I don't have to be here.'

Harrison remained opposed to any live show, particularly one that he viewed as 'expensive and insane'. Starr was adamant that he was not going abroad. Lennon vacillated between being up for anything and opposing everything. 'I'm warming to the idea of an asylum,' he remarked.

Harrison was vexed by yet another issue. As she had been during the White Album sessions, Yoko was impervious to all hints that her presence was unwanted, while Lennon revelled in the discomfiture of his friends. She often distracted him by kissing him or whispering in his ear during a take, causing him to miss a note or forget a lyric. It was virtually impossible for the cameras to get a shot of the four Beatles without Yoko being in the frame. It was obvious to everyone that Lennon, like Harrison, wanted to be anywhere but there.

At other times, Yoko would be Lennon's voice in group discussions about how best to break the impasse, but the others knew better than to take him on. McCartney reflected: 'He would have used that as an excuse to leave the band.' Harrison preferred straight-talking, having, months earlier, told Yoko that she gave off 'bad vibes'. Lennon struggled to control his temper then, but now, little more than a week into the project, the gloves were off.

On 10 January, Harrison's tolerance snapped. Lennon was sabotaging the sessions, putting his own self-interest before that of the band, was continuing to patronise him personally and was treating them all with contempt. He railed bitterly at Lennon for his put-downs of George's new songs, and brusquely added that he was leaving the band.

'When?' asked a startled Lennon.

'Now,' snapped Harrison. 'See you round the clubs. Put an ad in the *NME*.'

Reflecting on the incident later for the *Beatles Anthology* project, Harrison attributed his departure to a number of factors, among them the presence of film cameras, which he found particularly annoying when The Beatles weren't getting along. 'They were filming Paul and I having a row. It never came to blows, but I thought, "What's the point of this? I'm quite capable of being relatively happy on my own and if I'm not able to be happy in this situation, I'm getting out." It was a very, very difficult, stressful time, and being filmed having a row as well was terrible. I got up and I thought, "I'm not doing this any more. I'm out of here."'

Cameraman Les Parrott was part of the team assembled by Lindsay-Hogg and up-and-coming film-maker Tony Richmond. Though he didn't witness this particular bust-up Parrott was sussed enough to know something was amiss when Lennon, McCartney and Starr returned to their instruments. 'Well, George was missing for a start,' he told me. 'There was no reason for any of the crew to be told he had walked out or anything. But it was pretty awkward. We all knew something had happened and it was pretty serious.'

As for Yoko: 'She was a blob in black,' Parrott added. 'Always there. You could tell the others resented it. Especially George. You had the feeling he wanted to say something. He used to just glower at Yoko.'

Lennon and McCartney's immediate response to Harrison's departure was to launch into an ear-splitting jam. Yoko eased herself into Harrison's chair to lend her own inimitable vocals. It was the only time the cameras caught her smiling. Lennon betrayed the depth of his feelings towards Harrison by casually suggesting they had a ready-made replacement in Eric Clapton, Harrison's closest friend. 'If he's not back by Monday, we'll get Eric in,' he declared. 'He's just as good and not such a headache.'

As it turned out, they wouldn't have to approach Clapton, who would most certainly have refused to fill the gap left by his closest friend. But at that precise moment, The Beatles were victims of their own indifference and as close to breaking up as they had ever been. The candle that once shone so bright was nearly out.

*

Incorporated in May 1967, Apple Corps, its Granny Smith logo inspired by a Magritte painting, was Paul McCartney's vision for the world's first multi-media company. The band envisaged, in the parlance of the day, a happening – 'Western communism', they called it, a way of amassing cash and using it to become patrons of the alternative arts. They imagined Apple as a support network that would link artist to audience under various guises.

First came the Apple Boutique, peddling the regulation '60s Hobbit-styled satin and velvet clothes, overseen by a team of Dutch designers called The Fool. Beatle wives dutifully modelled the stock for *Rolling Stone*. Lennon and McCartney even flew to New York for a media blitz to launch the venture. Impulsively, McCartney declared: 'We're in the happy position of not really needing any more money. So for the first time, the bosses aren't in it for profit. If you come and see me and say "I've had such and such a dream," I'll say "Here's so much money. Go away and do it." We've already bought all our dreams. So now we want to share that possibility with others.'

Derek Taylor, the group's urbane press officer, recalled: 'They said they had set up this company and that anyone who had a dream could come and see them in London and they would make it come true.' Taking them at their word, London Airport immigration was crammed with Americans identifying The Beatles as sponsors.

Apple's philanthropic side was mainly McCartney's baby, but Lennon was, initially at least, willing to lend a hand. He bristled

at criticism in left-wing magazine *Black Dwarf* that Apple was a
sell-out and that they only *sang* about revolution. He replied: 'We
set up Apple with money we as workers earned, so that we could
control what we did.' Except that The Beatles, in terms of managing
a business, couldn't control anything. Their manager, Brian Epstein,
had supervised everything for them, insulating them from everyday
reality.

Three months after Apple was formed, Epstein was dead from
a drug overdose. Chaos quickly usurped order. By January 1969,
upwards of £20,000 a week was leaving the company, and no one
could account for where it went. 'Apple,' said Lennon, 'was like
playing Monopoly with real money.' The Beatles accused everyone
of ripping them off, while giving carte blanche to every opportunist
to do just that. Such as Magic Alex Mardas, a young Greek
entrepreneur who had assiduously courted Lennon and was the
money-eating inventor of an electronic pulsing apple and the aptly
named 'Nothing Box'.

Or Stocky, the Massachusetts artist who sat on a filing cabinet
and drew pen-and-ink drawings of genitals. Some California
hippies even set up a commune in an empty office. 'Apple,' said
Taylor, 'had an aim, but it didn't have enough order or structure.
There were lots of vague phrases like "get it together" and "be there
and just see what happens".'

Harrison was working with Ravi Shankar, the Indian sitar
maestro who was also his mentor in most other things. McCartney,
more mainstream, was recording not just Mary Hopkin but also
James Taylor, a young, honey-toned American singer-songwriter;
Lennon was well down the road of indulging Yoko's avant-garde
whims. By January, The Beatles were attempting to fight on too
many fronts as well as fighting among themselves.

The first casualty was the boutique. The Beatles announced
they would give the clothes away. When they threw the doors
open everything disappeared, carpets included. 'All our buddies
that worked with us for years were living, drinking and eating like
fucking Rome. It was just hell, and it had to stop,' raged Lennon.

Apple had by now become, in the words of Epstein's de facto replacement Peter Brown, 'a mausoleum waiting for a death'.

Faced with the realisation that Apple was decaying from the inside out, drastic action was called for. When the evidence was presented in the bluntest of terms by a young accountant named Stephen Maltz, it was the wake-up call The Beatles never dreamt they would hear.

McCartney now had cause to regret his New York declaration. 'I wanted Apple to run,' he said. 'I didn't want to run Apple.' Maltz's warning was also his kiss-off to The Beatles, with whom he had worked throughout the Beatlemania years. He knew it was akin to a resignation note when he told them: 'After six years' work, for the most part of which you have been at the very top of the music world, in which you have given pleasure to countless millions throughout every country where records are played, what have you got to show for it? Your personal finances are a mess. Apple is a mess.'

The company may have largely been McCartney's brainchild, but they were all accountable to the bottom line. In Maltz's calculations, they had only earned 'a pitiful' £78,000 in 1968 and Apple's spending was out of control. In the eighteen months up to January 1969, it had blown £1.5m – the staggering equivalent of £30m today. The Beatles had already spent £400,000 earmarked for investments by the accountants mostly on undeserving or far-fetched schemes. Apple even owned an upmarket London townhouse that no one could remember buying. Individually, they had hugely overdrawn their personal company accounts – Lennon by £64,000, McCartney by £60,000, and the other two each owed around £35,000.

Bill Oakes, Brown's personal assistant, reckoned trying to control the company's spending was like riding the back of a tiger. 'John was always the most profligate spender. George was perhaps the most thrifty, but it is still ranging between £2,000 and £10,000 every week,' he said. 'Some [of the accountants] questioned why Mr Lennon was spending so much money on "sweets". I had to point out they weren't really "sweets".'

Lennon was the first to feel the effects of the oncoming storm. He had always been consumed by an inner dread of ending up penniless 'like Mickey Rooney', forced to eke out a pittance on the cabaret circuit, singing songs like 'She Loves You' well into his middle age. The prospect now seemed perilously close. His divorce settlement with Cynthia had allegedly cost him £100,000. He had hired expensive lawyers to help extricate Yoko from her second marriage to American film-maker Tony Cox.

To complicate matters further, in January, Pete Best, the drummer they had fired while on the cusp of fame, brought a multi-million-pound defamation case against his former friends over a 1965 article, which suggested he had been axed due to a 'pill-popping' habit developed during their musical apprenticeship in Hamburg. The matter was quietly settled out of court later in the month.

It was obvious that The Beatles desperately needed a company doctor. To that end, Lennon set up a meeting, at McCartney's suggestion, with Baron Beeching. Dr Richard Beeching was notorious in Sixties Britain as the man who had taken a cost-cutting scythe to the country's nationalised rail network.

The meeting was short and far from sweet. Beeching cast a perfunctory glance at the Apple books Lennon had brought with him and curtly told him that he should 'stick to making records'.

Other potential saviours such as Lord Arnold Goodman, an advisor to Harold Wilson's Labour government, and media magnate Cecil King were discussed and discarded.

For McCartney especially, this was a fraught period. Not only did he have the Apple crisis to deal with, but in the studio he was the one bringing in the more fully formed songs. Fate, however, had offered up a potential solution. Linda Eastman, his girlfriend of the last ten months or so, had fallen pregnant just as filming began on 'Get Back'. She had been living with McCartney in his home in St John's Wood since late October, having abandoned her slightly erratic career as a photographer with *Country Life* magazine in New York. Her coltish looks and unfashionable dress sense rankled with the fans who huddled constantly outside his home and the Apple offices. McCartney, though, the last bachelor Beatle, was properly in love for the first time.

Linda came from New York wealth and, like Yoko, had attended Sarah Lawrence College. Her father, Lee, was a successful showbusiness lawyer whose client roster included some of the most famous names in the world. The family, part of America's post-war nouveau riche, wanted for nothing. Her brother John was already enrolled as a partner in the family business.

Paul later recalled: 'I remember when I first met John Eastman, I asked him, "What do you want to do? What's your ambition in life?" He said, "To be the president of the United States of America," which fairly soon after that he didn't want to do. They were very aspirational.'

For McCartney, always the most class-conscious of The Beatles, Lee Eastman provided him with an entrée into American high society, and, suddenly, the solution to The Beatles' problems seemed to present itself. Eastman had already offered him advice on how to make serious money by investing in music publishing and buying up the copyrights of other artists, adding that he should even consider setting up his own, stand-alone company.

At some point in early January, Eastman notionally agreed to map out a financial road for Apple's recovery, but McCartney quickly acknowledged that his bandmates would surely capsize the whole idea before discussions could take place. 'He would have been good business-wise, but of course he would have too much of a vested interest,' he recalled years later. 'He would have looked after me more than the others, so I can understand their reluctance to get involved with that.' Even so, a seed had been planted in Lee Eastman's mind.

It is worth recollecting that, to the public at that time, Apple seemed to be a huge success. The music label was thriving. In addition to everything else, McCartney understood the importance of keeping Apple's financial woes private. Like Harrison and Starr, he was well aware that a loose remark could spark disaster. Lennon, however, had a more cavalier approach. In an interview published in *Disc and Echo* on 18 January, conducted by Ray Coleman, a confidant of many years' standing, he casually laid bare their travails in sixty-two words.

He told Coleman: 'We haven't got half the money people think we have. It's been pie in the sky from the start. Apple's losing money every week because it needs close running by a big businessman. If it carries on like this, all of us will be broke in six months. Apple needs a new broom and a lot of people will have to go.'

It was a provocative statement, one that would set in motion a dire chain of events. Even in those pre-internet days, Lennon's remarks quickly echoed all over the globe. Wire services clattered out the story and newspapers had a field day with headlines that spoke of 'Beatles Cash Crisis'.

Derek Taylor quickly discerned the implications. He said later: 'By 1969 it was real madness. We didn't know where we were . . . Apple was like Toytown and Paul was Ernest the Policeman. We couldn't have gone on and on like that. We had to have a demon king.'

Across the Atlantic, sitting in his office off New York's theatre district at 1700 Broadway, a pudgy, thirty-eight-year-old man, dressed in his customary turtle-neck sweater and sneakers and pulling on a pipe, read the stories with relish. Instinctively, his accountant's mind was already reeling off the numbers. Without having to say it out loud, Allen Klein knew it meant just one thing: Gotcha!

*

George Harrison's walkout on Friday, 10 January, had turned out to be more than a fit of pique. In fact, he felt so frustrated over the impasse between all four that he succinctly summarised matters in his diary for that day: 'January 10. Got up. Went to Twickenham. Rehearsed until lunchtime. Left The Beatles. Went home.'

Over the weekend, discreet calls were made to coax Harrison

back into the fold. Eventually, he agreed to a meeting between all four of them on the Sunday night at Ringo Starr's house – the one place always considered neutral ground – and laid down the conditions for tearing up his resignation. But the meeting quickly broke up and Harrison again stormed out. This time it seemed like there was no way back. Not even Starr, always the architect of arbitration, could smooth this one over.

Unlike McCartney, Harrison didn't have a reverse gear when it came to inter-band diplomacy. Lennon, numbed and dilatory due to his heroin habit, sat in stony silence whenever his bandmate berated him over their plight. Now, though, with The Beatles' very future – and all their fortunes – on the line he would have to listen.

Over the years, tiny details have emerged of what happened during this attempt at appeasement at Starr's house. But what has become clear is Harrison's unbridled rage at Lennon's abandonment of his own sense of self. One by one, he itemised his complaints. Lennon had very little decent new material to offer up for 'Get Back'. He was fed up with being treated like some star-struck kid. Yoko had now become his mouthpiece in the studio and at band meetings when, if anyone was being brutally honest, she had no right to be there. His deferment to Yoko at every God-given opportunity was no longer tolerable.

Lennon's artistic and emotional withdrawal, his increased dependence on Yoko and his sullen, stoned passivity had left them all in a state of abject surrender. It was a make-your-mind-up moment. When Lennon refused to even engage in the discussion, Harrison angrily picked up his jacket and headed for the door. The more things changed, the more they stayed the same.

One discussion caught on tape during the month reveals Starr trying to drum some common sense into Lennon over his lover's constant presence at the sessions. But Lennon says, 'Yoko only wants to be accepted, she wants to be one of us.' Starr for once spoke for the three other band members when he said softly, 'She's not a Beatle, John, and she never will be,' before Lennon, digging his heels in, managed to get the final word: 'Yoko is part of me now. We are John and Yoko, we're together.'

*

Sporadic conversations recorded between McCartney and Starr in the canteen at Twickenham before John and Yoko's arrival often revealed McCartney's frustration at being trapped in a no-win situation and his desperate attempts even then to try and find some kind of compromise. All his well-founded attempts to hold The Beatles together after Epstein's death were in serious danger of rupture. His partner, and the man whose validation he cherished above everything else, had replaced him with someone he couldn't quite fathom out. And he knew that confrontation would mean only one thing – Lennon would tell him to screw The Beatles. Bubbling under the surface, of course, was also the sight of a decaying Apple. But twenty-four hours after the meeting at Starr's house broke up in acrimony and the same day that Lennon's comments to Coleman became public knowledge, there was no way of avoiding the elephant in the room.

'Yoko's very much to do with it and she's very much to do with it from John's angle,' McCartney declared in a hushed conversation with 'Get Back' director Michael Lindsay-Hogg during a break in the session. 'There's only two answers. One is to fight it and fight her and try to get The Beatles back to four people without Yoko and ask Yoko to sit down at [Apple] board meetings. Or the other thing is just to realise she's there and he's not to split with her for our sakes. But it's really not that bad, they want to stay together, so it's alright, let the young lovers stay together, you know. But it shouldn't be "can't operate under these conditions, boy". It's like we're striking because work conditions aren't right. Fuck that then. And John knows that. If it came to push between Yoko and The Beatles, it's Yoko ... okay, so they're going overboard but John always does. But maybe if I can compromise they will compromise and maybe bend towards me a bit. But it's silly neither of us compromising.'

Joining in the discussion, Lindsay-Hogg and Linda Eastman both got to the kernel of the problem – a lack of honest communication between all four. Lindsay-Hogg added: 'It really would be terribly dispiriting if it doesn't get together.' Unwittingly, McCartney had touched on an issue that had been overlooked – John and Yoko were a couple in love and like any young lovers (John was still in his twenties, after all) they wanted to be free to show affection without feeling judged by others.

Harrison, meanwhile, away from the studio poured all his anger into a new song, 'Wah-Wah'. Written on the day he walked out, the lyrics mined the same vein of frustration about the band as 'I Me Mine'. When the song was heard on his debut album, *All Things Must Pass*, eighteen months later, no one was under any illusions about the target of his vitriol.

Sessions continued over the next couple of days, but little work was done. McCartney and Lennon finally realised that they had belittled Harrison once too often. Now it was Harrison who had the future of The Beatles in his hands. His ally, Derek Taylor, used all his charm to persuade him that he would be 'doing the decent thing' by coming home and at least completing 'Get Back'. But he was not ready to return quietly.

At a second band meeting on Wednesday, 15 January, which lasted five hours, an uneasy truce was reached, provided everyone agreed to Harrison's rules: No more crazy talk of a live show in far-flung foreign shores. And definitely no more Twickenham. This time no one faced him down. McCartney reputedly apologised for his authoritarian behaviour. Lennon kept quiet, for now. Another five days would pass before all four were in the same room again.

The one thing they all agreed on was not to return to EMI Studios in Abbey Road, which for them had become little more than a sound-proofed prison. The obvious solution was to opt for the new, 72-track state-of-the-art studio being constructed in the basement of the Apple offices by Alex Mardas. But when they saw the studio, it was clear that it was not fit for even the simplest purpose. Glyn Johns summed it up as a 'disaster area'. Engineer Dave Harries said,

'They actually tried a session on this desk, just one take, but when they played the tape back it was all hum and hiss.'

The band sent an SOS to George Martin, the man they had largely frozen out of the 'Get Back' project, to use his influence to let them borrow a mobile recording unit from EMI. On 21 January, all four were back in the round in the Apple basement. That same day, Starr was buttonholed by *Daily Express* showbiz reporter David Wigg for BBC Radio's *Scene and Heard* programme, and responded to media claims of fist fights and bitter arguments amongst the band.

Were they all still as close? 'Yes. You know, there's that famous old saying, you'll always hurt the one you love,' he said. 'And we all love each other and we all know that. But we still sort of hurt each other, occasionally. You know . . . where we just misunderstand each other and we go off, and it builds up to something bigger than it ever was. Then we have to come down to it and get it over with, you know. Sort it out. And so we're still really very close people.'

He also downplayed Lennon's comments that Apple was a corporate basket case. 'We have spent a lot of money, because we don't earn as much as people think. Coz if we earn a million then the government gets ninety per cent and we get a hundred thousand. And we, we didn't sort of realise how much we were spending, you know. Like, someone pointed out, to spend ten thousand you have to make a hundred and twenty. But we just spent it as a hundred and twenty.

'So what we're doing now is tightening up on our own personal money and on the company's money, you know. We're not just giving as much away on handouts and things like that, you know, and as many projects. We're gonna cut down a bit till we've sorted ourselves out again and do it properly as a business . . . but it's not that we're broke. On paper we're very wealthy people. Just when it gets down to pound notes, we're only half wealthy.'

The twenty-first of January was an ad hoc session that passed without incident, but the next day saw things kick into a higher gear thanks to a happy accident. A few months earlier, attending a Ray

Charles concert at the Royal Festival Hall, Harrison had caught sight of a faintly familiar pianist hammering out funky R&B solos.

Billy Preston looked nothing like the scrawny kid from Houston whom Harrison had last seen in 1962 in Hamburg in the days of The Savage Young Beatles. Then, he and Preston, the youngest member of Little Richard's band, had established a rapport. Now, seven years later, Preston was a key (and physically imposing) part of Ray Charles' band.

Harrison put out the word for him to get in touch, unaware that Preston had already decided to catch up with his old friends from Hamburg. He rang Apple and was invited to 3 Savile Row. Footage shows him arriving at the studio on 22 January and being greeted warmly by The Beatles. Out of shot, Harrison might have been seen smirking.

Preston's presence immediately saw an improvement in behaviour – the same way Clapton had put everyone on point when Harrison brought him in to play lead guitar on 'While My Guitar Gently Weeps' for the White Album. Preston might have been unaware of the band's internal strife but he was not in the least fazed by their fame. He was simply delighted to get the chance to join in the jams on a no-questions-asked basis. His natural chirpiness was instantly infectious and spread itself to the band.

'I think they had lost a bit of the joy of making music,' he reflected later. 'There wasn't much bickering in the studio, because they were concentrating on music. But when we'd break for lunch, they'd start to talk about business. I was surprised to learn they'd gotten ripped off so many times. I learned a lot from them about that kind of thing.'

Preston could play anything from straightforward rock 'n' roll to blues-tinged gospel songs to syncopated jazz. Those sessions were not the most relaxed that The Beatles had ever played, but Preston's effervescence and instinctive playing did much to enliven it. 'Billy was brilliant – a little young whizz-kid,' McCartney recalled in *The Beatles Anthology*. 'We'd always got on very well with him. He showed up in London and we all said, "Oh, Bill! Great – let's have him play on a few things." So he started sitting in on the sessions, because he was an old mate really.'

Preston's keyboard skills injected life into new songs like 'Get Back', 'Don't Let Me Down' and 'Let It Be' as well as sharpening their focus and discipline on other acoustic numbers such as 'Two Of Us' and Harrison's 'For You Blue'. He added rudimentary keyboard textures to a song then called 'Bathroom Window', later retitled 'She Came In Through The Bathroom Window'. He said, 'Everyone was pitching in with ideas. They just let me play whatever I wanted to play.'

By the end of the week, Lennon was so enthused by Preston's involvement that he floated the idea of him becoming a full-time Beatle. McCartney was quick to shoot the idea down with the remark that 'It's bad enough with four Beatles.'

They now had five days left, more or less, to finally nail down usable tracks for the album while devising a spectacular end to the film. No one, though, could find a way through that quandary. Harrison remained steadfast in ruling out a live show. Besides, added Starr, they were in no shape to play live in front of an audience for a whole gig: a couple of songs, maybe, but an entire show would be hugely embarrassing.

Most of the day was spent fine-tuning songs that actually made the grade. And, despite the maelstrom of the past few weeks, some of them were almost over line. Lost amid the bickering was the fact that there had been some moments when it all came together joyously. Just not in the one-take, no-overdubs ethos that had been the guiding principle of 'Get Back' from the outset.

On Monday, 27 January, day sixteen of the album sessions, the band ran through some fourteen takes of 'Get Back', one of which included Lennon's mock introduction about Sweet Loretta Fart, thinking she was a cleaner, but actually being a frying pan. And they remained on the same page during new takes of 'Let It Be', 'The Long And Winding Road', 'Don't Let Me Down' and 'I've Got a Feeling', all of which crept closer to standard. Lennon, especially, was in good spirits after hearing that Yoko's divorce from Cox had just been made official. 'Free at last,' he hollered, casually forgetting that it had cost him thousands of pounds in legal fees. And that night he and Yoko had a furtive appointment that, ultimately, would set in motion a domino effect on all their futures.

*

'Nervous as shit' was how Lennon later described his frame of mind as he and Yoko walked into London's upmarket Dorchester Hotel that evening. He felt strangely vulnerable and the reason was simple; he was heading for a secret rendezvous with a man who revelled in his self-styled image as a music industry shark, a guy whose long-avowed obsession 'to get' The Beatles made it sound like they were prey waiting to be devoured. And now Allen Klein, the fearsome manager of The Animals, The Kinks, Donovan and, most notably, the Rolling Stones, had the chance to bite down on his biggest victim yet – John Lennon, the de facto leader of The Beatles.

Klein knew the band was perilously adrift after Lennon's public admission that Apple's financial woes had left them in serious danger of going bust. To Klein, this meant the biggest band in the world, one that had made – and squandered – untold millions, was ripe for the picking.

In the story of The Beatles, Klein is cast as Satan incarnate, a character whose breath reeked of sulphur. On his desk in New York sat a plinth parodying the Twenty-third Psalm: 'Yea, though I walk through the valley of the shadow of death, I will fear no evil, 'cause I'm the biggest bastard in the valley . . .' Naturally, his reputation had preceded him, and Apple staff had been instructed to shield The Beatles from his increasingly aggressive phone calls. When he finally got through to Peter Brown, the closest thing the band had to a manager, his overtures were instantly rebuffed. Brown recalled how Epstein had shown Klein the door several years earlier for dismissing as 'a crock of shit' the deals that Epstein had brokered for his charges.

Klein, now, was persistent. Sending a message through Stones intermediary Tony Calder he reached Derek Taylor, who, eager to get the aggressive American off his back, persuaded Lennon that he had nothing to lose by meeting him, especially when The Beatles needed someone to manage Apple.

McCartney, Lennon knew, had already sounded out his prospective father-in-law Lee Eastman about taking on the job. Eastman's first solution would be to delegate the task to his son John, who had already made a cursory examination of the band's finances. He had also held an initial meeting earlier in the month with Epstein's brother, Clive, over the possibility of The Beatles buying Nems, the Liverpool family firm that still banked a healthy twenty-five per cent management fee as part of the deal drawn up in 1967 before Brian's death.

Taylor, while acknowledging the part he had played in bringing Klein and Lennon together, always seemed to have retrospective regrets. He recalled: 'Klein is essential in the Great Novel as the Demon King. Just as you think everything's going to be all right, here he is. I helped to bring him to Apple, but I did give The Beatles certain solemn warnings.'

Lennon had, in fact, met Klein briefly in December during filming for the Stones' *Rock And Roll Circus*, but their conversation had been perfunctory. So much had happened in the seven weeks since. Lennon – and, especially, McCartney – knew that the Stones made more money than The Beatles despite selling fewer records – and there were five of them! So when Lennon arrived at the Dorchester with Yoko, he told himself to keep an open mind.

To their surprise, they found an Ordinary Joe shorn of big-business artifice, dressed in casual clothes and projecting an air of humility. Lennon recalled: 'He was sitting there all nervous. He was all alone, he didn't have any of his helpers around, because he didn't want to do anything like that. But he was very nervous, you could see it in his face. When I saw that I felt better.' Klein then got to work, using flattery as his weapon. He knew exactly which Lennon buttons to press. He emphasised the uncanny ways in which his own rough childhood had parallels with Lennon's.

Klein never knew his mother, who died when he was young. Lennon's mother Julia had died in a road traffic accident when he was seventeen. Klein's father, a Jewish-Hungarian immigrant, worked in a butcher's shop, and since he couldn't afford to raise four children on his own, had placed the infant Allen in an orphanage, where he remained until he was at least nine (some sources say older). Eventually he was placed in the custody of an aunt (just like Lennon had been).

And now? He owned a yacht and worked from a plush corner office on the forty-first floor of a West Side office building in the Big Apple. He could afford to gloat about his success because he had earned it. It came as a result of a ferocious work ethic, utter fearlessness and a brain that devoured audits like a calculator. He worked by the rules of Brill Building business: he consistently helped his clients – chiefly by forcing audits on unwilling record companies, which almost invariably turned out to be hiding a few beans themselves – while helping himself.

Lennon was seduced.

Klein pointed out that there were *four* Beatles. McCartney wasn't anybody's leader! Where did he get off, treating the others as if they were merely sidemen? It was just what Lennon wanted to hear. Lennon also believed Ono was fully his equal as an artist, and that she wasn't being paid proper respect – not by the other Beatles, not by society.

Klein had arranged for the hotel to serve Yoko the macrobiotic rice he knew she liked, and he lavished attention upon her throughout the dinner. He told Yoko he would find funding for her art exhibitions, and he would get her films distributed by the film studio, United Artists. Not only that, he guaranteed (preposterously) they would pay her a million-dollar advance.

According to Lennon's later recollections, Klein also underscored his deep understanding of The Beatles by telling him that he knew precisely which songs Lennon had written and quoted large chunks of his lyrics. Only three people know whether this is true and two of them are now dead. But it seems on the surface to smack of

Lennon spin, even allowing for Klein's lasting impression on the couple. 'He knew every damn thing about us, the same as he knows everything about the Stones,' Lennon claimed.

Then, of course, came the question of Lennon's own finances, and the real reason that had drawn him to the Dorchester. By quoting Lennon's 'Apple-is-going-bust' comments back at him, Klein touched on John's deepest fears – that he would end up on Skid Row. And he knew how to fix that in the same way he had once made Bobby Darin and Sam Cooke millions – by carrying out forensic examinations of the EMI and Apple books to get Lennon what he was rightly owed.

The first thing he would do was sideline John Eastman's idea that they should buy Nems for a cool million. Klein told John: 'I'll get ya Nems – and it won't cost ya a penny. I'll get it for nothing.' Quoting his favourite mantra – 'Fuck You Money' – he assured Lennon that initially he wouldn't charge him a penny. He just wanted permission to look into his affairs and see what he could do on his behalf.

In his own account of the meeting, Klein said: 'I didn't propose anything, I don't work that way. I just asked him "How can I help you?" That's all, and after we broke the ice, it was a very personal sort of meeting. We were trying to get to know each other. He was scared to death about the money situation. How would you feel, sitting there damn near broke after having made millions and millions of pounds and about to end up with nothing except memories?'

Lennon would later describe Klein as 'the only businessman I've met who isn't grey right through his eyes to his soul'. That night, he sent a memo to EMI chairman, Sir Joseph Lockwood: 'Please give Allen Klein any information he wants and full co-operation.'

If McCartney was ever aware of Lennon's meeting with Klein in advance, he has never let on. When all four Beatles gathered at Apple the next day, Lennon wasted little time in blurting out the news: Klein was the right man to lead The Beatles back from the brink. 'I don't give a bugger about anyone else. Allen Klein's the man for me,' he said.

He later explained to *Rolling Stone*: 'I had to present a case to them, and Allen had to talk to them himself. And of course, I promoted him in the fashion in which you will see me promoting or talking about something. I was enthusiastic about him and I was relieved because I had met a lot of people, including Lord Beeching, who was one of the top people in Britain and all that.

'Paul had told me, "Go and see Lord Beeching," so I went. I mean I'm a good boy, man, and I saw Lord Beeching and he was no help at all. Paul was in America getting Eastman and I was interviewing all these so-called top people, and they were animals. Allen was a human being, the same as Brian was a human being. It was the same thing with Brian in the early days, it was an assessment; I make a lot of mistakes character-wise, but now and then I make a good one and Allen is one, Yoko is one and Brian was one.'

In later years he would offer a more telling observation: 'He was the only one that Yoko liked.'

Klein was thus now convinced that he could seize the Ultimate Prize: management of the biggest band in history. After John and Yoko had left the Dorchester, he stayed up most of the night, poring over newspaper cuttings about their finances and Apple's future, while rehearsing a sales pitch that would pick apart John Eastman's suggestion that The Beatles lay out a million pounds to buy Nems.

When Klein met all The Beatles the next day, he was high on braggadocio, low on detail. Over a couple of hours, he set out his stall to save Apple while making each of them richer than Croesus. Fuck You Money! Harrison and Starr, while not rushing to early judgement, committed themselves to at least hearing more, but McCartney's disdain for Klein was instant and uncompromising. He was the first to leave the meeting, signalling he had heard enough. It was a grievous, tactical blunder because it ceded the higher ground to Klein and allowed him to impose a chokehold on Harrison and Starr.

He told them bluntly they were being royally screwed by the business establishment: Lockwood at EMI, Clive Epstein at Nems,

Dick James at Northern Songs. All of them (allegedly) creaming off the top, and that's before we talk about the leeches bleeding Apple dry: Peter Brown, Neil Aspinall, Derek Taylor, Alistair Taylor, all their Liverpool buddies-turned-hangers-on.

Klein's words, coated in a thick, expletive-filled Brooklyn brogue, zeroed in on their darkest fears. With Lennon already in his corner, victory was a foregone conclusion. Harrison and Starr gave tacit approval for Klein to, at least, examine their financial affairs as well as Lennon's.

For Harrison, the pull of Klein's working-class aesthetic won him over. 'Because we were all from Liverpool, we favoured people who were street people,' he said. 'As John was going with Klein, it was much easier if we went with him too.' McCartney, though, remained unwavering in his opposition: 'I didn't trust him,' he said.

It was for now an awkward stand-off but, unknown to all of them, a fateful die had been cast. A meeting was scheduled for the following Saturday – the first day of February – to try to map out a future course. Office politics, however, would have to be put on the back-burner. The reason? Astonishingly, they had a gig to play.

*

After weeks of arguing, all four Beatles had finally agreed to film a live performance to bring the curtain down on 'Get Back'. Even Harrison had finally relented. Over the years, a handful of people have claimed ownership of an idea that ticked the simplest of boxes: Why Don't We Do It On The Roof? Starr, Glyn Johns, Lennon, McCartney have all been credited with being first to suggest climbing the stairs of 3 Savile Row. Michael Lindsay-Hogg had mixed feelings. He said: 'There's no balls to the show at all … I think we are being soft. You are The Beatles, you aren't four jerks.'

In any event, on 29 January it was decided that the impromptu show should take place the next day. All they would have to do was build a makeshift stage on the roof of the premises, run the electric feeds from the basement studio mixing desk, set up the cameras

... and go for it. The fact that they would be playing to an invisible audience five floors below on the street played into Lennon's idea of the absurd. So, too, was the possibility that they could be busted for causing a public nuisance – the West End Central Police Station was only a few doors away, after all. That clinched it, especially for Starr: 'I thought it would be great if we were all hauled off in handcuffs. Brilliant ending.'

Fine, but what to play? Again, they felt insecure about performing new material in case they screwed it up. In the end they felt only five songs were up to scratch – 'Dig A Pony', 'I've Got A Feeling', 'Get Back', 'Don't Let Me Down' and 'One After 909', a jaunty pre-Beatlemania number that they had frequently exhumed at Twickenham and Savile Row. There were to be no Harrison songs. Nor would they make a pass at 'Let It Be' or such acoustic songs as 'Two Of Us'. Similarly ruled out were any of the other golden oldies and rock 'n' roll staples they had flogged to death throughout January.

On the morning of the show, Apple staffers Kevin Harrington and Mal Evans began hauling all the instruments (including Preston's Hammond B3 organ) up from the basement via a small lift. Elsewhere, sound technicians, including a twenty-year-old tape operator named Alan Parsons, recruited from Abbey Road to help Glyn Johns, worked with the camera crews to get everything in place. Downstairs, beside the front door, a secret camera was installed to catch any possible police intervention.

'I think the reason for the rooftop session was to generate a little excitement,' says Parsons, who would go on to achieve fame as one of rock's best-known producers. 'They were sick of just playing the same tunes over and over again. They just wanted to get a solid performance recorded, and I think that, until they did go on the roof, they hadn't really achieved that. Or at least they didn't think that they had. They announced it just the night before. It was just, "Let's go up on the roof tomorrow morning." So we worked late into the night to get it happening. Part of my job was to run multiple cables from the basement up to the roof.'

Parsons also had to deal with the wind lest it wreak havoc with the microphones. 'Glyn sent me out to buy some pantyhose to stick over the mics to minimise the wind noise,' he later told *Guitar Player* magazine. 'I walked into this department store and said, "I need three pair of pantyhose. It doesn't matter what size." They thought I was either a bank robber or a cross-dresser.'

Les Parrott, the cameraman, recalls the logistical problems presented by playing on the rooftop, which was extremely damp as a result of recent heavy rain. He told me: 'The first thing they had to do was get a builder in. He had a look on the roof and [had to] to get half a dozen Acrow props [telescopic tubular steel props] to make sure the ceiling didn't cave in on the accounts department which was directly underneath.

'It was just a pitched roof so they put down these Acrow props and then placed the wooden beams on top of them. Then it was a big deal to get sufficient power up to the roof for the lights and their amps. They were running feeds back down to the basement studio. That is why one of the numbers on the roof didn't get fully recorded because they were changing tapes down in the basement.

'Then someone said – it might have been Paul – "We should get a helicopter to film it as well." Then the next thing you hear someone say, "Oh, there's a girl in accounts and she has a lot of helicopters." Eh? Turns out she was related to Bristow's Helicopters. So they rang Bristow Helicopters and they said, "Yeah, yeah what do you want?" But the space was only 1,600 square feet so it would all have been a bit pointless really, not to say pretty dangerous. You have this image in your head of everyone on the roof either being hit by rotor blades or being carried away by the downdraft. Can you imagine it?'

By noon, the stage and The Beatles were ready. There were last-minute doubts, Starr's nerve especially beginning to waver. Typically, it was Lennon, who led from the front. 'Fuck it,' he said. 'Let's do it.' What then followed was something akin to miraculous. For forty-two minutes The Beatles looked and sounded like the rock 'n' roll gods they were.

Lennon, wearing a three-quarter-length fur coat as protection against the biting cold and with his long hair blowing in the wind, took centre stage. To his right stood McCartney, heavily bearded and wearing his favourite black Tommy Nutter suit; his Hofner bass still had the setlist from The Beatles' last live performance, at Candlestick Park, taped to its underside. Starr had borrowed his wife Maureen's red plastic mac as a shield against the elements for one of his best-ever performances on the drums. Only Harrison, wearing mint-green trousers and a black fur coat, and playing his custom-made Fender Rosewood Telecaster, gave off the air of a reluctant conscript. He can be seen only providing back-up vocals to five Lennon-McCartney numbers.

But it was a happy occasion for Preston. 'I didn't need to be out front or anything like that,' he said. 'I was an invited guest but it was one of the best moments of my career. I got to play on the last live performance of The Beatles and, let me tell you, it was magical.'

Altogether, The Beatles played five versions of 'Get Back', two rollicking run-throughs of 'Don't Let Me Down', 'I've Got A Feeling', 'One After 909' and two passes at 'Dig A Pony'. At one point, when the tapes are full, they even strummed an irreverent version of 'God Save the Queen'.

Several friends and family were given a front-row seat to watch history being made. Most of them squatted down beside the chimneys, anxious for a decent vantage point. The only key ally missing was Neil Aspinall, who was in hospital having his tonsils removed.

On the street below, dozens of passers-by gazed upwards, most of them unaware who was playing. Others quickly joined the dots. Up above and in the band's eyeline, a knot of secretaries and office workers, some perched precariously on chimney-tops, watched the scene in wide-eyed wonder. Not everyone was happy, though: bowler-hatted accountants harrumphed at the unwanted noisy lunchtime intrusion and complained to the local constabulary. Squatting at Lennon's feet was Kevin Harrington, who held a cheat-sheet of lyrics – but, even so, Lennon frequently fluffed the lines to his own songs.

Somehow, though, it all worked out. All the backstabbing bitterness of the previous month was cast aside for a short time. Then, all too soon, it was over, with Lennon's immortal ad-lib carried away on the January breeze: 'I'd like to say thanks on behalf of the group and ourselves and I hope we passed the audition . . .' But not before, as they all predicted, the police intervened to warn them to turn down the volume or pull the plug.

One of those on duty was a young constable called Ken Wharfe, who eighteen years later would be appointed as the personal protection officer to Diana, Princess of Wales. On that day, he was just another traffic cop following his sergeant's orders to tell The Beatles to 'cut out the bloody noise'. Wharfe returned to the scene on the fortieth anniversary of the rooftop concert.

'I arrived as a young cop from Piccadilly Circus and there were about fifty or sixty people spread around the roof. One of the things I remember was the music was fantastic and every available roof space was taken up by people. They were sitting on chimney stacks to get a better view. And despite my instructions to arrest The Beatles, no one would have done that, because it would have ended perhaps the greatest concert that had ever happened. Thirty minutes later, I left absolutely buoyant having witnessed one of the greatest bands in the world. I don't think the police were ever going to stop The Beatles [playing]. It was a great party atmosphere. There was no disorder. I remember John Lennon making quips like "I'll come quietly" and things like that. It was a lucky day for me and a lucky day for London that they had this free concert by The Beatles on the roof.'

Someone else rubbing his eyes in disbelief was Chris O'Dell, an American whose friendship with Derek Taylor had helped her land a job in the Apple press office, clipping newspaper files.

She said, 'I was lucky to have been there because the roof was actually very weak at the top of Apple and so they told all of us that we couldn't go up there. None of the employees could. I always got to know the right people so I got to know the cameraman. And he said, "Come up, you can help me." So I went up and I just sat there thinking, "God, I hope nobody realises that I'm not supposed to be here". But it was . . . it was freezing cold. That is, I mean that I remember more than anything – how cold it was up there. But also it was just so exciting to think originally the idea was that they were going to . . . they were doing it so that everybody in the whole West End of London could hear the music and in fact the amps weren't that big. So the people on Savile Row could hear it, and it was fun to watch them looking up trying to figure out, what was that?

Those who were there were indeed witnessing musical history being made. Parsons said, 'That was one of the greatest and most exciting days of my life. To see The Beatles playing together and getting instant feedback from the people around them, five cameras on the roof, in the road, it was just unbelievable. The only regret I have is that I intentionally set up behind all the cameras on the roof, so there is not one picture of me up there!'

Harrington remembers the whole thing passing in a blur. 'When you look back on it now it was an incredible thing just to be there,' he said. 'It really was historic. But at the time you're just trying to make sure everything goes okay. I was used to seeing them so I wasn't, like, starstruck or anything. But it's only when you look at the pictures that you think, I was really there.'

For Lindsay-Hogg, the rooftop brought a bittersweet combination of relief and a feeling of what might have been. He recalled: 'They'd been through everything together. It was kind of like a marriage and people were starting to not get along as they had when they first got married. But when they got up on the roof they really loved it. It was cold but they had a very good time together. It proved to them that they were such a great rock and roll band. They could still connect and they could connect as beautifully as they'd always done.'

Of course, the real wonder of the rooftop concert was the fact that it happened at all. Given the tumultuous events of the previous seventy-two hours, no one expected Lennon and McCartney to share the same space, let alone actually sing harmonies together as they used to. It was a measure of the musical bond that could still be resurrected on occasion. When they came off stage, all four felt the adrenaline rush of playing before an audience again. But that was as far as it went.

The next day, appropriately the last one of January, they were back at Apple, with Preston again present, to record 'Let It Be' and 'The Long And Winding Road' as well as another version of 'Two Of Us', all songs considered out of reach for the rooftop show.

And then 'Get Back', the most tortuous recording of The Beatles' career, was left to languish on the shelf. All that was left at that moment was the lingering memory of Lennon's parting shot as the amps were finally turned off and The Beatles shuffled off the stage for the last time.

Lindsay-Hogg said, 'Since you know it's their last time playing in public, and since you know they didn't know themselves it was the last time, it's kind of beautiful and heartbreaking at the same time because if anyone ever passed any audition it was them.'

The real question though, was this: was it a rebirth or a requiem? The answer would be quick to arrive.

Allen Klein's divisive pitch to take over the management of The Beatles quickly won over John and Yoko but arguably caused the biggest schism between Lennon and McCartney.

FEBRUARY 1969

High noon for The Beatles, Allen Klein and John Eastman arrived on the first day of February, a Saturday, at Apple. At one end of an oak-panelled table alongside Klein stood John Lennon, George Harrison and Ringo Starr. Staring them down on the other side were Paul McCartney and his future brother-in-law. It was a straightforward face-off between two very different adversaries. Park Avenue privilege poured from Eastman, a scion of the family law business. Contempt for the class system, meanwhile, oozed from Klein.

It was the first time Eastman had set eyes on the three 'rebel' Beatles. The euphoria of the rooftop concert was already dust in the wind. And the battle for what author Peter Doggett would later call the 'soul of The Beatles' had now shifted inexorably from the studio to the boardroom.

In the aftermath of the initial confrontation between The Beatles and Klein on 28 January, each side had pondered their next move. Klein, with three Beatles locked in, had dissected every contract they had ever signed, especially those that contained Brian Epstein's imprimatur. He had pored over the small print contained in their royalty agreements with EMI in Britain and Capitol in America. And he scrutinised agreements with United Artists Corporation over their film commitments.

Then there was Lennon and McCartney's publishing deal with Northern Songs. The two principal Beatle songwriters still received a relative pittance under a deal struck in 1963 with music publisher Dick James and his business partner Charles Silver. Six years later, they were still shackled to more or less the same miserly terms while James and Silver, as the majority shareholders of a highly prosperous company, raked in a fortune. What Klein found was that virtually every deal they had ever made was a rip-off in some shape or form. And thanks to a crippling ninety-five per cent tax rate for the UK's highest earners, and a business that was tanking financially, The Beatles were cash poor.

Klein had also uncovered duplicity closer to home. Encouraged mainly by Lee Eastman, McCartney had been secretly asking fellow Apple director Peter Brown to buy shares in Northern Songs, an act that made a mockery of his gentleman's agreement with Lennon that their holdings in their company would always be split 50–50. Klein knew he had scored a vital scoop, but for now he did not even tell Lennon. The information might come in handy further down the road, he mused, if for any reason he needed to gain a tactical negotiating edge over the Eastmans and McCartney.

Lennon, Harrison and Starr saw Klein as a heavyweight, someone to take seriously, but they viewed Eastman as a greenhorn. Lennon was also irritated that Lee Eastman hadn't taken the trouble to fly over for this meeting. Perhaps the old man thought the son would strike up a better rapport with people closer to his own age. Maybe he thought the kid could handle it, a career rite of passage. Either way, Lennon took the snub personally.

And when Eastman junior began describing the band finances as 'Kafkaesque', Lennon could be heard sneering loudly. The remark only stiffened his belief – and that of Harrison and Starr – that young Eastman was a conservative intellectual, a pawn of Paul's.

Top of the agenda was Eastman's proposal for The Beatles to buy Nems outright for £1m using an advance against future royalties from EMI. The Beatles already held ten per cent of Nems stock, but the deal would end the twenty-five per cent management fee the Epstein family still took from the band (and would continue to take until the deal expired in 1976). McCartney also floated the idea of The Beatles buying the block of shares Nems held in Northern Songs. Klein pushed back, dismissing both propositions as 'a piece of crap' while excoriating Eastman as 'a fool' and 'a shithead'. Nothing personal, you understand, but of course that's exactly what it was.

First, Klein insisted, they would need to earn at least £2m before tax in order to repay EMI. Secondly, it would be corporate suicide to spend money acquiring another company when Apple's finances were so exposed. Eastman quickly sensed that this was a fight he and McCartney would not – could not – win. As the meeting descended into a slanging match, Eastman tried to ingratiate himself with the others by taking on Klein at his own profanity-littered game. He denounced his rival as 'a perfect asshole' and called attention to a number of federal investigations currently taking place in the States into the finances of ABKCO Industries, the company Klein had founded with his wife Betty a year earlier as an umbrella firm involved in management, music publishing, film, TV and theatrical production. But he was no match for Klein's persuasive pitch.

'They always sided with the underdog,' recalled Derek Taylor, referring to Lennon, Harrison and Starr. In the end, a fragile truce was set in place to allow tempers to cool over the weekend. They agreed to hold another meeting on Monday, 3 February.

McCartney was gripped by fear at the prospect of Klein having any say in the future management of The Beatles. He felt more than a little betrayed by his three friends. Hadn't he done everything possible to try to accommodate John and Yoko while everyone else denounced them as publicity-mad freaks? He had even allowed them to move into Cavendish for a while when Lennon's marriage to Cynthia ran into trouble. And he had maintained a diplomatic silence as he watched his friend become enslaved to heroin. And this was how he repaid him?

Stinging even further was the fact that Yoko had by now clearly replaced McCartney as Lennon's creative partner on every level. He felt isolated, hurt and was wondering if all this grief really was worth the effort of holding The Beatles together.

But McCartney had one last card to produce: a letter from Mick Jagger, warning them all to steer well clear of Klein or commit 'the biggest mistake you can make'. He invited Jagger to Apple to deliver his damning verdict directly to the others,

McCartney was aware that the Stones had learned that Klein had incorporated the band in the States using the same name as their

British company, Nanker Phelge. Spoken out loud, no one had any reason to doubt they were not the same company. But the USA-registered Nanker Phelge was, in fact, wholly owned by Klein; and so all of the Stones' US royalties and publishing money ended up in Klein's pocket, with the Stones, effectively, his employees.

But when Jagger arrived at Apple he found Klein himself in the Apple boardroom alongside all four Beatles. It was a trap, set by Lennon to embarrass McCartney and Jagger. Intimidated by the scene before him, Jagger reneged on his promise to speak the truth about Klein. No accurate accounts of what he said have ever emerged, except for McCartney's oft-repeated quote that Jagger told them: 'He's all right if you like that sort of thing.'

Some in the Stones' orbit at that time, including Jagger's then lover, Marianne Faithfull, have offered an extraordinary alternative explanation. She later suggested that Jagger had shamelessly stacked the deck to ensure The Beatles fell under Klein's control, thus providing the Stones with a potential escape route from his clutches. Other accounts say Jagger found the courage, a few hours later, to warn Lennon to avoid Klein. 'He's all right but it's hard to get your hands on the money,' he is said to have warned.

Either way, when The Beatles, Eastman and Klein reconvened on the Monday, with Starr arriving from the first day of shooting *The Magic Christian*, a decision had to be made. The inevitable majority vote gave Klein an initial mandate to examine Apple's finances. It was dressed up in a press release to suggest that the job would be managed by ABKCO, but no one was in any doubt as to where the real power now lay.

In his inflammatory *Rolling Stone* interview after The Beatles had officially disbanded, Lennon revealed the full depth of his hatred for the Eastmans and all that they stood for, as well as an unresolved ambivalence towards Klein.

'We almost signed ourselves over to the Eastmans at one time, because when Paul presented me with John Eastman, I thought, "Well . . . when you're not presented with a real alternative, you take whatever is going." I would say, "yes," like I said, "Yes, let's do

'Let It Be'. I have nothing to produce so I will go along," and we almost went away with Eastman. But then [Lee] Eastman made the mistake of sending his son over and not coming over himself, to look after The Beatles, playing it a bit cool.

'Finally, when we got near the point when Allen came in, the Eastmans panicked; yet I was still open. I liked Allen but I would have taken Eastman if he had turned out something other than what he was.'

As a sop to McCartney, Apple would retain the Eastmans to offer legal advice over the future direction of the company. The agreement with Klein, though, was purely verbal. McCartney refused to sign any formal document that could tie his fate to the New Yorker. The ceasefire was conditional on Klein and John Eastman agreeing to share key information. In reality, neither party, each seething with contempt and mistrust, had any intention of playing by those rules.

Having been given a three-to-one mandate to disentangle The Beatles' finances, Klein began untying one of the key links in the chain. His first appointment later that same day was with Clive Epstein, who arrived at the Dorchester with the band's long-time accountant, Harold Pinsker.

Epstein had little of his late brother Brian's theatrical flair and found himself in a situation not of his own making. He had zero in common with The Beatles; he loathed the rock world and all its long-haired, druggy associations. By now he was desperately looking for an escape route from the ties that bound his family to the biggest band in the world. The obvious exit strategy was to sell Nems – now reincorporated as Nemperor Holdings – to the highest bidder, an arrangement that could see him return to his former life in Liverpool and pay the eye-watering death taxes due on Brian's estate.

In January, he had already rebuffed approaches for Nems from Triumph Investment Trust, an aggressive London merchant banking firm, which had offered £1.3m, to be paid over two years. But out of loyalty to Brian's 'boys' who, he felt, should have first refusal on any opportunity to buy out the company, Epstein stalled for time.

He had met John Eastman the previous month and laid bare the terms of the Triumph offer. At that precise moment The Beatles were in pole position to buy Nemperor for £1m in cash, provided of course that EMI agreed to give them an advance against future royalties. But Klein had baulked at the plan, arguing in typical swaggering style that he would get the company for nothing because Nems owed The Beatles a shedload of money. It was the first of many bitter stand-offs between the Americans and their respective Apple coalitions.

Aware that other vultures were already circling over the body of Nemperor, Klein persuaded Epstein at that first meeting to hold off on any move to sell the company until he had the chance to examine the band's finances.

An uneasy agreement was brokered under which Epstein cautiously agreed to do nothing for three weeks. It was, though, a non-binding accord.

Much of all the delicate, forensic work Klein undertook during February would be crucial. But no matter how well intentioned, it had little chance of progress with the Eastmans (John reported almost daily to his father) carefully watching his every move and ready to undermine him to McCartney at every turn.

On 14 February, the whole pack of cards surrounding the Nemperor buy-out discussions came crashing down. John Eastman had, inexplicably, without any authority from any of The Beatles, sent a letter to Epstein.

It read: 'As you know, Mr Allen Klein is doing an audit of The Beatles affairs vis-à-vis Nems and Nemperor Holdings Ltd. When this has been completed, I suggest we meet to discuss the results of Mr Klein's audit as well as the propriety of the negotiations surrounding the nine-year agreement between EMI, The Beatles and Nems.'

'Propriety of the negotiations' – the words burned deep into Epstein's soul. The smear against his deceased brother, a man whose very name stood for honesty and integrity, a man whose principled stewardship of The Beatles had provided a bulwark against the worst of the industry's predators, shocked him to his core. Bad enough to have to deal with Klein – in fact, the slur smacked more of his tactics than Eastman's – but now here was someone else trying to drag the family name through the mud.

He wrote a furious reply. 'Before any meeting takes place, please be good enough to let me know precisely what you mean by the phrase "the propriety of the negotiations surrounding the nine-year agreement between EMI, The Beatles and Nems." But his mind was made up. By the end of the day he had reopened the lines of communication with Leonard Richenberg, the straight-talking managing director of Triumph Investment Trust, and signalled his desire to work out a deal to flog the family silver – and cut 'Brian's boys' out of the deal.

Three days later Triumph owned the seventy per cent of the company held by Queenie Epstein, the family matriarch. The ten per cent holding that still belonged to the four Beatles had virtually zero corporate value, since they would remain as minority shareholders in a company owned by faceless City fatcats, Lennon's biggest dread.

Eastman's astonishing letter exposed his lack of negotiating experience and political shortcomings. With a few strokes of his pen, he had shattered the delicate alliance between Epstein and Klein. And, in doing so, he pushed up Klein's stock even further in the eyes of his three Beatle backers.

Klein learned about the deal in a frantic phone call from Neil Aspinall at Apple. Secretly, Klein was delighted at the unexpected turn of events. Eastman subsequently insisted the letter had been sent at Klein's behest, a claim that Klein always denied.

Epstein was in no doubt as to where the blame lay. In *Apple to the Core*, he told authors Peter McCabe and Robert D Schonfield: 'Eastman spent a week negotiating for Nems on the basis of the loan EMI was prepared to make The Beatles. But he loaded the offer with so many conditions and warranties that he ended up talking himself out of the deal. In my opinion, he was a little too young to be negotiating at that level.'

Aspinall, meanwhile, as an Apple director, had been ready to write a seven-figure cheque to Epstein before Eastman junior's extraordinary intervention capsized any hopes of a deal to purchase Nems. 'It's fair to say that had we got Nems, a lot of our later financial problems would never have occurred,' reflected Aspinall, who had been with the band throughout the decade, first as a roadie and now as an inner-circle confidant. 'It cost The Beatles a lot more to free themselves from Triumph later. You could say the deal was crucial.'

Ironically, though, Epstein's decision managed to do what neither Klein nor Eastman could ever have done – it united all four Beatles on a common cause. They were dismayed to see their management contract fall into hands of merchant bankers, the hidden face of the establishment. And it galled them to think that a quarter of all their earnings outwith music publishing would now be siphoned off by capitalist vultures, none of whom had any interest in them as artists but instead saw them as a giant corporate cash cow.

Klein threatened lawsuits against all concerned, and Lennon was prepared to give carte blanche to go to war with Triumph. At a meeting near the end of the month, the brash American demanded Richenberg unlock the golden handcuffs that bound The Beatles to Triumph. Not surprisingly, he showed Klein the door. 'For all I knew he might have been a nasty little gangster,' recalled Richenberg. 'I only agreed to see him because Clive Epstein asked me to see him for Lennon's sake.'

With February drawing to a close, Klein now fixed his crosshairs on EMI's sixty-eight-year-old chairman, Sir Joseph Lockwood, by demanding that in future all Beatle royalties be paid directly to Apple. Caught between two warring factions, Lockwood opted for the Swiss option of neutrality and simply froze all Beatle cash until the relevant parties mediated a truce. Right then, though, a ceasefire looked impossible. Conversely, a trilateral war of attrition between The Beatles, EMI and Triumph Investment seemed inevitable.

*

Musically, February would turn out to be The Beatles' most fallow recording period since the last few months of 1966. At that time, despite intense media speculation, there was never any question of a split. Now, however, it seemed as though all the joy had been snuffed out. And with a new generation of bands emerging, The Beatles risked looking passé even though the staggering sales of the White Album and 'Hey Jude' – their most successful single ever – suggested that their place in the public's affections remained intact. Ranged against that, though, was a drip-feed of rumours over their future.

Geoffrey Cannon in *The Guardian* wrote at the time: 'Unlike the Rolling Stones, who have developed the same rich preoccupations, The Beatles are an essentially versatile band; and they are now past their own limits. Other versatile bands have developed through never being identifiable in terms of set personnel,' as he cited The Byrds, and Frank Zappa's Mothers of Invention. Cannon then turned to other musicians – Eric Clapton and Mike Bloomfield – who had refused identification with one band. 'The notion of what essentially constitutes a rock music band is now in flux, and George Harrison and Paul McCartney do often get together and play with musicians they respect. But this is done privately: and that's what's wrong. If Harrison wants to play with Eric Clapton, he should say so on record. The Beatles should jump from being a first-generation band to embracing the creative flux of the richest third-generation bands.'

Harrison was due to go into London's University College Hospital on 8 February to have his tonsils removed, followed by eight days of recovery. Though he had experienced indifference from Lennon and McCartney too many times, he now felt emboldened, almost reborn, spiritually and professionally. His latest contributions to the 'Get Back' sessions had sounded good. Even Lennon had joined in on 'For You Blue', a jaunty bottleneck blues number. For the first time Harrison counted the songs in his bottom drawer and was amazed to discover that there were nearly thirty. The idea of putting out a proper solo album – not a self-indulgent project like *Wonderwall Music*, the intentionally non-commercial, Indian-flavoured film soundtrack album, released three months earlier – drifted through his mind. Yes, one or two numbers lacked lyrics, but now, stuck in hospital, he had the peace and quiet to get them down.

One such song was 'Something', which he had been carrying around since the White Album sessions began winding down. Though the opening line, 'Something in the way she moves', was a straight crib from a James Taylor tune, everyone who had heard him run through the song reckoned it had potential. But he couldn't figure out the words needed to sufficiently impress Lennon and McCartney. Now, though, this spell in hospital, might give him the opportunity to finish the words.

For the first three weeks of February, meanwhile, Lennon and Yoko kept themselves to themselves at the Montagu Square flat they were leasing from Starr, piecing together some avant-garde tapes that explored the human condition. Now, more than ever, they looked like each other's mirror image. This was the season of dangerous curiosity, of reckless experimentation. Behind closed doors, as Yoko later attested, they imagined themselves as Sixties versions of Robert Browning and Elizabeth Barrett, those star-crossed lovers of the Victorian age. It was a fantasy image, fuelled as much by the pain-numbing chemicals now coursing freely through both their bodies. Nine months had passed since their friendship had gone from quixotic to compulsive. It had shifted quickly through the gears from lust to outright obsession from the night the previous May that had seen them consummate their relationship after making the tapes that formed *Two Virgins* and precipitated the end of his seven-year marriage to Cynthia, his college sweetheart. Adultery did not sit well with his image as a Beatle. Especially with a twice-married Japanese artist whose main claim to fame so far had been a bizarre film of people's backsides. Memories of Japan's conduct during World War Two still hung in the air, which gave free rein to appalling racist remarks being hurled in Yoko's direction.

Barry Miles – then a close friend of McCartney's, and the

architect behind the Zapple label subsidiary of Apple, which focused on avant-garde spoken-word recordings – often saw at first hand how the other Beatles and the band's inner circle reacted to Yoko's presence.

He told me: 'John railed against anyone who suggested that the other Beatles and the staff at Apple hated Yoko because they were racists. That was never the case as far as I could tell. They didn't hate her. But the problem was they didn't love her either.'

Now the months of public opprobrium, coupled with John's detachment from his bandmates and his attachment to heroin, had forced the couple into a kind of quarantine. But midway through February, they received a letter that would change Lennon's life, and public image, for ever.

Peter Watkins was in the vanguard of a new wave of British TV directors whose gritty approach to filmmaking brought uncomfortable truths into people's living rooms. His groundbreaking 1964 BBC docudrama *Culloden* was praised by critics for its graphic realism and cinéma vérité style. *The War Game*, screened a year later, used the same hand-held camera techniques to illustrate the after-effects of a nuclear attack on Kent to such a chilling degree that it was banned by the corporation.

Watkins was also on the fringes of the London underground movement, many of whose followers detected like-minded, anti-authoritarian tendencies in Lennon, whose own anti-war declarations, especially on the subject of the conflict in Vietnam, had often swum against the tide of popular opinion.

Watkins wrote to Lennon, pointing out how the 'shadowy establishment figures' behind public corporations were still trying to control people's lives during humanity's most liberal and radical decade. Lennon would recall: 'It was a very long letter stating just what's happening – how the media is really controlled, how it's all run, and everything else that people really know deep down. He said: "People in your position have a responsibility to use the media for world peace." And we sat on the letter for about three weeks, thinking: "Well, we're doing our best. All you need is love, man."

That letter just sort of sparked it all off. It was like getting your induction papers for peace!'

Lennon was the archetypal rebel without a cause. Without Watkins' intervention, who knows what path his life might have taken? It seems reasonable to consider whether he would have been driven to write such anthemic songs extolling human brotherhood (and sisterhood) as 'Give Peace A Chance' and 'Imagine'.

For his part, Watkins downplays the part he played in Lennon's creative rebirth, an awakening that helped light the beacon for a movement that would unite millions of young people all over the world and, in no small way, help bring about the end of the Vietnam War.

In an email to me he wrote: 'Yes, in 1969 I sent John Lennon and Yoko Ono a statement about our responsibility as public communicators. I sent the same statement to a large number of other "public communicators" in the UK. I do not have the original text of what I wrote, but I think it was along the lines of our shared responsibility as "communicators" to address serious issues facing our society.

'I imagine that I was driven to write that statement as a counter-reaction to the banning of *The War Game*. Subsequently, John and Yoko gave interviews to the media about the effect that my statement had on their work. And I also received a note from them: "Thanks for your letter. We agree. We're trying. What next?"'

That, indeed, was a very good question.

*

McCartney, meanwhile, was desperately trying to head off an internal crisis. He had been forced to take stock of his life. Linda's pregnancy was now confirmed, their baby due in August if all went to plan. But his prospective joy at becoming a father for the first time was tempered by the turbulence swirling around the group. He continued to tinker away without much enthusiasm at new songs such as 'Another Day', 'Back Seat Of My Car' and 'Junk', a promising relic left over from their sojourn in India the previous spring.

He had been drained by the mental toll the 'Get Back' sessions had exacted on him. Worse, Klein was starting to invade his dreams. 'I used to have nightmares that Klein was a dentist and he was chasing me with a drill,' he said.

He fulfilled the occasional Apple obligation outwith business, breaking cover to appear at a launch party alongside Jimi Hendrix and Donovan atop the Post Office Tower in London on 23 February to mark Mary Hopkin's debut album *Postcard*. On the surface, he was his usual amiable self, working the room and talking up the talents of one of Apple's prized recording artists. But his interest in the young Welsh singer was already waning. He had produced her Apple debut hit single, 'Those Were The Days' – it unseated 'Hey Jude' at the top of the UK charts – and overseen the tracks on *Postcard*, which included songs written by Donovan and one by Harry Nilsson.

Hopkin herself would recall: 'I was aware that it was disorganised. I think everyone involved in Apple would agree on that. I think they were just finding their feet; it was early days for them, and a lot of them were new to it anyway. Derek Taylor mentioned in an interview that my management set-up was pretty dreadful. I had no one to represent me at the time. Eventually, my brother-in-law took over as manager, but there was no one at Apple. Paul's priority was The Beatles and that was only natural.'

Ringo Starr was for his part hoping that the movies would make him a big star. He'd leapt at the chance of taking part in *The Magic Christian* in order to put clear blue water between himself and the band after the toxicity of 'Get Back'.

A longtime fan of *The Goons*, he and Peter Sellers had been friends for several years before appearing together on set. Only seven months earlier, the actor had offered Starr the use of his luxury yacht moored off Sardinia as a bolthole when the drummer could no longer stand the ill-feeling that was poisoning the White Album sessions. It was while on the yacht that Starr started writing

'Octopus's Garden', a song destined to become a whimsical delight on *Abbey Road*. For the next three months, Starr dutifully turned up on set every minute he was required. He didn't even mind the rigid 9 a.m. curtain call. But Sellers' frequent mood swings were harder to fathom. 'I knew [Sellers] quite well, but suddenly there he was going into character and I got confused,' he would recall. 'The amazing thing with Peter was that, though we would work all day and go out and have dinner that night – and we would usually leave him laughing hysterically because he was hilarious – the next morning we'd say "Hi, Pete," and we'd have to start again. There was no continuation. You had to make the friendship start again from nine o'clock every morning. We'd all be laughing at six o'clock that night, but the next morning it would be "Hi, Pete," then "Oh God". We'd have to knock the wall down again to say hello. Sometimes we'd be asked to leave the set because Peter Sellers was being Peter Sellers.'

Sellers proved to be difficult throughout the shoot. Denis O'Dell was called upon several times to get him back on track amid the tantrums and suicide threats. And he later acknowledged the part Starr played in keeping Sellers on message.

'Ringo was the ideal person to keep Peter in check,' he wrote in his own Apple memoirs. 'Ringo was more famous, and had a more equable outlook on life, which could not help but have a calming influence on those around him. Although Peter would never adopt his laidback attitude to acting, I'm sure Ringo's presence was beneficial. Even Peter Sellers would have felt ridiculous throwing a tantrum in front of Ringo Starr.'

Sellers admired the Beatle's acting talent. Starr said: 'He always said I was a natural mime and that I can speak with my eyes. He would always say, "It's your eyes, Ring, it's your eyes. They'll be two hundred feet big up there on the screen, you know."'

Away from extracurricular activities, 'Get Back', the film project McCartney hoped would be their salvation, remained firmly in limbo. More than three hundred hours of footage was in the can but none of the band could face going through the reels. That was

Lindsay-Hogg's job. Then there was the music – take upon take of lifeless, sub-par performances. 'The most miserable sessions on earth,' Lennon later called them. 'It was the worst recorded shit of all time'.

Again, no one could bear to listen to any of it, even though songs like 'Let It Be', 'Don't Let Me Down', 'I've Got A Feeling', 'Get Back' and 'Two Of Us' would later emerge almost unscathed. That was Glyn Johns' job. And in late February, he was tasked with sifting through the tapes to turn them into an album that they could all at least bear to hear.

'It was obviously a fascinating experience,' Johns said later. 'I was a Beatles fan, everybody was, and felt The Beatles were wonderful, but having been so incredibly busy at the period of time up to then, I didn't really know any Beatle records, although I'd obviously heard them on the radio from time to time – I don't think I'd actually bought one, although I may have bought *Rubber Soul*, but anyway . . . the point is that I admired them, but they weren't necessarily my cup of tea as far as what I wanted to do, although I was extremely flattered that they should ask me to work with them, and so I did.

'The point I'm trying to make with all this preamble was that by the time I actually got into a room with them, although I was quite used to working with famous people, and was very rarely fazed by anyone I met, no matter how much I admired them, actually being in a room with The Beatles for the first time – all four of them with nobody else there – was pretty weird, and I suddenly realised how extraordinary the whole situation was, having never given it a lot of thought before. The time I worked with them was at the end of their career, obviously, and the *Let It Be* thing was something of a fiasco. It proved, however, to be an extraordinarily educational period for me – it obviously couldn't have been anything else, but that was why I wanted to do it, because I knew I'd learn something.'

'The extraordinary thing,' he added, 'is that they proved up to that point that they were the masters of the "Produced Record", yet the stuff I did with them wasn't "produced" in that way at all, it was all recorded live in a room, in a rehearsal situation. And for that, I think it has great value, because I originally put together an album of rehearsals, with chat and jokes and bits of general conversation in between the tracks, which was the way I wanted *Let It Be* ('Get Back') to be – breakdowns, false starts.

'Really, the idea was that at the time, they were viewed as being the be-all-and-end-all, sort of up on a pedestal, beyond touch, just gods, completely gods, and what I witnessed going on at these rehearsals was that, in fact, they were hysterically funny, but very ordinary people in many ways. And they were capable of playing as a band, which everybody was beginning to wonder about at that point, because they hadn't done so for some time – everything had been prepared in advance, everything had been overdubbed and everything. And they proved in that rehearsal that they could still sing and play at the same time, and they could make records without all those weird and wonderful sounds on them.'

That became an obsession with Johns. 'I got the bit between my teeth about it, and one night, I mixed a bunch of stuff that they didn't even know I'd recorded half the time – I just whacked the recorder on for a lot of stuff that they did, and gave them an acetate the following morning of what I'd done, as a rough idea of what an album could be like, released as it was. There was one thing that only happened once, a song that Paul played to the others, which I believe he later used on one of his ensuing albums, called "Teddy Boy", and I have a tape of Paul actually teaching the others this song. I loved it, and I was hoping they'd finish it and do it, because I thought it was really good. But my version does go on a bit, and they're just going round and round, trying to get the chord sequence right, I suppose, and the best bit is where John Lennon gets bored – he obviously doesn't want to play it any more, and starts doing his interjections. They came back and said they didn't like it, or each individual bloke came in and said he didn't like it, and that was the end of that.'

Lennon was still keen for Billy Preston to stay inside the fold. He had received an Apple contract and was now a bona fide member of the band's own musician's union, superior to a session player but never a fully fledged affiliate. Preston was naturally keen to maintain his Fab Four CV but had a number of obligations to fulfil back home in America before he could give The Beatles his full focus.

But on 22 February he found himself at Trident Studios working out the keyboard chords to a new Lennon song, a proto-heavy-rock song known at this point simply as 'I Want You'.

The end of the 'Get Back' recordings also blew the full-time whistle on Alex Mardas's attempt to install a recording studio in the Apple basement. Geoff Emerick, a former EMI engineer who had worked closely with The Beatles up to the White Album, had been employed by Apple at the start of the month to rip out all the bizarre wiring and cables and more or less build a new studio from scratch. That work was ongoing, which meant the band had to temporarily relocate to Trident Studios.

Not surprisingly, 'I Want You' was at this moment a work in progress. During one jam, Preston took the lead vocal and steered the song into much funkier territory. Raw and unvarnished, 'I Want You' was a musical distillation of Lennon's unceasing lust for Yoko and consisted of just thirty-four words, with the title repeated no fewer than sixteen times.

So far as Harrison was concerned, there had been signs that the band's dark horse was ready to come up on the inside fence. One song in particular instinctively felt right. Harrison knew that in terms of melody, 'Something' was more than just a throwaway. The Beatles had made two passes at the song on 28 January before tossing it aside. Even George Martin had dismissed the song as lightweight and derivative. But Harrison's non-Beatle friends loved the tune. Now, if only he could write lyrics to match the song's irresistible melody, possibly the best he had ever come up with.

Furthermore, the middle eight also needed work. However, it was only when Harrison was laid up in a hospital bed that the fog finally cleared.

On 25 February, his twenty-sixth birthday, he stole quietly into Abbey Road to record demos of three songs – 'Something', 'Old

Brown Shoe' and 'All Things Must Pass' – which The Beatles had half-heartedly tried to record during the 'Get Back' sessions. Harrison liked them so much that he privately reckoned they might be wasted on The Beatles. He had already mentioned to Lennon that he was mulling over the idea of a solo album. Still, he was in two minds as he committed the songs to tape on 8-track. The truth probably lies somewhere in between. It is likely that the recordings were meant as demos for the other Beatles to learn their parts from.

On 'Old Brown Shoe', Harrison recorded two takes with vocals and piano, onto which he overdubbed two electric guitar tracks. One of these guitar overdubs was played low on the fretboard, and was later adapted by McCartney for the bass part on The Beatles' recording, while the other was higher and included a solo.

Harrison then recorded two takes of 'All Things Must Pass', singing live to his tremolo guitar accompaniment. A second track also featuring guitar and vocals was then polished off. 'Something' also featured vocals and electric guitar, with a piano overdub. The songs were mixed and cut to acetate discs for Harrison to listen to at home. At this point he was considering handing 'Something' to Joe Cocker to record, the Sheffield singer with the rasping vocal having already enjoyed a massive hit with his cover of 'With A Little Help From My Friends'. For now, however, all three demos remained locked away in an unmarked mental compartment beside at least two dozen more. As The Beatles' winter of discontent gave way to the first snowdrops of spring, an emboldened Harrison was already starting the process of folding away all his yesterdays. At last, he thought, here comes the sun . . .

Paul McCartney and bride-to-be Linda Eastman prepare to leave for their wedding ceremony on 12 March.

Standing in front of the Rock of Gibraltar, on 20 March, the newly married Lennons proudly show off their wedding licence before heading to Amsterdam for the world's most public and bizarre honeymoon.

The last time John Lennon stood on a concert stage in full view of an audience was The Beatles' last moment as a touring band. Pausing only for the pop world's first selfie – Lennon had left a time-lapse camera mounted on Starr's drum kit to document the significance of the occasion – the band sprinted along the diamond contours of Candlestick Park, home to Major League Baseball's San Francisco Giants, for the safety of the windowless 'meat wagon' – the nickname a metaphor for the claustrophobia of their own fame – that protected them from 25,000 screaming fans. And it was Lennon, typically, who minutes later called a permanent halt to The Beatles' incessant record-tour-record-tour treadmill.

Now, nine hundred and sixteen days after that final performance, Lennon was back on the boards (the January rooftop show having hardly qualified as a real show). Yet hardly anyone among the four hundred-strong audience inside Lady Mitchell Hall in Cambridge University recognised the Beatle in their midst on Sunday, 2 March.

Lennon's hair reached halfway down his back. Clad in black denim jeans and jacket, he looked deathly pale and his famous horn-rimmed glasses made his thin face seem owlish and slightly threatening. And right now, in this setting, he was way out of his rock 'n' roll comfort zone. This was, after all, Yoko's gig, with Lennon her mere wingman. Still, it was a rare moment, only the second time any Beatle had ever performed on stage without the others.

Months earlier, Yoko had accepted an invitation from poet Anthony Barnett to play at an event called Natural Music: International Avant-Garde Concert Workshop, a freeform jazz showcase featuring some fifteen prominent musicians, notably John Stevens on percussion and piano and Danish saxophonist John Tchicai.

Yoko said: 'Near the date, they called me, asking if I was still coming . . . they didn't know if my plans had changed or not. "Tell him you're coming with a band," John whispered from the side. John and I thought it was a riot, but we didn't know how they would take it at the other end of the phone. Was it all right to bring a rocker? But the guy held his ground well. It was Cambridge, so the greeting committee was cordial but cool. John took that in, of course.'

The curious thing, of course, was that Johnny hated jazz. But on the day he put his misgivings to one side and took up position with his back to the audience and coaxed feedback and atonal noises from his Epiphone Casino guitar while Yoko announced a piece called 'Cambridge 1969' and started to howl and shriek into a microphone.

'He joined me on the stage and played underneath my vocal,' said Yoko. 'He played an incredibly creative avant-garde guitar that no one in the world had ever heard before and since. The audience didn't react to it. I was probably the only musician who was totally impressed by it.' By any stretch of musical imagination, it was a bizarre performance, light years away from The Beatles. After about twenty minutes, in the spirit of the event, Stevens and Tchicai gingerly joined in before the whole thing wrapped some nine minutes later.

As it happened, the entire performance was recorded by the Cambridge University Tape Recording Society. Lennon and Yoko's segment was also recorded by Apple engineers and would be released the following month on the experimental album *Unfinished Music No. 2: Life With The Lions*. Sadly, it was not filmed. As a piece of cinéma vérité it would have been fascinating.

Barnett, however, was furious at the way the duo had seemingly hijacked the entire event for their own egotistical purposes.

I contacted Barnett to ask him for his version of events. Initially, he held firm to a near fifty-year vow of silence on the matter while making clear the fact that his anger had not dissipated in any way. But my correspondence spurred him to go on the record for the first time.

'I do not have to tell you how disgraceful John's attitude was and Yoko's is,' he wrote. 'What prompts me to open up now, forty-seven years later, is that every so often I am approached to tell the story. Till now I have done so only to a limited extent. A trawl through the web brings up references in books, interviews and online, a few all right, most garbled, others plain wrong. So there is reason to set the record straight.'

Much of his disdain springs from the fact that Apple's subsequent release featured only the Lennons, with the rest of the cast reduced to the role of extras at what, after all, was their own show. And when Lennon and Yoko released the recording, they resisted all efforts by Barnett for a contribution to help offset the £130 losses the event had incurred. Then, as he tried to organise the release of the tapes on a double album through Polydor, the exercise was capsized by wave after wave of record-company red tape.

Fifty years down the line, the upshot is Barnett never received a penny but still retains ownership of the original audio reels of the show. His recollections, however, are at odds with those of a number of other witnesses. In a 2010 interview for the *Cambridge News*, Tchicai betrayed none of Barnett's antipathy: 'John was very pleasant, quiet, calm. Both of them were like this. I remember seeing them come in an old Rolls-Royce with a chauffeur wearing funny clothes, it was some kind of military uniform. I also recall John had a big alarm clock and when they started performing, he set it to ring at a certain time . . . that was the signal for the end of their part.'

Wingman he may have been to Yoko, but the significance of the occasion never left Lennon. Cambridge '69 may have been as far from his rock 'n' roll roots as it was possible to get, but it afforded him a tantalising glimpse of an alternative future. In 1980, days before his death, he told the BBC's Andy Peebles: 'That was the first time I had appeared un-Beatled. I just hung around and played feedback and people got very upset when they finally recognised me. "What's he doing here?" It's always "stay in your bag". So when she tried to rock, they said, "What's she doing here?" And when I went with her and tried to be the instrument and not project, like a sort of [Ike] Turner to her Tina, only her Tina was different, avant-garde Tina – well, even some of the jazz guys got upset.'

In another interview, he credited Yoko's freeform approach with liberating him as a guitarist. 'What she'd done for my guitar playing was to free it the way she'd freed her voice from all the restrictions. I was always thinking, "Well, I can't play like Eric Clapton or George Harrison or BB King." But then I gave up trying to play like that and just played whatever I could, whatever way I could, to match it to her voice.'

Paul McCartney found out about the Cambridge performance the same way as everybody else – by reading about it in the papers the next day. As he read the reports he couldn't help but feel a stab of pain. News of Lennon's impromptu stage return offered hope to all those promoters who had long ago accepted that The Beatles would never again play live. Quickest out the traps was Sid Bernstein, the American former GI who had risked everything on booking them for the Carnegie Hall in the days when they were still an unknown quantity across the pond and Beatlemania was picking up speed. The 'sold-out' notices at their gigs there told him he had scored the biggest act since Elvis, and he subsequently promoted their stadium shows at Shea in 1965 and 1966. Bernstein was adamant that gave him an 'in' with the band and even though three years had passed, he reckoned he had first refusal. Midway through March, he flew to London and turned up unannounced at Apple, convinced that his charm offensive would succeed. In his pocket he carried a $4m cheque for four gigs in Miami, Los Angeles, Chicago and New York. But Bernstein never even got past first base. None of the band would meet him.

'The Beatles are the biggest draw in the world but they are letting their fans down by refusing to play their new songs in public,' he said that month. 'It would be a bigger comeback than Elvis.'

Of a more pressing nature was the fate of the moribund tapes for 'Get Back', which were still languishing in the Apple basement. A decision had to be made – either scrap them for good or attempt a last-ditch salvage job.

On Monday, 10 March, Lennon and McCartney delivered the same ultimatum to Glyn Johns. When he said he would take on the challenge, they promptly handed over a boxful of tapes. 'I had to do it,' recalled Johns. 'Picture the scene. You are there with John Lennon and Paul McCartney and they are asking me to bring some kind of order from chaos. It was a huge task but you just couldn't say no, could you? I have always loved making records and that was what they were asking me to do.'

In the meantime, McCartney and Harrison were drawn back to the studio along with Preston to help an old mate. Jackie Lomax, who played with Merseyside band The Undertakers, had been one of the first names on Apple's A&R roster. McCartney, Harrison and Starr had played on his first Apple single, the Harrison-penned rocker 'Sour Milk Sea', which had flopped. With his debut album, *Is This What You Want?*, due for release, a new single was needed. Harrison had briefly considered giving Lomax the now lyrically complete 'Something' before changing his mind and deciding finally to offer it to Joe Cocker, who included it on his second album after it became the standout track on *Abbey Road*.

On 11 March, McCartney and Harrison set aside their business differences to play on Lomax's cover of The Coasters' 'Thumbin' A Ride', a favourite of McCartney's, the Beatle reckoning it would be perfect for Lomax. The second song committed to tape was 'Going Back To Liverpool', which, however, would remain locked in the vaults for years. McCartney's decision to play on the session later seemed strange – he was due to get married the next day.

McCartney arrived at Marylebone Registry Office to do the decent thing by the now four months pregnant Linda. It was the third Beatle shotgun wedding after Cynthia Lennon and Maureen Starkey. Linda was a reluctant bride, slightly fearful over the future direction her life would take as a Beatle wife and the bitchiness her new status would attract from jealous fans. She herself acknowledged: 'I was an unfashionable woman who married a Beatle.'

McCartney had already tipped off a select few friendly journalists about the occasion before Apple made it official with a press release to catch the final editions of the Fleet Street papers. Years later,

Paul offered up a possible explanation for his decision to head to the Apple Studios the night before his wedding and leave his bride-to-be at home, listening with her young daughter Heather to the catcalls from the small knot of fans gathered outside.

In *Many Years from Now*, he admitted: 'We were crazy. We had a big argument the night before we got married and it was nearly called off. We were very up and down, quite funky to the eventual image of "Twenty-five years of married bliss! Aren't they lucky for people in showbiz?"'

Then again, it could have been his reported last-minute purchase of a £12 wedding ring that ticked Linda off.

At the wedding, the only major hitch was the late arrival by train from Birmingham of Paul's best man, his brother Michael. When the couple emerged as man and wife, after 'giggling' their way through the ceremony, they were met by dozens of sobbing fans. One told the BBC: 'I just had to be here, but I still can't really believe it. Paul was always my favourite.'

None of the other Beatles were invited. McCartney claimed he simply couldn't remember if he had told them. 'It didn't seem important,' he said in 2001 during a family-produced *Wingspan*. 'It was really about the two of us.' In *Many Years from Now*, he was more candid. 'We were all pissed off with each other. We certainly weren't a gang anymore.' Harrison certainly knew since he and Pattie were invited to the lunch that followed at the Ritz. It's inconceivable that the others weren't aware of his plans.

As it turned out, while the McCartneys were tying the knot, John and Yoko were at Abbey Road, finessing *Life With The Lions*, Starr was still tied up with his film and Harrison was putting the finishing touches to the Lomax songs. At the Ritz, the guests included Princess Margaret and her husband Lord Snowdon. But Harrison's plans for the day were sent into disarray when a phone call from Pattie was put through to the Apple studio.

She was at Kinfauns, their bungalow home in Esher, Surrey, playing genial hostess to a group of visitors from Scotland Yard's drug squad. She recalled the events in her memoir *Wonderful*

Tonight: 'Suddenly I heard a lot of cars on the gravel in the drive – far too many for it to be just George. My first thought was that maybe Paul and Linda wanted to party after the wedding. Then the bell rang. I opened the door to find a policewoman and a dog standing outside. At that moment the back doorbell rang and I thought: "Oh, my God, this is so scary! I'm surrounded by police."

'The man in charge introduced himself as Detective Sergeant Norman Pilcher from Scotland Yard and handed me a piece of paper. I knew why he was there: he thought we had drugs, and he said he was going to search the house. In they came, about eight policemen through the front, another five or six through the back and there were more in the greenhouse. The policewoman said she would follow me while the others searched and didn't let me out of her sight.

'I said: "Why are you doing this? We don't have any drugs. I'm going to phone my husband." I rang George at Apple. "George, it's your worst nightmare. Come home."'

The officers clearly thought the Harrisons would be at Paul's wedding. The timing was not a coincidence.

After conferring with Derek Taylor, Harrison calmly told Pattie to let the police do what they had to do. But by the time he arrived home, he was furious. And when he glimpsed a newspaper photographer lurking in the garden, it only confirmed his suspicions of a fit-up. As he marched into his house, it quickly became clear that the police, using a sniffer dog called, with no hint of irony, Yogi had found what they came for. A large chunk of cannabis, discovered in a shoe, would serve as Exhibit A when the matter came to court.

Pilcher had already busted Mick Jagger, Brian Jones and Donovan, as well as Lennon and Yoko the previous year. National treasures or not, The Beatles were no longer protected from the law.

Taylor recalled: 'I was with George in the office when that call came through. It was the end of a long day at Apple. Pattie rang and said, "They're here – the law is here," and we knew what to do by then. We phoned Release's lawyer, Martin Polden [Release had been formed in London to provide legal assistance to those who had been busted for drug offences]. We had a routine: he came round to Apple, and we all went down to Esher, where the police were well ensconced by then – and I stood bail for George and Pattie. They went off to the police station. We were all extremely indignant because it was the day of Paul's wedding, a poor way to celebrate it.

'George kept his dope in the box where dope went, and his joss sticks went in the joss stick box. He was a man who ran an orderly late-Sixties household, with beautiful things and some nice stuff to smoke. In my opinion he didn't have to be busted because he was doing nobody any harm. I still believe what they did was an intrusion into his personal life.'

Harrison never denied having drugs at home but it didn't require a leap of faith for him to believe the hash had been planted. He said, 'I'm a tidy man. I keep my socks in the sock drawer and stash in the stash box. It's not mine.' After being released from a local police station, the Harrisons returned home before heading to the McCartneys' wedding reception.

When he narrated the day's events to his fellow guests, no one could quite believe it. But what is the point of being a Beatle if you can't use your fame to your advantage? Spotting Princess Margaret, George made a beeline for her. 'We got busted today,' he told her. 'Can you do anything?' Royal rebel she may have been, but even the party-loving Margaret knew where to draw the establishment line. Possibly fearing headlines of the 'Queen's sister helps Beatle George escape drug charge' variety, she grabbed Snowdon by the arm and left.

The affair strengthened Harrison's conviction that it was time to quit The Beatles. He told the *Daily Express's* David Wigg that month: 'All I'm doing is acting out the part of Beatle George and we're all acting out our parts. Even if it's being a Beatle for the rest of my life, it's still only a temporary thing.' He would ultimately be proved correct on both counts.

*

David Nutter instantly recognised the voice on the other end of the line when the phone rang early at his London photographic studio on Wednesday, 19 March. It belonged to Peter Brown, one of the key movers and shakers in the days when London was still swinging. Brown was among a select group, including Cilla Black and her husband Bobby Willis, who had financially backed Nutter's brother Tommy, a Savile Row tailor whose flamboyant fashion sense was his golden ticket to the capital's showbiz elite. As a director of Apple, and Brian Epstein's former right-hand man, Brown's biggest calling card was his membership of The Beatles' high command.

Nutter told me: 'Peter called me up at my studio. He just said, "I need you to come to Gibraltar tomorrow and bring your camera." I had no idea what it was for, but I had no reason to distrust Peter or have any reservations. I knew that Apple would probably take care of all the expenses et cetera. Yes, I was obviously intrigued but Peter made it clear that secrecy was paramount and he didn't want to say too much on the phone. And the reason for that was simple . . . I think that my phone was tapped.

'I was involved with *Oz* magazine [a radical, late-Sixties, left-wing publication] and I always got the feeling I could hear clicks on the phone. They were tapping everybody's phone, probably even The Beatles'. So maybe Peter sensed that and thought it was better not to go into any details. But it was all very cloak and dagger.'

The reason for the covert arrangements became clear at 8.30 the following morning when Nutter stepped off a privately chartered Hawker Siddeley jet piloted by Captain Trevor Copleston and onto the tarmac at Gibraltar. In the lounge he came face to face with Brown. Next to him were a couple dressed in matching cream outfits, John Lennon and Yoko Ono, who was also sporting a wide-brimmed floppy white hat. It was only then that Nutter was told why he was there. The couple were getting married – in secret, of course – and his job was to record the civil ceremony for posterity. Brown would be on best man duties, just eight days after he had acted as a witness at the McCartneys' wedding.

Nutter said, 'I was in shock. I couldn't believe it. My brother knew John and made clothes for him. His shop was opposite Apple. So I suppose I got the job through him in a way. But that was the first time I had met John. At that time John was probably the most famous person in the world but I never was very starstruck. I was never in awe of everybody really because I was used to meeting lots of famous people. John was just a nice, North Country English person. He was very down to earth and we could all have a laugh. He was lovely. I was very pleasantly surprised at how non-starry he was.'

Lennon and Yoko had spent a few days in Paris's Plaza Athénée Hotel before apparently deciding on the spur of the moment to follow McCartney's example. 'Intellectually,' he said, 'we didn't believe in getting married, but one doesn't love someone just intellectually. For two people marriage still has the edge over just living together.' More likely, they were both just jealous of Paul and Linda's wedding-day publicity.

Lennon's initial idea was for his wedding to be blessed by a suitably qualified captain on a cross-channel ferry called *The Dragon*, which sailed from Southampton. But that was swiftly scrapped due to difficulties with Yoko's visa while European countries such as France and Holland required a minimum two-week residency for any couple wishing to get hitched on a whim. Brown, in tandem with Apple's expensive lawyers, brokered the perfect solution. In Gibraltar there was no need for anyone to abide by any outmoded residency requirements. All they needed were passports and the necessary papers. It was the last place on earth anyone would expect to see John and Yoko getting hitched. Lennon said, 'We chose Gibraltar because it is quiet, British and friendly.'

With Brown and Nutter in tow, the wedding party made its way to the British consulate. After a brief wait, with Lennon nervously smoking a cigarette, the elderly registrar, Cecil Wheeler, carried out the formalities before pronouncing them man and wife. Nutter was roped in as an official witness, his name being misspelt on the marriage certificate.

The couple, of course, knew their cover would soon be blown. Some local photographers, spotting a financial opening, rushed to picture the newlyweds before they could board the plane that would take them to Paris. The cat was quickly out of the bag. Nutter joined the Lennons on the flight to Paris, his reward being dozens of exclusive pictures of a surreal day.

He said: 'The interesting thing was he never talked about The Beatles. It was all about other stuff he was doing with Yoko. In fact, if you didn't know any better you would never have thought he was a member of The Beatles. He saw himself more as a conceptual artist, which of course was what she was. He was all about her exhibitions. He wasn't very Beatle-y at all. He was beginning to strike out on his own and carving his own identity as a solo artist. We bonded over old English comedies. We had a good old laugh on the plane but the jokes went right over Yoko's head.'

Public reaction was mixed. One letter, in the *Daily Express*, alleged that Lennon had somehow committed treason by marrying a Japanese woman. The fans were, naturally, deeply divided. The Beatles' American fan club made an appeal for tolerance: 'Please try to understand that we should at least give Yoko the same chance we are giving Linda and that Maureen and Pattie got. If it makes John happy I guess we should be enthused as well.' Linda McCartney would soon have good reason to treat those words with wry contempt.

On 21 March, without fanfare, Allen Klein was formally announced as business manager of Apple. Other than in the highbrow business pages of *The Times* and the *Daily Telegraph*, it barely rippled the surface compared to the acres of newsprint devoted to the McCartneys' wedding, But it was a significant power grab nonetheless.

'Everything changed when Klein took over . . . for a start Paul wasn't there,' recalled Neil Aspinall. The official announcement was made while McCartney was still on honeymoon, visiting his new in-laws in the States. A few days earlier, when the matter had been put to a vote, he had dispatched his solicitor, Charles Corman, to offer a token protest. It was a futile gesture. 'I didn't trust him and I certainly didn't want him as my manager,' was his succinct summing-up of Klein later. McCartney decided to stay away from Apple whenever Klein was there.

Klein had drawn up a cost-cutting plan to pull the company back from the brink. On the hitlist this month were several eye-catching company names: Aspinall, Peter Brown, Ron Kass, the head of Apple, Denis O'Dell, office manager Alistair Taylor and his namesake Derek, whose open-door press office was more like a never-ending bacchanal. Prominent they may have been, but their Apple salaries were nowhere near the super-tax bracket occupied by their employers. As Brown later noted, no one got rich while riding The Beatles coat-tails. Rather, Klein was more concerned with the influence some of them had over Lennon, Harrison and Starr. He was a master of the black art of manipulation and knew full well the value of playing one person against another. But Klein was canny enough to bide his time before turning the full weight of his arsenal on the key players at Savile Row. For example, the Lennons' caviar account at Harrod's remained untouched, as did Starr's open-ended credit line at such noted London gambling joints as the Playboy Club and Les Ambassadors Club. And Taylor's shelves continued to be replenished with the finest produce, from vintage wines and Scotch to the best weed in London.

Klein had outflanked the Eastmans and McCartney while continuing to mollify Lennon, Harrison and Starr with a succession of dubious 'FYM' – fuck you money – promises. The debacle over Nems continued to eat away at him, though. For all that John Eastman's letter may have shredded any hopes of a deal with Clive Epstein, Klein still hoped to bring Leonard Richenberg and Triumph back to the negotiating table. He remained convinced that he could yet win back Nems, and save The Beatles a fortune in the process.

But there was, of course, a flipside to his ambitions. On his watch The Beatles had lost control of Nems while EMI had frozen £1.3m in royalties from sales of the White Album pending the legal outcome of his contretemps with Richenberg. It wasn't the prettiest picture.

As always, Klein was ready to do what he did best – hustle on behalf of his clients for an improved royalty deal. He used a well-practised combination of bully-boy methods and scare tactics to browbeat cowering record company executives into coughing up the money that rightly belonged to those who were making it in the first place. It was a strategy that had worked successfully for Bobby Darin, Sam Cooke, The Animals, Donovan and, more recently, the Stones. Now, as he prepared to declare war on Sir Joseph Lockwood at EMI, he had the biggest bargaining chip of all.

'These boys want to work but you have to motivate them,' he said as he prepared to sit down with Lockwood and EMI's lawyers in the middle of March to renegotiate the band's royalties deal with EMI and Capitol in America. The unspoken threat was that The Beatles could go on strike and, in the words of one observer, sing the national anthem backwards unless Klein got his way. But what Klein didn't know was that another major battlefront was about to open up.

Dick James had become a millionaire several times over thanks to the Lennon and McCartney hits that made up Northern Songs. But, of late, Lennon's public antics had appalled him, and now Harrison had been busted. Their behaviour was causing the stock price to wobble and James felt his primary obligation was to the three thousand shareholders of Northern Songs. So now, at the age of forty-nine, he was looking for a lucrative exit plan. Like Clive Epstein, loyalty to 'the boys' counted for more than a fat bank account, even though both were mutually bound to each other. But for months a cold chill had blown through his relationship with The Beatles. Since Brian Epstein's death, he was no longer given a free pass to sit in on studio sessions at EMI. Indeed, Lennon had forcibly shown him the door when he called in unexpectedly at Twickenham during the rancorous rehearsals for 'Get Back'.

The Beatles now saw him as just another 'suit' making money off their talent – a point made by Harrison in his witty putdown 'It's Only A Northern Song'. Their deal with the company was due to expire in 1973 and every instinct told James they would not renew it. Northern Songs without The Beatles would be like a vineyard that had finally dried up. Moreover, a permanent split could see the value of the company stock potentially crashing through the floor. And, in James's view, they had sold their soul to a diabolical man who was the direct opposite of Brian and his impeccable manners and genteel disposition. Klein, with his spitball tactics and expletive-driven outbursts, was the last person on earth he wanted to do business with.

James's path had often crossed that of Lew Grade during the Fifties, when the former was an aspiring crooner singing the theme tune to the popular British television show, *The Adventures of Robin Hood*. Grade was one of three pioneering brothers who formed a trident at the heart of British showbusiness. He ran Associated Television Ventures, a key plank of the ITV broadcasting network, and by the mid to late Sixties he was keen to expand the company's portfolio. The two men had remained on friendly terms when Dick's singing career faded and he went into music publishing.

Occasionally, Grade had thrown out a line to James about ATV buying Northern Songs. Enticing as they were, such overtures were always kicked into the long grass. Now, though, the landscape after Brian Epstein had been harshly redrawn. Midway through March, Dick James picked up the phone to call Lew Grade. Was he still interested in buying Northern Songs?

*

After their wedding, the Lennons had remained in Paris, hanging out with the likes of surrealist painter Salvador Dali and enjoying a degree of anonymity not afforded them in London or New York. Another sixteen years would pass before they would experience this inconspicuousness again.

Lennon was mulling over the idea of turning their nuptials into a song, 'The Ballad Of John And Yoko'. It was, as he freely admitted, more rock 'n' roll journalism than rock 'n' roll music. But from now on that was how he planned to live his life with her. And to do that they would need to place themselves at the heart of the world's media coverage. Their lives would become an open book for everyone to read. But how to do it . . . and for what purpose?

Lennon had long been identified as the maverick Beatle, a hero of the rapidly growing counterculture. The Cold War stand-off between America and Russia continued to stoke global tensions, but it was the Vietnam War and the burgeoning peace movement that would give the Lennons their most influential platform. The Beatles had long opposed the war between the Communist-backed Vietcong and the pro-Western Vietnamese Army, in the process trampling over Brian Epstein's diktat to avoid all things political. 'We didn't like the war and we told Brian that,' he recalled. In 1968, students had rioted on the streets of Washington, Belgrade, Berlin, Boston and Paris in protest at the war. There had been violent clashes between police and demonstrators at that year's Democratic National Convention in Chicago. The world's youth – or at least those in the West – were searching for a leader who could rally them together against political repression.

Peter Watkins had urged the Lennons to use their fame for something more meaningful than selling records. Lennon had been further spurred by an encounter in Paris with a Dutchman called Hans Boskamp, who worked for a record company and who talked him into holding a peace protest in Amsterdam. Boskamp recalled: 'He was incredibly preoccupied with the Vietnam War. When he said to me, "I want to do something, demonstrate against the war," I said, "Then you should go to Amsterdam. In Amsterdam, the Flower Power movement is in full swing." "That's a good idea," he said.'

And so early in the morning of Tuesday, 25 March, having a few days earlier summoned chauffeur Les Anthony to bring the white Rolls-Royce from London to the French capital, John and Yoko checked out of their hotel and drove to Amsterdam, a city Lennon had not been in since 1964. Apple had already sent an advance notice to the hotel telling them to expect a VIP and requesting the presidential suite on the fifth floor for a week. But they were completely unprepared for the day the Lennon circus hit town. Within minutes of their arrival, the Lennons had sent postcards to the local and international media inviting them to come the next day with the promise of 'a happening'. The press quickly joined the dots: John and Yoko in bed on honeymoon. It could only add up to one thing, couldn't it? After all, they had already appeared naked on the front of their first album. And this was Amsterdam, the anything-goes permissive capital of Europe.

John was shrewdly aware of how the 'bed-in' concept might titillate a voyeuristic media with its implicit promise of sexual exhibitionism. It guaranteed one thing – an audience. Of course the media fell for it. The next day dozens of journalists and photographers laid siege to room 902 in the hope of seeing the newly-weds taking Yoko's concept of performance art to a salacious new level. What they found were two people with beatific smiles dressed in neatly pressed pyjamas, each clenching a rose and announcing that they would be staying in bed for a week to promote world peace. In case they missed the point, crude hand-drawn posters with the words 'Bed Peace' and 'Hair Peace' were tacked onto the windows. Lennon's conversion from cynical rock star to St John the Peace Evangelist raised plenty of eyebrows within his inner circle, but his altered image seemed real enough to those who had noticed a change in him despite the borderline warfare at Apple. Peter Brown said, 'We hoped that John's pacifist stand would deflect some of the hostility that John and Yoko were experiencing in the press but characteristically John made peace a holy crusade and turned his honeymoon into a side show.'

The posters in the room were a play on words for Yoko's own art shows such as the one titled 'Cut Piece', which invited members of the public to take a pair of scissors to her clothes. But Lennon knew he had tapped into the zeitgeist, and the charge was electrifying.

He had learned that when the mass media takes an idea, they will amplify and simplify it. So he and Yoko realised that a message needed to be uncomplicated, yet novel and provocative.

Hour after hour, day after day, they fielded any questions from reporters and, in so doing, they shifted the debate from what level of American bombing of Vietnam was acceptable to the broader issue of war versus peace.

Lennon explained: 'We thought, the other side has war on TV every day, not only on the news but on the old John Wayne movies and every damn movie you see: war, war, war, war, war, kill, kill, kill, kill. We said: "Let's get some peace, peace, peace, peace in the headlines, just for a change." We thought it highly amusing that a lot of the world's headlines on 25 March 1969 were "Honeymoon Couple In Bed". Whoopee! Isn't that great news? So we would sell OUR product, which we call peace. And to sell a product you need a gimmick, and the gimmick we thought was "bed". And we thought "bed" because bed was the easiest way of doing it because we're lazy.

'It took us a long train of thought of hope to get the maximum publicity for what we sincerely believed in, which was peace.'

Keenly aware that they were being mocked worldwide, Lennon said, self-deprecatingly, 'We are happy to be the world's clowns . . . we stand a better chance under that guise, because all the serious people like Martin Luther King and Kennedy and Gandhi got shot.' Yoko, asked if she would be a dutiful wife, responded: 'No, but if that means bringing him his slippers all the time, I shall just do what I have to do.'

Lennon's antics raised the ire of those on the left and the right of the political spectrum. To the left, his pacifism seemed misplaced; they had never forgotten his uneasy compromise on his White Album song, 'Revolution', in which he had warned that he would never be an advocate of violence as a blunt tool to right the world's wrongs.

But if the left was hostile, the establishment press was outraged by the bed-ins. 'This must rank as the most self-indulgent demonstration of all time,' one *Daily Express* columnist wrote. To John and Yoko, for whom the bed-ins were deeply personal, the stark criticism cut to the bone.

Among their visitors was Fraser Watson, a member of an Apple-signed Scottish band, White Trash, who recalled their reactions to some of the more vicious media comments.

'It was very hurtful to them,' Watson told me. 'They genuinely thought they were doing a good thing. And remember this was the ultimate peaceful protest. There was no harm in it whatsoever. No one got arrested and no one got hurt, so what was the problem? So they gave people a laugh. When was that ever a crime?

'The amazing thing to me was how easy it was to get into the room. We just turned up because we had been appearing on this Dutch TV show but had run out of money. So we knew if we could get to John we could get to Apple and at least get enough money to bring us back home. He was in great form. He seemed genuine enough to me when he was going on about peace. But you try saying the same things twenty-four hours a day for six or seven days. It's bound to come across as a bit cynical but I have no doubt whatsoever that John and Yoko were totally sincere in what they were doing.'

Amidst all the earnestness, there were moments of levity. Scottish journalist Rick Wilson was working for a magazine in Amsterdam when he got the call to head to the Hilton. He recalled the scene before him in the *Guardian* in 2017: 'To be honest, I didn't understand then, and still don't, what that now-legendary "bed-in" was all about. It was to do with spreading a message of peace, but there were also undertones of helping the world's less fortunate, which didn't gel with John and Yoko's arrival in a white Rolls-Royce and their week-long stay in that citadel of American capitalism, the Hilton Hotel.

'There were about thirty of us, reporters and cameramen, summoned up to room 902, which looked out on to the roofs of a less colourful residential part of Amsterdam. Both dressed in pyjamas, John and Yoko were sitting on a big bed looking remarkably like each other. The Dutch may be extremely good at languages, and particularly English, but they are shy about showing the level of their proficiency to each other. So I ended up asking many of the questions in an attempt to find out what this was all about.

' "Why Amsterdam?" "It could have been anywhere really," said John. "But this is just one of those cities, you know. The youth thing and all that. And the beds here aren't bad at all . . ." "Why not Saigon or Dallas if peace is the cause?" "Because I'm dead scared of Saigon or Dallas. There's less chance of getting shot or crucified here." "Why the hair theme?" 'We intend to grow our hair even longer for the peace cause. Everybody should do it, all over the world – if only to bring about more awareness. But we're doing it with a sense of humour, too, because we think the world needs to laugh more." "Yes, people should first take their pants down before they start fighting," added Yoko.'

Although nothing was off limits, questions about The Beatles remained largely below the radar. Enquiries about their future were largely straight-batted by Lennon, who repeatedly gave the impression that his old gang were – clear business difficulties aside – still united under a common flag.

Three days into the bed-in, however, peace and love gave way to something darker. Lennon, a voracious newspaper reader, had ordered a number of British publications for his room every day. On 28 March, his eye was drawn to a *Financial Times* headline: 'ATV takes control of Northern Songs'. 'Uncle' Dick James had secretly sold his stake in the Lennon and McCartney songbook to Lew Grade.

Lennon was outraged at what he considered the worst kind of betrayal, perpetrated by two old men in suits.

Back in London, James was braced for the reactions. Unlike Clive Epstein, who was a member of Northern Songs' board because of the small shareholding Nems held in the company, James no longer felt loyalty to the band that had given him a millionaire's lifestyle. Dissent and mistrust had long ago fractured his relationship with Lennon and McCartney, so he reckoned he was entitled to map out a perfectly legal pathway to free himself from an increasingly bitter marriage.

The ATV deal had been worked out several days earlier. Both parties had arrived for discussions with their lawyers in the expectation of bruising negotiations. In the end, James and Grade comfortably agreed a price for the shareholding in his name and that of his business partner/accountant, Charles Silver. Grade recalled: 'I just said, "Let's settle this between us." In the end we agreed everything over a cup of tea. When the lawyers came in it was all done.'

Grade, with his ever-present Havana cigar, was the type of old-school impresario The Beatles despised. So James was fearful of the reactions of Lennon and McCartney, but it was Harrison who got to him first, accusing him of an act of betrayal at a meeting in which he was backed by Neil Aspinall and a mildly inebriated Derek Taylor. At least Clive Epstein had the decency to offer them first refusal on Nems, said Harrison.

Asked why he had not consulted the songwriters before deciding, James said, 'To telephone John and Paul would have been difficult. The call would have gone through a number of people and there was a need to keep it confidential.' He tried to placate the guitarist by pointing out that it was not as serious as he was making out, only to get the response, in broad Scouse: 'It's fucking serious to John and Paul is what it is.'

Harrison's intervention on behalf of Lennon and McCartney in absentia was puzzling. He had sold his small shareholding in the company months earlier, a token arrangement brokered by Brian Epstein when Northern was formed. Instead, he had set up his own publishing company, Harrisongs Ltd, and later formed another separate company, Singsong Ltd, in October 1968. (It would eventually be folded inside Harrisongs.) He had no personal ties to Northern.

So, while it might have been strange that he should speak for Lennon and McCartney, given the way they had treated him, Harrison was still a Beatle, still loyal.

James, for his part, refused to accept that he had done anything wrong. Who were they to saddle him with any guilt trip? The deed was done and there was nothing he nor Lennon and McCartney could do to stop it. Unless, of course, they were prepared to gain majority control of the company for themselves. That would mean buying enough shares to gain a fifty-one per cent majority. 'You are getting some very bad advice,' was James' parting shot. Harrison left knowing that another business battlefront had just presented itself.

Klein was enjoying a holiday in Puerto Rico when he received two calls – one from Lennon and the other from McCartney – summoning him on the first flight back to London. Initially, McCartney was indecisive. Who should he turn to? Klein or Eastman? Klein, no matter how much he disliked him, was a brutal and intimidating negotiator with a proven track record. But the Eastmans, father and son, were experts in the byzantine world of copyright ownership.

Ultimately, it came down to the Lennon-McCartney alliance to save the one thing that would bind them together for ever, their own copyrights. That meant, reluctantly, giving Klein the green light to ride into battle against Grade.

Contacted by the *Daily Express*, Paul offered this lone comment: 'You can safely assume that my shares are not for sale to ATV.' But Lennon had no such misgivings about the fight that lay ahead: 'They are my songs and I want to keep some of the end product . . . we are not going to sell and we advise all our friends to hang on to what they've got. Dick James? We don't think he was very nice. You'd have thought the first thing he would have done would have been to consult us.'

The Amsterdam bed-in continued for another two days before the couple called it quits and went on a spontaneous tour of Europe. As the month drew to a close, they had one last stunt to perform, setting up a brief base camp at Vienna's Hotel Sacher, where, yet again, an over-excited press corps arrived en masse. Ostensibly, the purpose of the visit was to promote Yoko's film *Rape*, which was due to premiere on Austrian television that night. But the real purpose was also to inform the world of the couple's new concept for total communication – Bagism.

Most of the journalists, just hoping to breathe the same air as a real-life Beatle, were dumbfounded by the couple's zany sense of self-parody and gift for self-publicity. John and Yoko stayed hidden inside a white bag, with John whistling a snatch of Johann Strauss's 'The Blue Danube'. It was hokum on an epic scale.

Yoko introduced Bagism as the natural extension of the bed-in. Eventually, one reporter broke the stunned silence, asking, 'Will you come out?' Lennon uttered an emphatic 'no' and added, 'This is a bag event – total communication.' To a wider audience, it seemed as if he had lost grip of his sanity, but again they overlooked the humour involved.

As Lennon later said, 'When we were in Amsterdam doing Bed Peace, halfway through the week we sort of realised a tag to put on what we're doing, which makes it easier for us and you to recognise what we're doing, by calling it Bagism. That means, if we have something to say or anybody has something to say, they can communicate from one room to another, and not confuse you with what colour your skin is, or how long your hair's grown, or how many pimples you've got.'

Asked by one reporter how his recent actions had changed the world, he responded: 'I couldn't give you a concrete example, except for a few good cartoons that came out of it and a good few reactions from readers' letters in England that I especially know about. Some old woman that said she's had the best laugh of her life. If the least we can do is give somebody a laugh, we're willing to be the world's clowns, because we think it's a bit serious at the moment and a bit intellectual. That's the least we can do, because everybody is talking about peace but nobody does anything about it in a peaceful way. If you donate your holiday instead of just sleeping with your wife and giggling, you might do something about it.'

*

Like everyone else, Harrison and Starr had watched as the Lennons' honeymoon circus continued to dominate the news. But if any of

The Beatles were worried about John's behaviour, they kept it to themselves. Starr, typically, had a wider perspective of the shift in public opinion towards the band. In an interview that month with music magazine *Hit Parader*, carried out during a break in filming on Cobham Common in Surrey, he said the cheeky, grinning moptops of Beatlemania were a thing of the past.

'No, I don't always understand [what the couple did], but then I am in a privileged position of being the person who is probably the closest to them and I can go and ask. I read the paper like anyone else and I think, "What's this? What's going on?" But then I can go and ask them what it's all about. People have really tried to typecast us. They think we are still little moptops, but we're not.'

With no group sessions in the diary, Harrison used the downtime to fine-tune a clutch of new songs, some of which had grown organically following his visit to Bob Dylan the previous autumn. The so-called Quiet Beatle was quietly confident that he was now finding his own voice. The demos laid down at the end of last month – 'Something', 'Old Brown Shoe' and 'All Things Must Pass' – had been added to a growing stockpile of strong compositions that were already beginning to form the outline of a possible solo album.

He said, 'I felt they were good songs. I didn't know if they were good Beatle songs but I liked them. I just wasn't sure about having to go through all the usual just to get them on a Beatles record. It was always a stressful process for me.'

As it happened, Harrison was already well down the road to finishing his second, deliberately non-commercial solo album. In February he had become the first musician in Britain to own a Moog IIIP synthesiser, a new-age electronic instrument that, with its swirling keyboard textures and white noise effects, would soon revolutionise rock music and be brought on board by the likes of Yes, Pink Floyd and Genesis, as well as The Beatles.

Harrison had first encountered it the previous year during a trip to California, where he was given a demonstration of its abilities by Paul Beaver, a Hollywood sound-effects specialist, and his collaborator Bernie Krause.

Knocked out by the instrument's seemingly limitless potential for creating new sounds and imitating others, he had immediately ordered one to be shipped to his home. Its arrival had been delayed for several months as Harrison haggled over a price – he reckoned he was Beatleproof when it came to actually paying for something, believing that his celebrity endorsement would entitle him to a substantial discount.

He was quickly captivated by his new plaything and spent hours programming it to reproduce the sounds he had heard in California, Krause having supplied him with a multi-track tape of the recording from the tutorial in America. Throughout March, he laboured to create and hone an eighteen-minute aural soundscape called 'Under The Mersey Wall'. In many ways, Harrison was dipping his toe into the unexplored waters of experimental sounds normally associated with Yoko.

When he wasn't so engaged in the studio, he could often be found at Twickenham watching Ringo on the *Magic Christian* set, enjoying hanging out with Sellers and comic surrealists like Graham Chapman and John Cleese. Harrison had already developed an interest in the art of film-making and was often seen deep in conversation with the film's Scottish director, Joe McGrath.

Both men shared a love of *The Goons* and McGrath told me: 'Yes, George was a frequent visitor and it was always good to see him. I had produced several of The Beatles' early videos so we knew each other. You could tell how close he and Ringo were. They had an almost telepathic understanding. He was very quiet and just stood on the sidelines while we were filming. I think he was just happy to blend into the background. Fame wasn't his thing.'

Nevertheless, the month ended with another reminder of the high cost of celebrity for Harrison. Nineteen days on from the police raid, he and Pattie appeared at Esher and Walton Magistrates' Court to plead guilty to possessing the cannabis they adamantly believed was planted in their house by police officers.

Despite his plea, there was no disguising his bitterness over the whole affair. They were each fined £250 and warned about the dire consequences of drug-taking. Only once did the Quiet One raise his voice – and that was to politely ask for the return of a key Crown exhibit, an ornamental peace pipe, which was a present from the Native American Church of Peyote Indians. Outside, justice having been done and with a criminal record now attached to his name, Harrison restricted his comments to: 'I hope the police will now leave The Beatles alone.' The Blue Meanies, though, were the last thing they would have to worry about.

Eastman and Eastman
39 West 54th Street
New York
New York 10019   18th April 1969

Attention Lee Eastman, Esq.

Dear Mr. Eastman,

    This is to inform you of the fact that you are not
authorized to act or to hold yourself out as the attourney
or legal representative of "The Beatles" or of any of the
companies which the Beatles own or control.

    We recognize that you are authorized to act for
Paul McCartney, personally, and in this regard we will
instruct our representatives to give you the fullest co-
operation.

    We would appreciate your forwarding to

        ABKCO Industries Inc.
        1700 Broadway
        New York
        N.Y.

all documents, correspondence and files which you hold
in your possession relating to the affairs of the Beatles,
or any of the companies which the Beatles own or control.

                    Very truly yours,

                    John Lennon *[signature: John Lennon]*

                    Richard Starkey *[signature: R Starkey]*

                    George Harrison *[signature: George Harrison]*

Signed by Lennon, Harrison and Starr, the letter that effectively outlawed Paul's in-laws from
The Beatles and widened further the rift with McCartney.

April was only two days old when Dick James arrived to face the music at McCartney's house in Cavendish Avenue, a short bus journey from EMI Studios in Abbey Road. He had already been harangued by George Martin over his decision to sell out Lennon and McCartney. The Beatles' gentlemanly producer recalled the angry exchange between the two of them in an interview with Ray Coleman.

'This can't be true! Martin had said.

'Yes, it is,' Dick replied. 'I have sold. I'm tired of being threatened by The Beatles, and being got at. So I decided to sell.'

Martin: 'Why didn't you ask The Beatles first?'

James: 'If I'd done that it would have been all over the place and then I could never have done the deal with Lew Grade.'

'I told him he was a rat,' Martin remembers. 'I felt he'd betrayed everything we'd done together and I felt I was in a position where I could say that.'

Martin's denunciation, however, was nothing compared to the sub-zero reception awaiting James at McCartney's house. He went alone, armed only with an unwavering self-belief that he was doing the right thing. He might naturally have expected Charles Silver, his right-hand man and chief ally in Northern Songs, to provide some kind of solidarity. But of the reclusive Silver there was no sign.

In the countless books written about The Beatles, Charles Silver remains the missing piece in the puzzle. He has never been pictured or interviewed about his role in the greatest melodrama in showbiz history. Instead, he is a furtive figure, lost in the margins, unknown to even The Beatles.

McCartney noted: 'We never met this Charles Silver guy, a character who was always in the background. He was "the money", that was basically who he was, like the producer on a film. He and

Dick James went in together, so Silver always got what was really our share. There were the two of them taking the lion's share, but it was a little while before we found out.'

Inadvertently, George Martin had touched on one of the biggest oversights in The Beatles' career. When the Northern Songs agreement was drafted, no one thought to include a clause giving Lennon and McCartney first refusal on the option to buy outright the company that was rightly theirs.

Unknown to them, Northern Songs had, in fact, been folded into the Dick James Music publishing stable as a subsidiary company. It was a dereliction of duty on Brian Epstein's part and a calculated move by James that would ultimately cost Lennon and McCartney untold millions and see their songs bartered down through the decades ahead in a corporate game of pass the parcel. And each time the music stopped, someone else took ownership of the world's most lucrative song publishing catalogue.

James, however, felt his conscience was clear, and all that was left was to endure the wrath of Lennon and McCartney that afternoon. By all accounts it was not a long conversation. The two musicians found their song publisher in an intransigent and unapologetic mood. No, he didn't think to tell them he was selling his shares as he didn't want to spook the market and see the value of the company's stock plunge; no, he didn't have any qualms about unloading his stake to Lew Grade, the bête noire of British entertainment; and, no, he didn't see his decision as a personal betrayal of them. Neither Lennon nor McCartney ever talked about this meeting, but James, in rare interviews, did offer a small insight into their reactions.

'Paul was annoyed, but John was inconsolable; he was hurt and I was very sorry.' In another account, he declared: 'Everything was very civilised. I explained why I had done what I had done, supported by the board. Paul sort of shrugged it off. John, who always placed great emphasis on respect and integrity for each other, was very cynical. I said: "Your financial gain will at least give you, regardless of what your earnings are from records, a substantial income." Although they were established at that time as certainly great catalogue-sellers, no one could really visualise how they would continue to sell in ten, twelve, fifteen years' time.

'I tried to point out to John that his capital gain, which wasn't like earnings from records, on which tax was astronomical because his royalties were subject to ordinary tax . . . the reward he would get from his shares was, in fact, a capital gain and that was at the lowest rate of tax you pay anywhere in the world.

'I endeavoured to give John that point of view and I said, "At least that means you can put some money by for your children." To which he retorted, quite cynically, "I have no desire to create another fucking aristocracy." That'll be the only four-letter word that you'll get from me, but that is verbatim what he said.'

Apart from James and Silver, Northern's board also included Clive Epstein and Geoffrey Ellis, both of whom held a small stake in the company. Minority shareholders they may have been, but both were entitled to feel part of the key decision-making process. Neither, though, was party to the discussions with Lew Grade, despite James's later claims to the contrary.

Rather than it being a unanimous and collective decision taken by all of the company's principals, it came down to a singular will. Like Allen Klein's ABKCO, Northern Songs was a one-man band, run largely on similarly arbitrary lines by Dick James. As long as the share price held firm, everyone was happy. But when it started to wobble amid fears that the Lennon and McCartney train was coming off the rails, beads of sweat started to form on his brow. Fortunes easily made could just as easily vanish. So, as he walked out of McCartney's house, having witnessed the hostile demeanour of his company's two greatest assets, he was convinced more than ever that he had done the right thing.

It was Peter Brown who later said, 'To John and Paul, Northern wasn't just a collection of compositions; it was like a child, creative flesh and blood, and selling it to Lew Grade was like putting that child into an orphanage.

'But Dick James had seen the writing on the wall; it was in Allen Klein's handwriting and James was determined to pull out. The value of Northern Songs depended on the willingness and ability of Lennon and McCartney to compose together. Already John and Paul had refused to sign an extension on their songwriting contract with Northern Songs and James had good reason to doubt the longevity of their relationship.'

Lennon made no mention of the confrontation, Northern Songs, Apple or The Beatles when he appeared on the *Eamonn Andrews Show*, a popular British TV news/discussion programme, the following evening. But the news about Grade's takeover attempt renewed speculation over the health of The Beatles' business interests and sparked a fresh wave of 'Fab Four to Split' headlines. In fact, The Beatles had not been seen in public together since the rooftop concert. By April, even their own sanctioned fan-friendly publication, *The Beatles Monthly*, was reduced to producing single shots of an individual Beatle looking vaguely interested.

Of course, they had not quite vanished: two weddings, one high-profile honeymoon, a dodgy drugs bust and now a Fleet Street feeding frenzy over Northern Songs had seen to that. But Apple press officer Derek Taylor recognised that the mask was slipping at a time when, more than ever, it needed to be held firmly in place. So he turned to an old photographer chum to help preserve the myth.

Taylor had befriended Bruce McBroom while both worked at the 1967 Monterey Pop Festival in California. McBroom had also worked with Peter Sellers on a film called *The Party*. By one of those curious twists of fate, the young American was in London at this time working as a stills photographer on the *Magic Christian* set at Twickenham, where he had struck up an amiable working alliance with Ringo Starr. Taylor got in touch to ask how much he would charge to take pictures of the biggest rock group on the planet.

Decades later, in his first-ever interview on the subject, McBroom admitted he did not play hard to get. He laughed down the line from Los Angeles, telling me, 'I can't remember what we agreed, but I do know I sold myself very inexpensively. I never heard any more until about a week later during a lunch break on *The Magic*

Christian. Peter Sellers said would I mind popping into his trailer for a minute? So I went over to his dressing room and Derek Taylor was there with all four Beatles. Of course, I knew Ringo, and Derek then introduced me to John, Paul and George.

'And I can tell you this, it was a mind-numbing moment to see all four of them right in front of you. We talked about what we could do if we did a photoshoot. It was not meant to be mean-spirited but at some point Paul McCartney said, "This is all really wonderful but we have had so many bad experiences with photographers ripping us off and releasing unauthorised pictures. I have to ask, how can we be sure that you are not going to do that?"

McBroom continued: 'I did not have an answer. There I am being interrogated by all four Beatles. Peter Sellers then came up behind me and said, "Boys, I would trust Bruce with my wallet." And that is how I got the job. Peter just defused the whole situation in a way that was so characteristic of him.

'The thing was that as far as The Beatles were concerned Peter was the big star. They really idolised him, having grown up listening to radio shows like *The Goons*. That was the backstory but Derek explained to me that there had been a lot of bad press recently and rumours were rife that the boys were breaking up. Which he said, of course, was untrue. So he told me they needed group photographs to rebuff those rumours. They wanted happy photos to put out to disprove the fact: they were all here, they were all mates and they would be continuing to work together. Little did I know or most of the world know they were already at odds. So that was the thrust of my assignment – to come up with happy photos of The Beatles together.'

On 9 April, Bruce met the band at Twickenham where a sound stage had been set aside for the photoshoot. McCartney was accompanied by Linda, who shadowed Bruce with her own camera, a habit he found slightly irritating.

He recalled: 'I didn't get any art direction from anyone. There were no wardrobe people or make-up experts. I was mentally trying to figure out what to do so, like any photographer, I put up a white background and lit it so that when they came in we would be ready to shoot.

'We made small talk before finally one of them said, "So, what do you want us to do?" So I said, "Why don't you all go and stand on the white sheet?" That was all my direction. All the shots were those four guys arranging themselves without any direction from anyone else. They were talking and joking and they just seemed to have an understanding of each other, which I never experienced again with a group of people. I don't want to say it was telepathic but you could feel how they reacted to each other.

'The whole thing was very unprepared. And that is the way I like to take pictures, which is not to tell people what to do but to let it all happen organically. And that way you capture them much more naturally and that is what happened with The Beatles.'

After breaking for lunch, McBroom suggested some outdoor shots, so they headed down to the nearby Madingley Club beside the Thames, where Bruce shot several more rolls of film. Spotting a small rowing boat, Lennon mischievously suggested they all get in and start rowing.

'In those days we were shooting still film, not digital,' the photographer added. 'I had been shooting colour but I wanted to shoot black and white the way I had done that morning. John was steering the boat back to its mooring and I called out to them, "Hey, guys, could you do that again?" And John said from a distance, "Look, people are always asking us to repeat ourselves but we never do. So, no, we won't be doing that again." And I totally got it. I suddenly realised why they hadn't wanted to tour any more and why their music always had to progress.'

His final shots showed all four Beatles leaning insouciantly against Lennon's white Rolls-Royce, though by this time boredom was clearly setting in.

'I never detected any attitude between them during the time I spent with them,' said McBroom. 'In one of the final frames, McCartney is looking really glum but by then we had been at it for about four hours. Looking back at the pictures now, George

Harrison looks a little detached from the rest, which may or may not have been significant. I got the impression that Paul was the spokesman for the group. George was very quiet. John was a free spirit. Ringo was a very zany, loose kind of guy. McCartney struck me as the businessman of the group but in a very nice way. It was a seminal moment in my career.'

For McBroom, it was mission accomplished. The Beatles loved his pictures, especially the moody black-and-white images taken at Twickenham, and immediately sanctioned their release to media outlets all over the world. He had managed to perfectly capture The Beatles in that twilight moment between finishing what would become *Let It Be* and starting what would become *Abbey Road*. And for an instant, the gossamer illusion of The Beatles as a working collective remained delicately preserved for an unsuspecting world.

*

McBroom's stellar images of four smiling Beatles could paper over the cracks but there was really only one way to disprove the lie that nails were being hammered into the band's coffin and that was by releasing new music. Eight months had passed since the release of 'Hey Jude', the longest gap in the group's studio history. The obvious solution was to record a single, but in the first few days of April neither Lennon nor McCartney was prepared to offer anything. Harrison had, of course, recorded several songs, including 'Something,' 'Old Brown Shoe' and 'All Things Must Pass'. But the indifference shown to his material – their version of 'All Things' especially was shockingly contemptuous – by Lennon and McCartney still burned deep. Hard-bitten cynicism was hotwired into Harrison's DNA. The quiet one was more often the droll one and that combination of mistrust and misanthropy was commonly woven into his songs. 'Here Comes The Sun', though, went to a more optimistic place. Still a work in progress, it had been sparked into life during a carefree, slightly guilty stroll round the manicured lawns at Eric Clapton's house in Surrey sometime around the middle of April.

Harrison, of course, hated the business machinations of Apple more than any of The Beatles. For him, music had always provided an escape, either from school or from Beatlemania at its height. Songs such as the optimistic 'Here Comes The Sun', alongside a fully realised 'Something', would eventually see him finally get his due and lasting recognition as a songwriter of note.

He said: '"Here Comes The Sun" was written at the time when Apple was getting like school, where we had to go and be businessmen: sign this and sign that. Anyway, it seems as if winter in England goes on for ever, by the time spring comes you really deserve it. So one day I decided I was going to sag off Apple and I went over to Eric Clapton's house. The relief of not having to go see all those dopey accountants was wonderful, and I walked around the garden with one of Eric's acoustic guitars and wrote "Here Comes the Sun".'

In Martin Scorsese's 2011 documentary, *Living in the Material World*, Clapton recalled watching the song take shape in his friend's hands. 'It was one of those beautiful spring mornings. I think it was April, we were just walking around the garden with our guitars. I don't do that, you know? This is what George brought to the situation. He was just a magical guy . . . we sat down at the bottom of the garden, looking out, and the sun was shining; it was a beautiful morning, and he began to sing the opening lines [to "Here Comes The Sun"] and I just watched this thing come to life.'

Back at Apple, meanwhile, Glyn Johns had been diligently sifting through the 'Get Back' tapes in an attempt to compile an album that would please everyone. At first listen, very few would pass Beatle quality control, but EMI were pressing hard for a radio-friendly 45.

Eventually, a compromise was reached: Lennon and McCartney agreed to release a single version of Paul's 'Get Back' on 11 April from the January tapes bracketed alongside Lennon's fevered hymn to Yoko, 'Don't Let Me Down', perhaps his most notable contribution to the January sessions.

As was often the case, acetate copies of the new single had clandestinely been given to a few, select Radio 1 DJs a few days earlier – in this instance, John Peel and Alan Freeman. But when McCartney heard 'Get Back' on the airwaves for the first time, his ears pricked up with a perfectionist's disapproval. It still didn't sound right, so, on 7 April, he sat down with Johns at Olympic Studios until a new mix of the song was tweaked to his satisfaction.

The single version of 'Get Back'/'Don't Let Me Down' owed its existence to the back-to-basics concept that kickstarted the January sessions: no overdubs, no studio trickery, no compromises. But the song that flooded into record stores broke every one of those taboos. The finished version ended up as an amalgam of two takes from 27 and 28 January and differed from what would be the album version with the distinctive coda replacing Lennon's quip – 'thank you on behalf of the band' – that would end the version on *Let It Be*.

'Get Back', The Beatles' nineteenth single, was unexceptional but, powered by Starr's inventive drumming, it became the first Beatles single to enter the UK charts at number one – a position it held for six weeks during a seventeen-week stay in the Top 20. In America, it hit the summit after two weeks, enabling the band to overtake Elvis Presley's record of sixteen chart-toppers. It was also the first Beatles single to be released in proper stereo and the first to fully credit an outside musician. The song's distinctive electronic keyboard solo ensured Billy Preston was given rightful commendation.

'I couldn't believe it when I saw my name out there,' he would recall. 'It was such an honour. I thought it was a good solo and I was just happy that they liked it. I wasn't looking for any kind of validation, but I knew they liked it.'

Equally unusually, the country blues lead guitar was played by Lennon, who was forced to learn the chords during the time Harrison had gone AWOL in January. 'Paul used to let you do a solo when he was feeling generous,' he said later, somewhat disdainfully.

For all their recent business headaches, Lennon and McCartney had been reunited by the same musical forces that had shaped their friendship from the start. They had spent more time together in the first two weeks of April than at any time since the end of January.

On the afternoon of Monday, 14 April, they met at Paul's house before heading to the EMI Studios for what was ostensibly a mixing session. McCartney immediately picked up on the excitement and impatience in Lennon's voice. Lennon had a new song swirling around inside his head and he wanted to get it down on tape straightaway. The title of the first fully formed song he had written for weeks might have given McCartney serious pause for thought. 'The Ballad Of John And Yoko (Christ You Know It Ain't Easy)' was too self-serving in its title to be a Beatles song. To his credit, McCartney did not flinch as Lennon ran through the tune on an acoustic guitar as he scanned his partner's handwritten lyrics. The last verse was incomplete so McCartney did what he always did with Lennon. He helped him finish it.

His only reservation concerned the words in parenthesis – an unnecessary provocation that he felt could inevitably resurrect the 'We're bigger than Jesus' furore of three years earlier. Not to mention the line that, to press the point home, added: 'They're gonna crucify me.'

With no little sense of irony, McCartney brought up the subject of the chorus: 'I said "Jesus Christ, you're kidding, aren't you? Someone really is going to get upset about it." He said, "Yeah, but let's do it." I was a little worried for him because of the lyric but he was going through a lot of terrible things. He came around to my house, wanting to do it really quick. He said, "Let's just you and me run over to the studio." I said, "Oh, alright, I'll play drums, I'll play bass." John played guitar. So we did it and stood back to see if the other guys would hate us for it, which I'm not sure about. They probably never forgave us. John was on heat, so to speak. He needed to record it so we just ran in and did it.'

A quick call ahead to Abbey Road ensured two other members of the studio team would be on hand to record the song, a candid piece of journalese about Lennon's life over the past few weeks. George Martin and Geoff Emerick agreed to man the engineering boards alongside John Kurlander as second engineer.

Kurlander told me: 'It was a strange session in the sense it was only John and Paul. At that point we didn't know if it was an album track or what. But there was a lot of urgency about the whole thing. They were in Studio Three instead of Studio Two, which was where The Beatles generally recorded. But what I do remember about it was just the sheer sense of fun we all had. John was in a great mood and that always helped. Plus, it really was just the two of them, no wives and no distractions. It was great.'

Over eleven takes, Lennon and McCartney hammered the song into shape. Paul handled the drums, bass and piano parts while John looked after the lead guitar. McCartney also underpinned Lennon's vocal with some lovely high harmonies to provide a call-and-response feel to the track. There was none of the forced laughter and awkward silences that punctuated the 'Get Back' sessions from January. For five hours, all the old antagonisms were pushed to one side. On one take, Lennon shouted up to the drum kit, 'Go a little faster, Ringo,' which brought the jokey reply, 'Okay, George.'

Listening to the playbacks later, Lennon was delighted with the outcome. He said, 'It's like an old-time ballad. It's the story of Yoko and I getting married, going to Paris, going to Amsterdam, all that. It's "Johnny B. Paperback Writer". The story came out that only Paul and I were on the record, but I wouldn't have bothered publicising that. It doesn't mean anything. It just so happened that there were only two of us there – George was abroad and Ringo was on the film and he couldn't come that night. Because of that, it was a choice of either remixing or doing a new song – and you always go for doing a new one instead of fiddling about with an old one. It turned out well.'

George Martin, though, was perceptive enough to know he had just glimpsed the future. 'It was hardly a Beatle track – yet it was a Beatle track,' he said. 'It was a kind of thin end of the wedge. John had already mentally left the group and I think that was just the beginning of it all.' McCartney was equally pleased but for different reasons. As well as completing a funky track, which would be The Beatles' next single, he felt he had reconnected with Lennon on a more personal level. He said, 'It always amazed me how even though it was just the two of us how it sounded like The Beatles.' Was there, he wondered silently, still hope for the band?

Any resentment Harrison and Starr may have felt over being excluded from 'The Ballad Of John And Yoko' was clearly not an issue. Two nights later, all four of them were back at Abbey Road for the first full band sessions in weeks, to polish Harrison's 'Old Brown Shoe', which would become the B-side of 'The Ballad Of John And Yoko'. Some minor work was also done on a backing track for 'Something', making it a Harrison-focused session, perhaps a guilty concession on the parts of Lennon and McCartney.

Enough common ground was found to agree a timetable for five more sessions for the rest of the month. Nothing too formal or rigid, more like a gentle push forward into a fragile and uncertain future. Some songs, such as Lennon's searing proto-blues, 'I Want You', and McCartney's Fifties pastiche, 'Oh! Darling', were, over the next twelve days or so, dusted off as the band breathed new life into that rarest of things: a track written by Starr with a little help from Harrison.

Whether by accident or design, 'Octopus's Garden' continued the nautical whimsy of 'Yellow Submarine', the 1966 *Revolver* track that had cemented the drummer's role as the Beatle most beloved by small children. Further work was also done on 'Let It Be'.

George Martin would undoubtedly have been aware of the work going down in Studio Two and Studio Three but diplomatically stayed away. He still carried the bruises from his brusque demotion during the 'Get Back' sessions. Besides, it was manners to wait until you were asked. In truth, though, the band needed him now more than ever.

The White Album sessions had been tense, but at least there was an endgame. With 'Get Back', they had drifted listlessly from one unfinished track to the next. The finish line never seemed close. Now here they were, all four back in their allotted slots but still lacking the schoolmasterly discipline Martin brought.

In his absence, The Beatles largely produced themselves with a hive of EMI staffers acting as worker bees in the background. Prominent among them were John Kurlander and Jeff Jarrett who mainly filled the engineering roles. Both men would become instrumental in the band's final recordings throughout 1969 but for now they had to adhere to the rules of 'speak when you're spoken to'.

Jarrett had worked at EMI Studios for a couple of years, helping out in particular with Pink Floyd, then a progressive young band from Cambridge. On 18 April, the day of the first run through for 'Octopus's Garden', he was assigned his first Beatles sessions and sought some advice from George Martin.

'I was really thrown in at the deep end,' Jarrett told Beatles author Mark Lewisohn. 'George informed me that he wouldn't be available. I can't remember word for word what he said to me but it was something like "There will be one Beatle there, fine. Two Beatles, great. Three Beatles, fantastic. But the minute the four of them are there, that is when the inexplicable charismatic thing happens, the special magic no one has been able to explain. It will be very friendly between you but you will be aware of this inexplicable *presence*."

'Sure enough, that's the exact way it happened. I've never felt it in any other circumstances. It was the special chemistry of the four of them which nobody since has ever had.'

*

On 10 April, ATV officially launched its bid for control of Northern Songs, firing the starting gun on three weeks of tempestuous and factional in-fighting that, perhaps more than anything, pulled The Beatles ever closer to destruction. At its heart lay the simmering business tensions between Lennon and McCartney that were finally brought to the boil by Klein's Machiavellian manoeuvres.

Even before hoovering up James and Silver's thirty-two per cent shareholding, ATV owned three per cent stock in the company. So now they controlled around thirty-five per cent, only sixteen per cent short of the magical fifty-one per cent needed to guarantee Grade majority control of the company and grant him authority over history's most lucrative song catalogue. As far as everyone at Apple understood, The Beatles' stockholding collectively amounted to around twenty-nine per cent. The deal between Northern and

ATV valued the shares at just over thirty-seven shillings – just under £2 in 1969 and approximately £23 today – a far cry from the seven-shilling (35p) valuation placed on the shares when the company floated on the stock market in 1965.

Grade felt confident enough to announce his intention to mount a full-blown takeover of Northern Songs. 'We are determined to buy Northern Songs,' he warned on Saturday, 12 April. 'Music is an essential part of our business and there's no denying the brilliance of The Beatles as musicians.' The company was valued at £10m by Grade's moneymen, a miserly appraisal according to the City's most seasoned observers. But Grade was not the type to spend one pound unless he could get five in return. Nor, in many ways, was Klein, who had been summoned back to fight the good copyright fight by Lennon *and* McCartney.

This unexpected crie de coeur stuck in McCartney's throat, as it saw him abandon his steadfast principle to never do anything for the benefit of Mr Klein or let him represent him. But for some, his reluctant gesture equated to Klein being his de facto manager in the war to come over Northern Songs. Privately, he wondered when someone would rip off Klein's mask to reveal what really lay beneath. On Sunday, 13 April, he had his answer.

The *Sunday Times'* fearless investigative team, Insight, published an excoriating profile of Klein's business activities. Over two broadsheet pages it dragged the American's dark past out into the light. Headlined 'The Biggest Wheeler-Dealer in the Pop Jungle', it pilloried him over a string of dodgy deals.

The story raised questions over alleged dubious share dealing involving the Cameo-Parkway record label (the forerunner of ABKCO), and disclosed that he faced a string of court cases in New York and was being investigated by the US tax authorities. But the top line concerned the claim that Klein had pocketed a $1.25m advance he had won for the Rolling Stones from Decca Records in 1965.

Much of the content had been leaked to the paper by an old foe. In February, during the bitter stand-off over the purchase of

Nems, Leonard Richenberg, the pugnacious chairman of Triumph Investment, had secretly commissioned a Bishop's Report on Klein, the corporate equivalent of a private investigation into someone's business activities.

The Insight article was the opening that Lee Eastman had been waiting for. Proof that his son John, and McCartney, had been right all along about Klein and his nefarious business practices, and that The Beatles – and Lennon in particular – were being taken for suckers.

Eastman was a man accustomed to getting his own way. He was furious with Klein for the way he had apparently bullied his son and son-in-law over Apple, Nems and now Northern Songs. From his point of view, Klein was already a failure: Nems had been lost with twenty-five per cent of The Beatles' earnings now tied up by faceless merchant bankers. Now Northern Songs was in danger of slipping away, while Apple remained a financial sinkhole.

Eastman senior arrived in London a few days after publication of the *Sunday Times* piece.

His first port of call was to Richenberg to find out whether there was any way for The Beatles to buy back Nems. But the merchant banker was no keener to do business with Eastman than he was with Klein and had no desire to quickly cash in on so prized an asset.

That same night, Lee Eastman sat down alongside all four Beatles for his first face-to-face with Klein, the two men eyeing each other with mutual loathing. Lennon had already been well briefed by Klein over Lee's 'phoneyism'. So when Eastman extended his hand with the words, 'I've always admired your work,' John could taste the hypocrisy. It was a lamentable blunder. The wafer-thin civility quickly gave way to outright hostility.

A few days earlier, Lennon had, to his glee, discovered that Eastman senior had changed his surname from, of all things, Epstein, to try to mask his Jewish background and help smooth his way into New York society. For Lennon, Yoko and Klein it became a verbal weapon with which to bludgeon Eastman. As the discussions became ever more fraught and angry, Lennon spat it out as only he could: EPSHTEEEN. It would have reeked of anti-Semitism were it not for the fact Klein was also Jewish.

Eastman swallowed the bait, giving way to his volatile side and branding Klein a 'swine' and a 'louse'. Klein stayed on the ropes and let Eastman punch himself out. 'I didn't think it was right to retaliate,' he later said wryly.

Lennon recalled that meeting in typically forthright terms: 'We arranged to see Eastman and Klein together in a hotel where one of them was staying. For the four Beatles and Yoko to go and see them both. We hadn't been in there more than a few minutes when Lee Eastman was having something like an epileptic fit, and screaming at Allen that he was "the lowest scum on earth", and calling him all sorts of names. Allen was sitting there, taking it, you know, just takin' it. Eastman was abusing him with class snobbery.

'What Eastman didn't know then is that Neil [Aspinall] had been in New York and found out that Lee Eastman's real name was Lee Epstein! That's the kind of people they are. But Paul fell for that bullshit, because Eastman's got Picassos on the wall and because he's got some sort of East Coast suit, form and not substance. Now, that's McCartney.

'We were all still not sure and they brought in this fella, and he had a fuckin' fit. We had thought it was one in a million but that was enough for me, soon as he started nailing Klein on his taste. Paul was getting in little digs about Allen's dress – who the fuck does he think he is? Him talking about dress! Man, so that was it, and we said, "Fuck it!"

'I wouldn't let Eastman near me; I wouldn't let a fuckin' animal like that who has a mind like that near me. Who despises me, too, despises me because of what I am and what I look like. This was supposed to be the guy who was taking over the multi-million dollar corporation, and it was going to be slick. Paul was sort of intimating that Allen's business offices on Broadway were not nice enough – as if that made any fuckin' difference! Eastman was in the good section of town. "Oh, boy, man, that's where it's at!" And Eastman's office has got class! I don't care if this is fuckin' red white and blue, I don't care what Allen dresses like, he's a human being, man.

'The more we said "no" the more (Paul) said "yes". Eastman went mad and shouted and all that. I didn't know what Paul was thinking when he was in the room; I mean, his heart must have sunk.'

Indeed it must have.

Ronnie Schneider, Klein's nephew, had been riding shotgun to his uncle at Apple and was convinced that in the battle with the Eastmans there would only be one winner. He recalled: 'I sat in a few of these meetings between John, Allen and the Eastmans and they were not pleasant because, you know, the attitude was competition. And Allen attacked competition.'

John Eastman later doubted that a simple case of name-calling would have been enough to spark his father's notorious temper. Rather, he reckoned his old man had reacted the way any father would when his son's reputation was trampled on by bullies. Years later, he preferred to draw a veil over some of the more lurid accounts that have been painted of this summit but out of personal and professional loyalty to Paul he kept his own counsel for more than forty-five years.

But in 2016, with McCartney's approval, he broke cover to deny the long-held allegations that the two camps tried to outdo each other by piling obscenity upon obscenity. Hard though the repudiation is to believe, he told McCartney's unauthorised biographer Philip Norman: 'We were in opposition right from the beginning. I'm a pretty patient sort of guy. In all our arguments, I never raised my voice once.'

A few days earlier, Lennon, McCartney, Klein and Yoko had met with Apple's merchant bankers, Henry Ansbacher & Company, to draw up plans to win control of Northern Songs. On paper, it looked a fairly even fight, and the bank's Bruce Ormrod was detailed to look after the interests of its celebrity clients.

Over the next week or so, a counter-proposal was presented to the Stock Exchange by Ansbachers. The Beatles were prepared to buy back 1,000,000 shares in Northern Songs, a move which, if successful, would push The Beatles' current thirty-five per cent shareholding over the magic fifty-one per cent line they needed to keep the company out of Lew Grade's grasp. They had no intention of seeking an outright buyout. That would leave both sides looking to snap up fifteen per cent of shares they required to declare victory. The idea was fine in theory, looked good on the bank's headed notepaper and scanned well in the column inches of the next day's *Financial Times*. There was just one problem. The Beatles would need to fork out the then eye-watering sum of £2m – money that they just didn't have. Their royalties from EMI continued to lie fallow in a High Court escrow account due to the ongoing litigation between Apple – or more accurately Klein – and Triumph over the still unresolved battle for Nems. The battle for control of Northern Songs opened the door for avaricious traders to move in and, possibly, just possibly, hold the short-term balance of power – and get rich in the process. Chances were that in the weeks ahead the share price would inevitably rise. So the idea would be to buy low and sell high to either The Beatles or Grade when the time was right. Enter, then, a tripartite bloc of City financiers known collectively as the consortium who owned around fifteen per cent of Northern shares – the precise figure both parties required. The consortium consisted of clients of three leading London brokers, Astaire & Co., W.I. Carr and Spencer Thornton and included theatre owners Howard & Wyndham, the Ebor Unit Trust, the Slater Walker Invan Trust and merchant bankers Arbuthnot Latham. For The Beatles, it then came down to a question of personal cash. In order to find the money to counter Grade, Lennon and McCartney were forced to conduct an audit of their own financial reserves. This mainly included the shares they held in Apple, their film production company Subafilms as well as the cash value of their own shares in Northern Songs. Twenty-four hours after the row with Lee Eastman, they were back round the table at Ansbachers to tally up how much money was in the kitty – and how far or far apart they were to finding the money needed to take on Grade.

Klein wanted everyone to pool their various shareholdings as collateral. McCartney, however, on the advice of Lee Eastman, refused to throw in his shares, deeming it a risk too far. Klein had already anticipated that McCartney would continue to play for time. So, as a sign of good faith, he announced that he would put up £640,000 worth of MGM shares held through his own company ABKCO Industries to boost the pot. The unexpected – and entirely out-of-character – act of altruism blindsided McCartney and the Eastmans.

But Klein's next comment exploded a chain of events that arguably did more than anything to sever the bond between Lennon and McCartney. Almost casually, he let slip the fact that John owned 644,000 shares in Northern Songs, worth around £1.25m. Then he dropped the bomb: Paul's shareholding had been tallied at 751,000 and was valued at £1.4m. There followed a few seconds of silence before all hell broke loose.

Lennon, unaware of Klein's clandestine machinations over McCartney's secret shareholding, quickly joined the dots and felt an overwhelming sense of betrayal. The man who for the past month had been preaching global peace flew into a red-faced rage at his songwriting partner, calling him a 'bastard'.

Various accounts over the years have suggested the two men almost came to blows. One unverified report has the volatile Lennon shaking his fist at Linda McCartney with Klein holding him back. Sheepishly, McCartney tried to defend his underhanded actions: 'I had some beanies and I wanted more.'

Lee Eastman, for once, had no comeback. On paper, it may not have mattered. At that point the combined shareholding of Lennon and McCartney could simply have been added together to be used as a shared purpose against a common foe, had McCartney not reneged on that proposal. But Klein's jaw-dropping revelation about Paul's insider dealings had left Lennon badly wounded.

It was a betrayal that cut deep, especially since their song publishing was the one thing about The Beatles Lennon felt most nostalgic about. Yes, there had been bitter fall-outs in the past, even when they were not much older than kids. But in the main these disagreements had been about music and, occasionally, Yoko. This was truly the day trust died between John Lennon and Paul McCartney.

In the months ahead, they would continue to work in the studio and fine-tune each other's songs. But Lennon would never forget the pain. 'It was the first time any of us had gone behind the other's back,' he recalled.

McCartney, in contrast, felt – and still does – that he had done nothing wrong. Yet it looked to any impartial witness that he was guilty of playing both ends against the middle. Like Lennon, he hated the idea of ATV getting its hands on his songs, but he wasn't offering any credible alternative. Lee Eastman's instruction to sit tight only further isolated McCartney in Lennon's eyes. After all, it was his recommendation that Paul clandestinely buy up Northern shares that had now created an almost fatal rupture.

Harrison and Starr were equally dismayed by McCartney's perceived treachery and Eastman senior's meltdowns. One thing was now clear; they didn't want Eastman anywhere near them. The next day, 18 April, Eastman received official notification on Apple-headed notepaper that he was outlawed from any future involvement in their corporate activities. The memorandum, a stinging rebuke, was another personal blow for McCartney – and a triumph for Klein.

In the meantime, The Beatles, minus McCartney's Northern Songs stock, launched their counter-offer in a bid to rally shareholders to their side. It included the veiled threat that Lennon and McCartney would stop composing altogether and not fulfil the six-songs-a-year minimum quota stipulated in their existing contract if ATV prevailed.

The overture to shareholders broke down as follows: The Beatles were prepared to offer 212p per share as opposed to ATV's offer of 196p per share, though, as with all things business, there were complications when you drilled down into the detail.

Key to the proposal was that Lennon and McCartney would renew their contracts with the company, thus ensuring that their songwriting goldmine would remain fruitful for City prospectors. As expected, Northern's share price rose as the consortium that held the balance of power sought assurances from both sides.

One overriding point of concern soon became clear – the prospect of Klein sitting on a newly constituted board for Northern Songs. Consequently, Apple was forced to hold a press conference on 28 April giving the City a guarantee that Klein would have no place on the board.

Throughout this period, Klein and Bruce Ormrod, of Ansbachers, continued to diligently woo the consortium of minority shareholders who held all the key cards. At one point, it looked as if the consortium would throw their hand in with The Beatles to give the band a controlling stake in Northern Songs. Then, just as quickly, the tide turned in the direction of ATV, who had set a deadline of 2 May for their offer to be accepted. Alarm bells notwithstanding, the clock was now seriously ticking.

Lennon was torn between two impulses and the stronger one was to walk away from The Beatles and, especially, McCartney. But twenty-four hours after screaming at Paul and allegedly hurling abuse at his wife and her family, he was, remarkably, talking in glowing terms about writing new songs with his partner. He was still savvy enough to appreciate that it was his day job that financed his increasingly costly lifestyle. He still harboured hopes that the abortive 'Get Back' sessions could be salvaged.

When Alan Smith, the editor of the *New Musical Express*, sat down with Lennon on 28 April, there was no evidence of any lingering fall-out from recent events. Oddly, he was instead extremely upbeat, talking about the band's next musical adventure, a medley of songs strung together to form a symphonic whole, and about a new song called 'Because'.

On the subject of business matters, he told Smith: 'If I could only get the time to myself right now, instead of all this Monopoly and financial business with Northern Songs, I think I could probably write about thirty songs a day. As it is, I probably average about twelve a night. Paul too . . . he's mad on it. It's something that gets in your blood.

'I've got things going around in my head right now, and as soon as I leave here I'm going around to Paul's place and start work. The way we're writing at the moment, it's straightforward and there's nothing weird. Songs like "Get Back", things like that. We recorded that one on the Apple roof but I'm not sure if that's the version that went out. We always record about ten versions. You get lost in the end. I'm not really interested in the production of our records.

'In fact, I wish I didn't have to go through that whole thing, going through the production and balancing the bass and all that. For me, the satisfaction of writing a song is in the performing of it. The production bit is a bore. If some guy would invent a robot to do it, then it would be great. But all that "get the bass right, get the drums right", that's a drag to me. All I want to do is get my guitar out and sing songs.'

He added: 'Paul and I are now working on a kind of song montage that we might do as one piece on one side. We've got two weeks to finish the whole thing so we're really working at it. All the songs we're doing sound normal to me, but probably they might sound unusual to you. There's no "Revolution Number 9" there, but there's a few heavy sounds.

'I couldn't pin us down to being on a heavy scene, or a commercial pop scene, or a straight tuneful scene. We're just on whatever's going. Just rockin' along.'

It was, of course, purely illusory, a fantasy suggesting a unity of purpose where there was none. Even so, the last day of April found the band back at EMI Studios for one of the strangest sessions of their careers.

After recording a new Harrison lead guitar overdub for 'Let It Be' Lennon and McCartney excavated an eighteen-month-old track. It was a curious choice. 'You Know My Name (Look Up The Number)', a Lennon creation, had absolutely no commercial value and bordered on *Goons*-like comedy. Yet McCartney would strangely later recall the session as one of his favourites.

A multi-part song containing a nightclub cabaret pastiche and a host of silly voices and effects, 'You Know My Name' had been initially recorded in the weeks after the completion of the *Sgt. Pepper* album and then left on the shelf. In truth, though, it was an old note which should have remained unopened.

On 25 April Lennon and Yoko squeezed in a whistle-stop visit to Montreux, where their film *Rape* was being screened on television. By now Lennon had assumed an almost Christ-like appearance, with his long hair and beard. And, in a further show of marital devotion, he had also changed his name from John Winston Lennon to John Ono Lennon.

'This image thing that people are always on about with The Beatles – image is something in Joe Public's eye,' he declared. 'That's why it's a drag when people talk about fresh-faced Beatles, like it was five years ago. I mean, we're always changing, like the TV clip of "Get Back". Now I've got the beard, Paul is clean shaven, and George is the one with the moustache. Even I can't keep up with our own image. I come into Apple one day, and there's George got a new head on him. So if that's the way it is with us, I tell you, the public doesn't stand a chance of keeping up with how we look.

'And anyway, who we are is up to ourselves personally. Music is what's important. As far as that's concerned in my case, Yoko and I stimulate each other like crazy. For instance, did you know she'd trained as a classical musician? I didn't know that until this morning. In college she majored in classical composition. I've just written a song called "Because". Yoko was playing some classical bit, and I said, "Play that backwards", and we had a tune. We'll probably write a lot more in the future.'

Those last words, when read by Paul McCartney, summoned up his worst fears for the future of The Beatles.

After filming had been completed early on *The Magic Christian*, Ringo Starr joined comic hero Peter Sellers on board the newly launched *QE2*, before the pair sailed for America.

On 13 May, The Beatles went back to the future for a picture session that was intended to perfectly bookend their career. The location was the fifth floor at EMI House in London's Manchester Square, the photographer was Angus McBean, and his task was to recreate the carefree spontaneity – or as near to it as possible – that he captured for their first album back in the breezy days of early 1963.

The intention was to use McBean's new image as the cover of their next album, which Glyn Johns was still laboriously stitching together. It now had the notional working title of 'Get Back', with the suffix 'With Let It Be and 11 other songs', a mirror-image nod to the wording of their 1963 debut, *Please Please Me (With Love Me Do And 11 Other Songs)*.

It all suggested that the band genuinely thought the album, notwithstanding a few tweaks by Glyn Johns, was in the can. The idea, according to McCartney, sprang from a group meeting at which they all agreed it would be cool to shoot a cover that 'went full circle'.

After checking out the original image for *Please Please Me*, McBean, then aged sixty-five, lined them up in the same order from left to right – Ringo, Paul, George and John – and had them leaning over the balcony, smiling in unison, as he snapped away from the stairwell below.

Exactly two thousand, two hundred and sixty-one days had passed since McBean had answered a favour from George Martin for him to photograph a young Liverpool beat group that he had high hopes for.

It's interesting to view the 1963 and 1969 images side by side. Lennon's face was now framed by a thick beard rising high on his cheekbones while his hair reached his shoulders (it would become even longer in the months ahead); Harrison had a moustache and hair as long as Lennon's; Starr, moustache and long hair; only

McCartney easily stood a fair comparison with his former chipper self, although the moptop of Beatlemania had been replaced by a slightly more hippie style. Harrison and Lennon both wore the dandy white pin-striped suits that had last seen the light of day on The Beatles' swansong tour in 1966. McCartney and Ringo opted for darker and more conventional outfits.

The cheerful breeziness of the original shot may have been missing, but McBean still managed to catch something special. In fact, this was his second attempt at getting the perfect shot. When all four Beatles congregated for the scheduled date a few days earlier, they discovered a new porch had been erected at Manchester House, making it impossible for McBean to recreate the original picture from the same perspective. So staff agreed to remove the porch, and the shoot was rescheduled.

McBean was amazed when he viewed the four Beatles through his viewfinder – and even more amazed that they were still together. He recalled: 'In 1963 I asked John Lennon how long they would stay as a group, and he said, "Oh, about six years, I suppose – whoever heard of a bald Beatle?" Well, it was just six years later that I was asked to repeat the shot with The Beatles as they now looked – very hairy indeed.'

Starr was so late, he added, that EMI staff were streaming down the stairs on their way home. 'I got the camera fixed up and John, fascinated by photography, came and lay down beside me to look at my viewfinder. I can still hear the screams of the EMI girls as they realised who they were stepping over to get out the door!'

The shoot capped a tumultuous two weeks for the band. In a conversation with music writer Paul Du Noyer years later, McCartney admitted that the whole experience had a haunting feeling of a cycle having been completed. He said: 'The most final we got was going back to EMI in Manchester Square and taking that photo. And we all felt spooky. This is full circle. We've started and ended.'

Having banished Lee and John Eastman from the Apple orchard, Lennon, Harrison and Starr now urged McCartney to accept the reality of their corporate situation. Klein was about to begin delicate talks with EMI and Capitol in America over The Beatles' low royalty rates, and they insisted that his negotiating hand would be strengthened by all four of them being on the same page.

McCartney again found himself torn between his Beatle brothers and his new in-laws. But when it came to Klein, he had to go with his gut. On Tuesday, 6 May, he had unveiled a new song that laid bare his contempt for the band's de facto manager. Entitled 'You Never Give Me Your Money', it was a radical departure for him. In the past he had occasionally let his private feelings seep into the public domain via love songs, but the lyrics were often so opaque that their true meaning – and intended target, such as former fiancée Jane Asher – remained hidden. This time, however, there was no ambiguity.

McCartney later claimed Lennon 'saw the humour in it', though that seems highly unlikely. If anything, the lyrics, direct as they were, read more like Lennon than McCartney. Kicking subtlety into the long grass, Paul tore into Klein for making false promises. Nems had been lost despite his claims he could get it 'for nothing', and their stake in Northern Songs was also under serious threat – yet all they ever saw was 'funny paper'.

In the second verse he reveals his relationship with Klein was so bad that he didn't even want Klein to have his phone number. The middle verse sees McCartney admitting he 'could see no future' because 'all the money's gone nowhere to go'. And the last verse has him imagining he could 'step on the gas and wipe that tear away' because, tellingly, the 'magic feeling' he once held so dear has gone. The song read like a no-holds-barred resignation letter. A year later, he would deliver the real thing. 'This was me directly lambasting Allen Klein's attitude to us: no money, just funny paper, all promises and it never works out', he said of 'You Never Give Me Your Money'. 'It's basically a song about no faith in the person, that found its way into the medley on *Abbey Road*.'

It was a classic bittersweet McCartney ballad that slowly built into a juggernaut rock rhythm. (Sadly, since it was part of the medley, it was denied any kind of radio-friendly airplay, thus depriving it

from the kind of exposure that a song like 'Yesterday' had enjoyed.)
The band laid down thirty-six takes of the song, including the
soaring three-part harmonies that helped make it a musical tour de
force and would, further down the line, shape *Abbey Road*.

Ian McDonald, the acclaimed musicologist and author of
Revolution in the Head, said of the song: 'The Beatles' future may be
gone, but McCartney is determined to salvage their spirit, and that
of the Sixties, for his future. "You Never Give Me Your Money"
marks the psychological opening of his solo career.'

Harrison had already committed a solo demo of 'Something' to
tape at the end of February before a full band version – enhanced
by Billy Preston on the organ – had been attempted on 16 April.
Now, on 5 May, The Beatles' dark horse finally had the bit between
his teeth for a song that would in time be hailed as a masterpiece to
rival anything penned by Lennon and McCartney.

During each take, the band tried to nail the song's musical
foundations before any vocals were added. Casting aside his earlier
indifference, McCartney finally acknowledged a special song was
forming. He said: '"Something" was out of leftfield. It appealed to
me because it has a very beautiful melody and is a really structured
song. Until then he had only done one or two songs per album. I
don't think he thought of himself very much as a songwriter and
John and I would dominate – again not really meaning to but we
were "Lennon and McCartney". Maybe it wasn't easy for him to
get into that wedge. But he finally came up with "Something" and
everyone was very pleased for him.'

George Martin would later declare: 'The trouble with George
was that he was never treated on the same level as having the same
quality of songwriting by anyone – by John, by Paul or by me. I'm
as guilty in that respect. I was the guy who said, "If he's got a song
we'll let him have it on the album" – very condescendingly. I know
he must have felt very bad about that.'

The hypnotic basslines that underpinned 'Something', as laid
down at Olympic Studios on 5 May, typified McCartney's team-
player approach to the band. Harrison, however, was not impressed,

complaining that the basslines were 'too fussy'. McCartney defended his playing in *Mojo* magazine, admitting the criticism rankled slightly and adding: 'I was just trying to contribute the best I could, but maybe it was his turn to tell me I was too busy.' It was the kind of putdown that perhaps underscored Harrison's growing musical confidence and his role within the band.

Geoff Emerick, who had been restored to his place as chief engineer on the session, acknowledged there had been a minor shift in the band's studio hierarchy: 'Paul started playing a bassline that was a little elaborate, and George told him, "No, I want it simple." Paul complied. There wasn't any disagreement about it, but I did think that such a thing would never happened in years past. George telling Paul how to play the bass? Unthinkable! But this was George's baby.'

The lengthy night-time sessions – they often ran from 7.30 p.m. until 4 a.m. the next day – ran parallel with energy-draining daytime business summits for Lennon, Harrison and Starr. By now Klein had been working for The Beatles for three months without an official contract. He also claimed to have spent around £60,000 of his own cash wheeling and dealing on their behalf. Now he was about to wade into renegotiations over the band's royalty remuneration. And he was still battling to salvage the debacle over the purchase of Nems by Triumph while seeking to outbid ATV for control of Northern Songs. So Lennon's understandable rationale was that if Klein was going to bat on behalf of all four musicians, he was entitled to a contract signed by all four.

Consequently, between 4 and 9 May, all the relevant parties pored over documents drawn up by Apple's lawyers to legitimise Klein's role and put him on the company payroll. Eventually, a fragile financial framework was brokered. Under the terms of the agreement, ABKCO, rather than Klein as an individual, would become exclusive business manager to Apple Corps Ltd on behalf of The Beatles and their group of companies. In return, his company would receive twenty per cent of all Apple income generated under his watch, a sum to remain in force as long as the contract stayed in place between all parties.

During the discussions, McCartney, wary of the bottom line, persuaded the others to include significant caveats. Klein would not be entitled to receive any portion of the band's record royalties unless he negotiated a new deal with EMI and Capitol. Even then, he would only be paid twenty per cent of that increased rate instead of the full whack. In addition, he would only be able to claim ten per cent of the income generated by Apple records. By any measure, it was a convoluted – some might say Klein-esque – package. But for Klein it was another sign that he had outflanked the Eastmans and McCartney to seize control.

Naturally, he tried to put a positive spin on matters. By offering to take a commission only on The Beatles' increased business, a change from his normal operating methods, it meant that if Apple kept losing money he would take nothing, thus incentivising him to work hard for his clients.

Despite this apparent philanthropy, some of Apple's legal team had serious misgivings about the proposed agreement. McCartney was unhappy that Klein would be receiving a fifth of Apple's newly generated income. But Lennon's patience, never his strongest quality, was wearing icy thin over the dawn-to-dusk business routine that was setting in. Lennon had a naïve approach to business – the debacle over Nems and the ongoing battle for Northern Songs was shunted to the margins – and to loyalty. Having brought Klein to the party, he felt the American was entitled to a slice of the Apple pie.

In the early hours of 9 May, three Beatle signatures were on the document that legitimised Klein's dream of becoming the manager of The Beatles and the Rolling Stones. There were no prizes for guessing which one was missing.

Twelve hours later, all four Beatles were at Olympic Studios along with Glyn Johns as they again listened to various playbacks of the 'Get Back' tracks that he had assembled from more than one hundred and fifty hours of tape. But he was aware of the gathering storm clouds in the room – particularly between McCartney and the other three – and tactfully found a reason to be elsewhere.

In his absence, the talk inevitably shifted from music to majority interest. Fed up with McCartney's procrastination over formalising Klein's contract and the terms of his salary, the other three demanded that all four sign the contract. Lennon presented McCartney with the A4 document that officially made Klein – or ABKCO, depending on your interpretation – an Apple employee. He insisted it be signed right there so it could be legally ratified by Klein's ABKCO board in New York the next day, a Saturday.

McCartney's gaze zeroed in on the one constituent part that was still an instant red flag: the money. 'I thought twenty per cent was too high,' he recalled. 'I said, "We're a big act, he'll take fifteen, believe me. Klein is the board and anyway no one does business on a Saturday. Let's leave it till Monday."'

It was a fudge too far. Lennon, Harrison and Starr lost their cool and unleashed an unsparing verbal assault on McCartney, leaving him bruised and bleeding on the canvas.

Klein was reportedly at Heathrow Airport waiting for a New York flight and the piece of paper that said The Beatles were finally his when Lennon reached him on an airport phone to say McCartney was refusing to play ball. Klein rushed to Olympic and joined in the free-for-all. By McCartney's own account, it was a brutal affair.

In his statement to the High Court some eighteen months later, he declared: 'It became clear to me that the other three had already signed the agreement the previous day without my knowledge.' Under company rules, three Apple directors constituted a quorum and their assent made the document legally binding. McCartney's intransigence over Klein remained but, pragmatic enough to know that a fait accompli had occurred, he repeated his insistence that he take a reduced commission. 'I thought The Beatles' fortune was on the line and I was the only one fighting to save it,' he recalled.

In an interview with BBC Radio Merseyside, he said: 'One thing in the business is that you get agents and things and sometimes you can get a bit carved up. We've been involved in a lot of contracts . . . that we've had to straighten out. We've become more business-minded but I still can't stand business. The four of us are really just a rock band. But when we sign a contract now we have to ask what does it mean?'

Elsewhere, he displayed the kind of public candour that Lennon would have been proud of: 'The thing is, I am not signed with Allen Klein because I don't like him. The truth is he only has three quarters of The Beatles and, in fact, he doesn't have The Beatles. He is definitely the manager of John, George and Ringo but I have told him that he doesn't manage me.'

The meeting at Olympic ended in familiar deadlock. Patience exhausted, the others in unison told McCartney to 'fuck off' as they angrily exited the building. It was a new low. Harrison would later observe: 'He was outvoted three to one. If he doesn't like it, it's a real pity because we're trying to do what is best for The Beatles as a group or best for Apple as a company.'

As he sat alone in the studio, McCartney, gripped by fear and loathing, had never felt so isolated during his time in the band. He was close to tears when he heard a tentative American voice at the studio door.

Steve Miller was a young Texan singer-songwriter, a mainstay of the San Francisco scene that upended American culture in the late Sixties, a guitar blues virtuoso who had been in London for some time and had drifted into the outer margins of The Beatles' social orbit. This had led to him sitting in at the Apple studio as the band recorded the single version of 'Get Back' and, on at least one occasion, jamming with them.

On this night Miller was hoping to get some studio time at Olympic to continue laying down a track for his forthcoming third album, *Brave New World*. The link between McCartney and Miller was Glyn Johns, who was engineering Miller's album while working on the 'Get Back' tapes.

McCartney recalled: 'Steve happened to be there recording, late at night, and he just breezed in. "Hey, what's happening, man? Can I use the studio?" "Yeah!" I said. "Can I drum for you? I just had a fucking unholy argument with the guys there." I explained it to

him, took ten minutes to get it off my chest. So he and I stayed
that night and did a track of his called "My Dark Hour". I thrashed
everything out on the drums. There's a surfeit of aggressive drum
fills, that's all I can say about that. We stayed up until late. I played
bass, guitar and drums and sang backing vocals. It's actually a pretty
good track . . . it was a very strange time in my life and I swear I got
my first grey hairs that month. I saw them appearing. I looked in the
mirror, I thought, I can see you. You're all coming now. Welcome.'

But Klein didn't need McCartney's signature on a piece of paper.
Lennon's endorsement carried the real weight in The Beatles, as his
sheer, indomitable strength of will always had. 'John was the leader
because he shouted the most,' said George years later when time's
passage had made reflections less acerbic.

In an interview that month, Klein's reciprocal loathing for
McCartney surfaced when he was asked if Paul's refusal to endorse
him was a problem. 'Well,' sneered Klein in his Brooklyn tone, 'I
can understand him wanting to go with his family. It is a problem.
But it's his problem.'

Even before the ink on his contract was dry, Klein had already
begun stripping Apple to its core. The company, he reckoned, not
without some truth, had become a hippie haven for every freeloader
in town. Apple owned cars no one could remember buying, had
a portfolio of addresses no one had ever visited – including a
townhouse in Mayfair – and retained a charge account at such
high-end stores as Harrods and Fortnum & Mason. On top of
that, staff salaries had to be taken into account – and that included
everyone from Derek Taylor in his generously stocked press office
to the likes of Neil Aspinall, Mal Evans and all the mini-skirted
girls perched behind a battery of secretarial desks and those who
manned the telephones.

Moreover, every Beatle had a gofer – and each one was on the
clock. And every gofer had an assistant.

Apple also ran a number of subsidiary companies, such as the
newly-formed experimental Zapple label. And, of course, there were
still those Beatle IOUs in the safe worth many thousands of pounds.

To make matters worse, there was no fresh money flowing into the coffers. EMI had for weeks refused to unlock around £1.3m in royalties until Apple's legal stand-off with Triumph Investment Trust over the purchase of Nems had been resolved.

In Klein's eyes, every penny was a hostage and every pound a prisoner as he set about his task. Sergeant Buzzkill was off the leash.

The swiftness and brutality of Klein's actions sent shivers through Apple. His assistant and nephew Ronnie Schneider, an equally brash American, acted like a Mafioso – an image he did nothing to contradict – as he helped carry out his uncle's bidding. Among those caught in the first wave of the purge were Alastair Taylor, the company's general manager, Ron Kass, the highly respected president of Apple Records, and Brian Lewis, who worked in contracts.

Magic Alex discovered the spell had been broken when he turned up at his lab in Boston Place to find the doors shut and padlocks firmly in place as his so-called inventions were hauled away for scrap. By then he had run up debts of £53,000 – a sum nearly twenty times his annual salary. He kept his silence for forty years before pouring out his rage to *The New York Times* while insisting history had dealt him a bad hand over his part in the story.

'I broke the locks and went in,' he said. 'I thought that there had been a burglary. None of my engineers were there. I therefore went straight to the Savile Row offices. When I walked in, the receptionist told me that Allan Klein had fired all the staff of all the Apple companies. She told me that I had been fired as well. I asked for John Lennon. He was not there, so I telephoned him in Weybridge. I said that all the equipment was missing and that I had been told that I had been fired. John Lennon replied: "Bullshit, no one can fire you. You are not an employee, you are a partner."

'Boston Place was ruined', he continued. 'They had removed all the equipment. I refused to have anything more to do with the venture. At John Lennon's request, Allan Klein telephoned me. He told me that his job had been to clean out the whole of Apple

Corporation. He said that the equipment that had been installed was now in the basement of Boston Place. I said that I wanted to have nothing more to do with it and I left Apple permanently.'

Back at Apple, three secretaries were shown the door in one afternoon. Dee Meehan survived but watched the executions take place. 'Klein just moved in and started firing people,' she recalled. 'He got rid of everybody he could possible clear out, either by taking their work away, so that there was nothing for them to do, or by making their jobs so uncomfortable they felt obliged to quit. He didn't like people who were close to The Beatles. As soon as Ron Kass went, everybody was worried . . . Klein was really mean. He fired people when they were on location. Tea-girls were dismissed, then it was discovered that there was no tea.'

Chris O'Dell was another who seemed to cling on by her fingertips but her intimacy with the whole meltdown helped her provide a measured assessment in the years that followed. 'Apple was bipolar', was her verdict. 'It had a split personality. They were losing money and things were getting out of control. There is this part of it that was supposed to be very business-like, it was supposed to earn money. The idea wasn't to turn millions and millions but it was supposed to support itself. The eccentric other side of it and the business side of it just clashed.'

Others, such as talent scout Peter Asher, were quick to see the writing on the wall and began making their own plans rather than work under Klein, or at least walk before they were pushed.

Alistair Taylor had been in from the start, having been standing at Brian Epstein's shoulder when he first saw the unkempt and leather-clad wannabes playing Liverpool's Cavern in November 1961. He had remained a loyal Epstein lieutenant before becoming Apple's general manager following Brian's death in July 1967. He famously appeared in a flyer for Apple as the one-man-band who now owned a Bentley.

He was especially close to McCartney, for whom he was on call twenty-four hours a day as a personal Mr Fix-It. But when Klein pulled the trigger, Taylor quickly found himself out of favour.

McCartney failed to return any of his calls. 'It was a hell of a blow,' said the mild-mannered Taylor, who never spoke to any of The Beatles again.

Kass was embarrassingly bulleted after Klein concocted a false story to suggest the then fiancé of actress Joan Collins was creaming off the top. He left without a pay-off but was given the lease to the Mayfair town house no one could remember buying.

Klein's scattergun approach to cost-cutting was just as much about cementing his own powerbase. To that end, he trained his sights on The Beatles' inner sanctum, which included Peter Brown, Neil Aspinall and Mal Evans, but each remained ring-fenced from his grasp. He felt that Aspinall, especially, was a big threat, having wrongly pigeon-holed the former roadie as a shameless sponger. At one point he had tried to get Aspinall to sign a contract, even chasing him round a conference table before Lennon intervened, telling Klein: 'Leave him alone. Look at the trouble I got into by signing pieces of paper. Neil's not stupid.'

Despite his closeness to Lennon, Brown was rightly or wrongly considered to be a Klein lackey, an assertion not helped when he carried out some of the dismissals himself. Overnight, he went from director to doormat. In his own memoir, Brown defended his actions: 'Some of the dirty work was left to me. I have been criticised for serving Klein in this task, but I unhappily agreed to do the job only because I hoped the news could be delivered with kindness and dignity instead of from Klein's mouth.'

They were indeed tempestuous times. Under normal circumstances, this would be familiar and comfortable terrain for Klein. Outwith personnel purges, he loved nothing more than taking on 'the men in suits' on behalf of clients he felt had been royally ripped off. And the strategy was simple – if they made more money, so did he. Greed and power, the oldest motivations known to man. Until now those battles had been waged on home turf, the courtrooms of his native America. British laws and British customs, however, provided a considerably different challenge, one that represented a steep learning curve.

Klein's power base at Apple was largely dependent on the support of Lennon. By May, he had Lennon's unqualified backing over 'sweeping out all the rubbish and the deadwood and stopped Apple from being a rest house for the world's hippies'. Having slashed staff costs, his next priority was the royalties agreement with EMI.

*

EMI's chairman, the genial Sir Joseph Lockwood, had, along with Brian Epstein and George Martin, ensured that The Beatles' fame reached every part of the globe. He had always kept his door open for 'the boys' in recognition of the fact that the group had turned EMI and its American partner, Capitol, into the world's most profitable record companies. Unrestricted access had been especially granted to Lennon and McCartney, and both men felt an informal and jovial affinity with Sir Joe, despite the generation gap.

Only twice had they butted horns. Lockwood had insisted Gandhi's image be removed from the *Sgt. Pepper* cover for fear of offending Hindus, and he had refused to distribute John and Yoko's 1968 album, *Two Virgins,* on the simple grounds of good taste.

Until his death, Epstein had been Lockwood's go-to guy when it came to renewing the band's EMI royalty contracts. The last one had been agreed in 1967 but the group had been so prolifically creative during this period that they had already fulfilled the terms of that deal by May 1969 – seven years earlier than required.

Which was why Klein knew he held all the aces as he prepared to do battle with EMI. On 7 May, two days before McCartney's bust-up with the other three at Olympic Studios, he and Lockwood sat round the boardroom table at EMI to discuss a new royalties agreement. Next to Klein, and looking slightly uncomfortable, were the four musicians and Yoko. (McCartney had argued for John Eastman to ride shotgun but had been shouted down.)

Klein wasted no time in getting to the point. No increased royalty meant no more records. It was that simple. But if Klein expected Lockwood, a veteran of many bruising boardroom battles, to simply kowtow to his despotic behaviour, he was mistaken. Lockwood said he was happy to renegotiate the terms of the 1967 deal provided it benefited all parties. Puffing on his pipe, Klein guffawed and said, 'You don't understand. We get everything, you get nothing.' Seconds later, the visitors were being summarily ejected from the premises. Only McCartney had the presence of mind to give Lockwood a sheepish backwards glance as if to say 'Sorry, guv, it's nothing to do with me.'

Within half an hour, Klein, showing uncharacteristic contrition, was on the phone to apologise.

There was, of course, an unspoken truth attached to the meeting; Klein and Lockwood knew they needed each other. Klein understood that within EMI Sir Joe's word was law and that he alone could make or break any deal. Lockwood was equally aware that much of his company's profits lay in the hands of the four musicians. A tense stand-off remained in place.

Running parallel to the EMI discussions at this time was the equally fraught stalemate with Triumph over Nems. That drama was this month due to be played out in the High Court in London as Triumph sought a judicial ruling on EMI's refusal to free up the £1.3m in royalties currently lying dormant in a Lloyds Bank escrow account. Having bought the company, Triumph was entitled to pocket an annual twenty-five per cent management fee – approximately £325,000 after expenses – for managing The Beatles, even though they didn't fulfil that role. And they were entitled to keep on doing that until 1976. Clearly, someone had to blink.

Days before the case was due to be heard in court, Triumph's Leonard Richenberg heard a familiar New York accent on the end of the phone offering a plea bargain. Richenberg was prepared to mull it over but by the end of the day Klein had changed his mind, saying, 'I'll see ya in court.'

Richenberg had by now grown weary at the prospect of a lengthy and costly courtroom battle, and eventually visited Apple to try and reach some kind of compromise without resort to QCs and judges. Triumph, he said, would surrender its entitlement to twenty-five per cent of the Beatle bounty in return for £750,000 and £300,000 of the royalties currently frozen by EMI. In addition, Triumph would receive £50,000 for Nems' twenty-three per cent stake in The Beatles' film company, Subafilms, as well as five per cent gross of the band's royalties from 1972 to 1976. In return, Nems would surrender all its rights in all contracts affecting The Beatles.

They received an option on the 4.5 per cent of Northern Songs' shares owned by Nems, then valued at £335,000. Triumph also bought The Beatles' ten per cent stake in Nems for 226,000 of its own shares, at the time valued at £420,000. When all the head-swirling sums had been calculated, both sides naturally proclaimed a victory of sorts. Even McCartney bought into the complicated outcome, which nevertheless would not be formally ratified for another two months.

The Beatles no longer had any connection to Nems, thus severing a connection that had gone back to the earliest days of Beatlemania. The deal, however, had come at a sum far exceeding £1m – the precise figure John Eastman had laid out to Clive Epstein back in February to keep Nems in the Fab Four family. And he wasn't slow off the mark in sending out a reminder of this to Lennon, McCartney, Harrison and Starr.

He wrote: 'Before memories become too short, I want to remind everybody that we could have settled the Nems affairs for very little. Klein killed my deal by claiming all sorts of improper acts of Nems, which his investigation would disclose and promising to get you Nems for nothing. We all know that no improper acts were found by Klein if, in fact, Klein made an investigation at all.'

Oddly enough, there was no mention of the letter he had sent to Clive Epstein in February questioning his late brother's integrity, which brought Triumph on to the board in the first place.

Shark though he was, Klein wisely refused to take the Eastman bait. He had bigger fish to land – Northern Songs. The struggle to retain the Lennon-McCartney catalogue was the third spoke in an ever-evolving corporate wheel – and the one that, perhaps, mattered most.

Klein knew he desperately needed a major negotiating coup to restore confidence in his abilities and to ward off any nagging doubts that might surface with Lennon, Harrison and Starr.

ATV had set a revised take-it-or-leave-it deadline of 11 May for its bid for majority control to be accepted. Both sides owned around thirty-five per cent each of the company's stock, give or take a few points. But the main focus of any last-minute pitch was not to reel in a few wayward strays but to convince the consortium of shareholders who still held the crucial fifteen per cent balance of power to join them. It consisted of clients from three top London brokers, W.I. Carr & Spencer Thornton, Astaire & Co., and Howard & Wyndham, who, as owners of several West End theatres, carried more clout and were seen as natural allies of ATV. In business, however, money always held sway before any old pals' act.

The consortium remained unimpressed by ATV's offer but were equally wary that a victory for The Beatles could see Klein, viewed by key City observers as a divisive figure, elevated to an influential place on a newly constituted Northern Songs board.

In an effort to placate the consortium, Apple announced that David Platz, a respected music publisher and the man in charge of Essex Music, would run Northern Songs if The Beatles bid got over the line ahead of ATV. But it didn't take the media long to discover that Platz had secret links to Klein and so wasn't quite as impartial as Apple suggested. The consortium had their own ideas over who would run Northern Songs, with no place for either Klein or Grade at the top table. That scenario, mapped out during several meetings with Apple, would have seen The Beatles potentially still owning the company but, crucially, having no say in how it should be run.

Backed into a corner, Lennon sensed that his grip on his copyright was slowly slipping away. Angry, frustrated and utterly fed up, he finally snapped. 'I'm not going to be fucked around by men in suits sitting on their fat arses in the city,' he famously declared after one meeting with consortium negotiators. It was an intervention, however, that helped to drive the consortium into the welcoming arms of ATV.

Alerted to Lennon's outburst and knowing how it would be received, Grade got in touch with Peter Donald, head of Howard & Wyndham, which was viewed as the most influential of the three consortium members. The two men agreed a deal for the entire bloc at, remarkably, a price lower than The Beatles' offer. It was virtually game over for Lennon and McCartney.

In his autobiography, Grade said: 'I had meetings with Klein [in May] for hours on end each day and didn't like the way it was going. I had a strange feeling about Klein because of all the delays so I called Donald and said, "I want to buy your fourteen per cent of Northern Songs, how much do you want for it?" We agreed a price and did the deal on the telephone.

'We now had fifty-four per cent of the company and therefore controlled Northern Songs. Klein called me late that afternoon and said, "Well, I have to admit it, you beat me to the punch. We're now ready to sell you the shares at the same price you paid Peter Donald." That, my friends, is how we acquired The Beatles' catalogue and got into the music business.' Of course, it was much more byzantine than that.

Klein retreated to the shadows to lick his wounds while Lennon and McCartney were forced to come to the grim and heartbreaking realisation that the songs they had written, the songs that had provided the soundtrack to a generation, were lost to those 'men in suits sitting on their fat arses in the city'. Songs like 'Yesterday', 'She Loves You', 'Day Tripper', 'Eleanor Rigby', 'Hey Jude' and 'A Day In The Life' would now yield a multi-million pound future harvest for faceless stock market speculators, City institutions and one tragic pop star, Michael Jackson, for years to come.

Over the next few months, Klein continued to cling to hopes of brokering a deal with Grade, but the truth was that he had been trumped. Northern Songs had followed Nems out the door. He still, however, retained one vital card that might at least redeem him in the eyes of his clients. EMI and Capitol had signalled they were ready to resume talks over renegotiating The Beatles' royalty rates. It was the one window of opportunity Klein had been waiting for.

*

Throughout May, Lennon remained seriously conflicted over the future direction of his career. Acrimony seemed to leap out of every corner, especially when it came to his increasingly polarised relationship with McCartney. One minute he was trying to rekindle a lost magic in the studio; the next he found himself in a boardroom hurling venomous insults at his erstwhile partner and his new 'bourgeoisie' American family.

'I quite fancy giving some live shows, but Ringo doesn't because he says, you know, "It'll just be the same when we get on, nothing different,"' he told one interviewer early in May. 'I can't give you any definite plans for a live show when we're not even agreed on it. We've got to come to an agreement. For a start, there's too much going on now for us to even talk realistically about going on tour.'

Despite worries about his personal finances, he splashed out a reported £145,000 on Tittenhurst Park, a twenty-six-room Grade Two-listed Georgian pile set in seventy-two acres of lush Berkshire countryside. The house had previously been home to Peter Cadbury, a non-conformist member of the famous chocolate-making family. Lennon commissioned extensive and expensive refurbishment work, including the installation of a state-of-the-art recording studio.

On the music front, 'Get Back' remained in limbo, unloved and unfinished; Lennon continued to look to Yoko to provide the creative counterpoint that had once been McCartney; Harrison, having stockpiled a bank of new songs, was already glimpsing a road ahead without The Beatles. Indeed, on 11 May he worked with Cream's bassist Jack Bruce on a song for his first solo album. Starr, his work on *The Magic Christian* finally in the can, saw movies as a potential new outlet to put his name up in lights instead of being seen as the lowest rung on a four-step ladder.

McCartney, preparing for fatherhood and getting acquainted with the role of stepdad to Linda's daughter Heather, headed for Corfu with his wife on a month-long break. Before departing, the

couple made a lightning trip up to Liverpool to see his dad. After
that, Paul was happy to shut out Apple, Klein and The Beatles.

The ninth of May – the date of the seismic bust-up between
McCartney and the others – was the last time they would be in the
studio together for the foreseeable future. That particular day also
saw the release of two Beatle solo albums; but anyone looking for a
Pepper or even a *Magical Mystery Tour* was browsing in the wrong
record store.

Harrison's *Electronic Sound* did exactly what it said on the cover. It
was no more than two lengthy tracks consisting of beeps and bleeps
inspired by his new Moog synthesiser. It reeked of self-indulgence,
the kind of arrogance that suggested a Beatle could commit any old
rubbish to tape and still think the fans would love it.

Lennon's *Unfinished Music No. 2: Life With The Lions*, meanwhile,
was the unofficial follow-up to *Two Virgins*. Side one contained
the music recorded in Cambridge in March. The flipside was,
by any measure, an even harder listen; it included a track called
'Baby's Heartbeat', which captured in Yoko's womb the heartbeat
of John Ono Lennon II, the child she had miscarried the previous
November.

Both albums were released on Zapple, the label that would soon
become part of Klein's kill list. And both had zero commercial
appeal. Neither of them troubled the loftier reaches of the British or
American charts, and nor were they meant to. But while Harrison
stayed off the grid, Lennon was happy to use the record to bring the
John-and-Yoko publicity machine out of mothballs.

Since the Amsterdam bed-in, he had been keen to maintain his
image – on student campuses around the globe, at least – as the
Maverick Beatle, the one most fully in tune with anti-authoritarian
agendas. Now he wanted to broadcast his peace message to a
transatlantic audience, one he was convinced would take him and
Yoko more seriously than did their European counterparts, who
dismissed them as eccentric buffoons.

In an interview on 8 May with David Wigg for the BBC Radio
One show, *Scene and Heard*, he said, 'The Beatles are treated like

Britain's children, you know. And it's okay for the family to insult us. But you try . . . see what happens if abroad starts insulting us. The British will stick up for us. And it's just like a family. And it's all right for them to slap our face, but if the neighbour does it, you watch out, you know. It's always been like that. And George was very depressed and it is depressing when the whole family's picking on you, you know. Whether it's because he did something wrong. I don't believe in hitting the child, you know. We do get hurt because Britain appreciates us least, you know. But we can't help that. But at least we can live here in peace you know, really.'

He also touched unflinchingly on a subject most rock stars veered away from: his own mortality. Asked how he would deal with a life shorn of fame and the trappings that come with it, he was characteristically honest. 'I'd like to live to a ripe old age, with Yoko only, you know. And I'm not afraid of dying. I don't know how it'd feel at the moment. But I'm prepared for death because I don't believe in it. I think it's just getting out of one car and getting into another.'

By May, American universities including Stanford, Harvard and Cornell were a hotbed of political agitation, sit-ins and a source of violent protests over Vietnam, civil rights, apartheid and nuclear weapons. Ranged against them was a five-month-old Richard Nixon Republican administration and a House of Congress in no mood for compromise with 'those little bastards', as the American president called them. 'The time has come for an end to patience,' said White House attack dog, Attorney-General John Mitchell. 'I call for an end to minority tyranny – and for an immediate re-establishment of civil peace and protection of individual rights.'

It was precisely the type of David v. Goliath setting that touched on Lennon's belief in power to the people. Then an opportunity arose for the Lennons to mix business with pleasure.

Starr, along with Peter Sellers, was due on board the newly launched Cunard liner the *QE2*, sailing from Southampton to New York. The all-expenses-paid trip was a gift from Commonwealth United, the company behind *The Magic Christian*, as a reward for helping to bring the film in under budget and ahead of schedule.

'All the sailors were from Liverpool so I went down to their quarters,' recalled Starr. 'I was with Terry Southern, who became a good friend, and we were on our way to the Bahamas. The *QE2*'s crew band had a little stage in their hangout room, so I got up and played with them. They played a Beatles number and I didn't stop in the right place, where it had a break, so they turned and shouted at me. I said, "I don't remember them all!"'

The Lennons also tried to book passage on the ship, a bold statement of Sixties Cool Britannia, with a view to holding another bed-in in the Big Apple, but an unexpected hitch scuppered their plans. When he enquired about a US visa, American immigration officials in London vetoed Lennon's request on the grounds that his 1968 conviction for drug possession made him an illegal alien and an unwanted visitor to the land of the free.

Undaunted, the couple, with John playing paterfamilias to Yoko's daughter Kyoko, from her marriage to Tony Cox, quickly made alternative arrangements to fly to the Bahamas which, as an oh-so-British colony, imposed no such legal restrictions on their arrival, and which lay just under two hundred miles off the Florida coast. They reckoned it was the perfect place from which to launch a new media blitz on the American mainland.

But the Bahamas largely existed in splendid isolation from the world's press and could in no way provide the window to the world the Lennons were seeking. That realisation dawned on them after just one night in the Sheraton Oceanus Hotel. The stifling heat also proved too much for Yoko.

So the couple, complete with twenty-six pieces of luggage, a two-man film crew and Yoko's assistant, Anthony Fawcett, were back in the air and heading north, this time to Canada. Upon disembarking at Toronto they were quickly ushered into a holding room by suspicious immigration officials for two hours. They were haughtily informed that the drug conviction that blocked their entry into the US also applied to Canada, though, commendably, they were granted ten days' access pending an appeal. That gave them enough leeway to head first to Toronto's King Edward Sheraton Hotel for an overnight stay before flying on to Montreal at 9.55 p.m. on 26 May where they arrived at midnight outside the equally patriotic-sounding Queen Elizabeth Hotel, and took over three suites on the seventeenth floor.

The Hilton-owned establishment, like the one in Amsterdam, was one of the grandest in the city and no stranger to celebrity. The Queen had already stayed at the hotel that, controversially in the French-speaking province, had been named after her. Other famous names in the register included Fidel Castro, Princess Grace of Monaco and Charles de Gaulle. But no one was prepared for the arrival of the John and Yoko peace circus.

Among the other late arrivals was Apple press officer-turned-minder Derek Taylor, who had flown in from New York after being among Starr's party on the *QE2*. For the next seven days, room 1742 was given over to peace as Lennon turned it into a big top for his own circus. This week would do more to shape Lennon's life – and his legacy – since that fateful summer of 1957 when he first clapped eyes on a fifteen-year-old Paul McCartney.

On the first day alone there were over fifty journalists, photographers, disc jockeys and camera crews all jostling for his attention. Mostly, they were serious and attentive and devoid of the cynicism that had largely accompanied the Amsterdam bed-in. Lennon was confident and passionate. His appearance was commanding, almost Messiah-like as he delivered sermon after sermon.

Inside the crowded suite, Lennon and Yoko sat peacefully holding hands, surrounded by pink and white carnations, record players, film equipment, empty glasses and busy phones. Two books lay on a table – Vladimir Nabokov's *The Defence* and a personally autographed copy of Jacqueline Susann's latest voyeuristic masterpiece, *The Love Machine*. (Earlier, Miss Susann, who had also written *Valley of the Dolls*, had dropped by to pass on her good wishes and to cash in on the publicity of the Lennon visit.)

Yoko wore a white blouse and cream slacks with no shoes, and Lennon, also barefoot, had on a white T-shirt with a green stripe on the sleeves, cream trousers, white socks with red and blue stripes, and, round his neck, a gold chain, from which dangled a crucifix. A pair of white sneakers lay on the floor beneath his knees.

The couple were at ease with the press. Lennon fielded sceptical questions about his peace-making efforts with adroitness and peppery wit. They were obviously sincere in their campaign for peace and non-violence but bitter about the United States' refusal to admit John. 'The whole effect of our bed-ins has made people talk about peace,' he said as he toyed with a white carnation. 'We're trying to interest young people into doing something for peace. But it must be done by non-violent means – otherwise there can only be chaos. We're saying to the young people . . . and they have always been the hippest ones . . . we're telling them to get the message across to the squares. A lot of young people have been ignoring the squares when they should be helping them. The whole scene has become too serious and too intellectual.'

What about talking to the people who make the decisions – the powerbrokers, suggested a cynical reporter. Lennon laughed. 'Shit, talk? Talk about what? It doesn't happen like that. In the US, the government is too busy talking about how to keep me out. If I'm a joke, as they say, and not important, why don't they just let me in? We are both artists! Peace is our art. We believe that because of everything I was as a Beatle and everything that we are now, we stand a chance of influencing other young people. And it is they who will rule the world tomorrow.' The room quickly became the backdrop to a varied cast of visitors that included the serious to the downright curious.

Among those swearing fealty were American comedian Tommy Smothers, civil rights activist Dick Gregory, Harvard professor cum hippie guru Timothy Leary, Beat poet Allen Ginsberg and DJ Murray the K – a leftover from the days of Beatlemania. There was a constant drip of open-mouthed students and shaven-headed devotees in saffron robes from the local Hare Krishna temple, whose bell-ringing and intermittent chanting added another surreal aspect to the proceedings. Less starstruck was a local rabbi, Abraham

Feinberg, with whom Lennon struck up a brief but respectful acquaintanceship. And in the middle, dressed in the same pyjamas they had worn in Amsterdam. were 'the world's clowns'. But there was nothing funny about the message, which by now was daubed on walls, pillows, scraps of paper and piles of doodles strewn on the floor as in Amsterdam.

Derek Taylor said, 'They made themselves completely available to anybody on Earth who wanted to come into their bedroom, provided they were not carrying a blood-stained axe. Maybe they came in thousands, it certainly felt like it. My job was to be around day and night while they were in bed.'

Across the pond, the Lennons' peace campaign was accepted with courtesy and a degree of reverence from a more liberal-minded press corps. Instead of sneers and finger-pointing (though one venomous and villainous exception was yet to appear), the message was treated seriously by print and broadcast outlets. Very few of them mentioned the dreaded B-word.

Montreal was only sixty miles from the American-Canadian border, or an hour's flight from New York, making it fairly easy for media big-hitters to make the pilgrimage. Ritchie Yorke, a young rock writer with the *Toronto Globe and Mail*, was still earning his journalistic stripes but he knew a good story when he saw one, and he persuaded his editors to let him join the Lennon entourage as it headed to Montreal. Yorke, who would become one of the couple's closest media confidants, recalled: 'It was an extremely colourful scene – a potted purple gloxinia plant, signs, placards, and proclamations covering the walls, John's guitar, candles, other burning objects and an expanding set of lyrics to a new and emerging Lennon song.'

Lennon had already accidentally hit on a simple but affecting new slogan, which scanned so well: 'Give Peace A Chance.' Like 'All You Need Is Love', it was a lightning-in-a-bottle-moment. Four words that perfectly caught the mood swirling inside room 1742 and the zeitgeist of 1969. Soon it became a rallying cry that was repeated to every newspaper journalist and radio broadcaster within earshot. The message became a mantra – and the mantra became a melody.

To begin with, all he had was a chorus: 'All we are saying, is give peace a chance.' At one point he toyed with the notion of keeping the song as lyrically sparse as 'I Want You'. Reaching for his Gibson guitar, he began to flesh out the text . . . Bagism . . . Shagism . . . Dragism . . . Madism . . . Ragism . . . Tagism. What did it matter if it read like garbage? What really counted was the message.

At one point the word 'masturbation' was to be slyly inserted, but he was fed up being burnt by the censors over his lyrics. The 'Ballad Of John And Yoko' single was due to be released in the UK on 28 May (complete with Yoko on the cover alongside the four Beatles) and would undoubtedly spark a furious reaction over the line 'they're gonna crucify me'. So he replaced the offending word with 'mastication', even though he hadn't a clue what it meant.

The problem now was what to do with the song he hoped would give him the same kind of street cred Bob Dylan had initially enjoyed as a 'serious' songwriter and political troubadour. In his heart, he wanted to write a song that would at least match Dylan's version of the traditional protest song 'We Shall Overcome'.

He was keen to record right away but a hotel bedroom in Montreal was a long way from Studio Two at Abbey Road. Surely someone, somewhere in Montreal should be able to record it? Calls were quickly relayed to Capitol Records of Canada, which, luckily, had a branch office in Montreal. Eventually, they reached a producer called Andre Perry, the company's go-to-guy in Canada's second-biggest city: 'Would you like to record a song with John Lennon?'

Meanwhile, music was also on the mind of Timothy Leary, the LSD advocate whose hippie refrain telling students to 'turn on, tune in and drop out' had made him the unexpected spokesman for mid-Sixties, disaffected American youth and, in turn, the scourge of their parents. In 1966, he had declared Lennon, McCartney, Harrison and Starr to be like the Four Horsemen of the Apocalypse who would usher in a new world order. His precise words were: 'I declare that The Beatles are mutants. Prototypes of evolutionary agents sent by God, endowed with a mysterious power to create a new human species, a young race of laughing freemen.' Proof, if any were needed, of the mind-altering qualities of lysergic acid diethylamide.

Leary had co-authored a book, *The Psychedelic Experience*, which was said to have borrowed liberally from the ancient *Tibetan Book of the Dead*. Lennon read Leary's work and used it as a lyrical and musical jumping-off point for 'Tomorrow Never Knows', the eerie closure to *Revolver* that signposted The Beatles' chemically-friendly future. Three years later, Leary and Lennon found themselves putting the world to rights in a Montreal hotel room.

At the time, Leary was running against Republican candidate – and future president – Ronald Reagan for the governership of California under the simplistic slogan of 'Come Together, Join The Party'. Without making any promises, Lennon loosely agreed to Leary's request to write a song framed around the campaign catchwords. But his interest in the subject matter, like his friendship with Leary, quickly waned, even if he did file away the notion of yet another song based on the concept of 'one world'.

For now, Lennon continued to preach peace to the masses while using the language of confrontation. He described the police and politicians as 'pigs', mirroring the rhetoric of the campuses, especially that of Berkeley in California where thousands of students had clashed with baton-wielding cops. Though some accused him of selling out by pushing peace and a non-violent solution, he knew he would face more pointed accusations of hypocrisy were he to suddenly advocate a violent overthrow of the American way of life.

Nevertheless, as he rallied his followers, his name began to be whispered ever more loudly in the upper echelons of American power. Inside the White House and behind closed doors at the FBI, Lennon was giving cause for concern. It was time to reopen and update the FBI file started in January by a Nixon administration mired in paranoia, the one marked 'John Lennon, musician'.

McCartney, meanwhile, remained in Corfu with Linda and stepdaughter Heather. Starr was taking to the life of an English playboy in New York with gusto before heading to the West Indies. Harrison and Pattie were bound for Sardinia, but before he left, he met Glyn Johns at Olympic to listen to his first proper pass at resurrecting an album from the mess that the 'Get Back' tapes had become.

The track listing read: 'One After 909', 'I'm Ready', 'Save The Last Dance For Me', 'Don't Let Me Down', 'Dig A Pony', 'I've Got A Feeling', 'Get Back', 'For You Blue', 'Teddy Boy', 'Two Of Us', 'Maggie Mae', 'Dig It', 'Let It Be', 'The Long And Winding Road' and a reprise of 'Get Back'. It was a rustic and homespun confection which, looking back, was similar to Dylan and the Band's *The Basement Tapes* (recorded between June and October 1967, but not officially released until 1975) and as far from the glossy production values of *Sgt. Pepper* and the White Album as you could get. It stuck rigidly to McCartney's initial vision of a stripped-down, live-in-the-studio album. The Beatles, naked. Or, as Lennon would later put it, the band 'with their trousers down'.

Harrison didn't have the authority on his own to sanction the compilation as the group's next album. He had long been overcome with indifference to 'Get Back', which he considered little more than a McCartney vanity project. The fact that Johns had only included one Harrison song – 'For You Blue' – hardly helped.

So, with no Beatles sessions pencilled in, 'Get Back' was gently returned to its dusty shelf in the Apple basement. And Glyn Johns, for the time being at least, quietly removed himself from the play.

Room 1742 of Montreal's Queen Elizabeth Hotel was turned into an ad hoc studio for the impromptu recording of John Lennon's anthemic 'Give Peace A Chance' with a peculiar cast of backing singers.

In the early evening of 1 June 1969, Andre Perry entered the ground-floor lift at Montreal's Queen Elizabeth Hotel and pressed the button to take him to the seventeenth floor. Lugging a 4-track tape recorder and a bag containing four microphones and two speakers, he stepped out of the lift when he reached the appointed level and walked along the corridor towards room 1742. No one barred his way or asked any questions as he arrived at the door, which already lay open. Seconds later he was face to face with John Lennon and Yoko Ono in a room swarming with people that included scandal-hungry journalists, celebrity liggers, prurient hangers-on and mantra-chanting devotees from the Canadian chapter of the Radha Krishna Temple. 'It was a circus, complete chaos,' recalled Perry, then Montreal's most in-demand record producer and a man with impeccable music credentials.

It had been a trying day for the Lennons. There had been the usual conveyor belt of interviews as the Montreal bed-in headed into day seven. The chilled-out ambience had turned toxic with the arrival of Al Capp, the American right-wing cartoonist and self-confessed 'Neanderthal fascist'. Capp, Richard Nixon's favourite satirist, lobbed racist insults at Yoko in the hope that Lennon would explode. Capp's shameful xenophobia was undoubtedly the lowest point of the Montreal bed-in.

But the highest point – and the most memorable – would take place just a few hours later with Perry's arrival.

His involvement had stemmed from calls made the previous day by flustered Capitol Records executives keen to make sure their VIP's every request was met. His task was simple – to turn 'Give Peace A Chance' from a simplistic, improvised singalong into a proper record. For two people who had never met, Lennon and Perry soon found themselves striking up an easy accord.

Perry told me: 'I guess he felt very comfortable with me. He just let me set up and said, "That looks fine." He was more concerned with working on the lyrics and trying to get the people who were in the room to participate really. We did a soundcheck and then we did two takes.'

The lyrics were pinned up on huge signs on the walls, like hippie graffiti. By now, around fifty people were shoehorned into the room, a supporting cast that became a backing chorus. Among them was American comedian Tommy Smothers, who would play acoustic guitar alongside Lennon, Timothy Leary and his wife Rosemary, civil rights activist Dick Gregory, poet Allen Ginsberg, local rabbi Abraham Feinberg, British DJ Roger Scott, who was working at local radio station CFOX, English singer Petula Clark and Apple press officer Derek Taylor, who would be comically name-checked in the song's lyrics alongside 'Bobby' Dylan and Norman Mailer.

Perry faced significant technical challenges to get the sound right. 'When I walked in there were two things that I knew,' he recalled. 'I knew that it wasn't going to sound right because the room was very small and also the ceiling was very low. The ceiling was about eight feet maximum. And it was made of sheet-rock and that would create a parallel wall, what we call standing waves where, if people slap their hands, you would hear this brrrrr-like reverberation. So I knew for a fact this was going to be ridiculous.'

He wasn't the only one slightly out of his comfort zone. Petula Clark, best known for her 1964 hit 'Downtown', had been a popular British singer for years but was far removed from Lennon's bohemian social orbit. Yet she found herself accidentally press-ganged into singing along to the chorus on 'Give Peace A Chance'.

Earlier that night she had got caught up in an Anglo-French controversy during a gig at the city's Place des Arts. She had been asked to do a show singing songs in French and English. But 1969 was a politically charged year. The 'Free Quebec' independence movement was at its peak and Petula's attempt to bridge the divide was met with jeers on both sides. The audience reaction left her dismayed and later she went seeking solace from a most unexpected source – John Lennon.

She recalled: 'I sang in French and the English-speaking audience were unhappy and quite vocal, and the French were particularly vocal when I sang in English. It was like open war. I was very hurt and I couldn't understand it at all. I really didn't know what to do and I needed to talk to somebody who I had no connection with, and John was in town with Yoko doing a bed-in for peace. So after the show one night I went over the hotel – no security, of course, I just walked in – and said I wanted to see John Lennon.

'So up I went, and there they were sitting in bed, and he was adorable. He could see I had a problem and he put his arms around me. I told him what it was all about and, well, he gave me some advice that I can't repeat. Anyway, he said it didn't matter, let them get over it, and he told me to go and have a glass of wine in the living room, and there were a lot of people in there. It was just chilling out, nothing weird. There were no drugs. Nothing like that. Just a nice, chilled-out atmosphere. There was some music being piped in, a very simple little song, and we started singing along with it, and it was "Give Peace A Chance". We were all being filmed and recorded, so I'm on "Give Peace A Chance".'

Clark was certainly on the record in spirit but whether she – and others in the room – was truly on it vocally may be open to conjecture. After the song was recorded, Perry took the tape away to his own studio for a playback and was left aghast by what he heard. Lennon's vocal track, with its busker-like spontaneity, and the acoustic guitars measured up fine, but the muffled background voices virtually made the track unusable.

'It sounded horrific,' he said. 'Lennon's voice was great and the energy was great and the guitars were great so I knew we had captured something. But the overall singing was not good. So being a producer I called some people, and asked them if they wanted to come down to the studio and overdub some things on a John Lennon record.

'They thought I was crazy, but they all showed up about ten o' clock in the morning. I didn't want to do a slick rendition that sounded like back-up singers in a studio doing harmony. What I wanted to reproduce was what I think Lennon was hearing in his head and the sound he heard in the room. It was supposed to be raw and unvarnished. It was supposed to sound like an amateur group and not finessed or anything. We did several overdubs and then my friends went away. I am also a drummer so I looked out a rubber garbage can and I did the old Beatles thunk, you know, to get the rhythm on this rubber can and slowly I built it up and put some tape echo on it.'

Having been up all night trying to salvage the recording, Perry took a shower before heading back across town to let Lennon hear the finished product.

'He looked at me and said, "It's no good, is it?" I said, "To tell you the truth, as far as the people in the room are concerned, no. But as far as your voice was concerned, it was good." So I told him I had kept some of the background to preserve the feeling of the room itself but that I had overdubbed stuff. So I gave him a choice – "Either you take what I recorded or you take the original back to Abbey Road and you do what you want with it." So he listened to what I had done and he just smiled and said, "That's fantastic."

'The funny thing is that in later years people said they could hear themselves singing and saying 'that was me banging the door'. But I would say only about thirty-four per cent of the original recording is what you hear on the record. The rest of it was overdubs in my studio. I wanted to give him some kind of option. You see, the point of the matter, it's not that we wanted to cheat or anything, it was a question of, like, not usable, the condition was absolutely terrible. What we did was take the original stuff that was there, and just added a few voices in a cleaner recording environment.'

Lennon's appreciation was genuine. When the record came out as a single a month later he insisted that Perry receive a special credit, and printed the name and address of his studio almost like a business card, giving him some unexpected, but welcome, exposure.

Fifty years after the experience, the Canadian admits he still finds it all quite surreal but says he was never daunted by the opportunity to record a Beatle. 'I wasn't a pop guy, I was a jazz musician. Obviously I knew who he was, I wasn't naïve, but I wasn't necessarily overwhelmed. I went round there to do a professional job. On reflection I think that's why he liked me. I wasn't overwhelmed by his fame or celebrity. I knew what I was doing. And I think he sensed it. He was a very intelligent guy but also the feeling I had from him was that he was very positive, very perceptive.'

Derek Taylor estimated that during the seven days of the Montreal bed-in, the Lennons conducted more than three hundred radio interviews and countless dialogues with print journalists. Among the many topics floated was the idea of a meeting between John and Pierre Trudeau, Canada's youthful prime minister, whose liberal attitude had drawn favourable comparisons with John F. Kennedy. The couple's astonishing media onslaught elevated their celebrity to new levels. But the uncomplicated access to room 1742 also made them easy marks for street-smart hustlers looking for a piece of the action.

For all his hard-edged misanthropy, Lennon was often effortlessly reeled in by fast-talking grifters like Allen Klein and Magic Alex Mardas. Happily, Allan Rock didn't fall into this category, although he nevertheless possessed a certain amount of callow chutzpah to bluff his way into the Lennons' inner sanctum on the same day as 'Give Peace A Chance' was recorded.

Rock was a geeky, bespectacled twenty-one-year-old and the leader of the students' union at Ottawa University in the country's capital, some one hundred and twenty-five miles from Montreal. He drove down to Montreal in his Volkswagen Beetle (it had to be, didn't it), bolstered by the firm belief that he could convince Lennon to speak at a seminar for world peace that his university was hosting the next day.

On the surface, it touched all the right buttons for Lennon – guaranteed media exposure, one-to-one communication with a like-minded youthful audience and the chance to again ramp up the message. Plus, with the bed-in now in its fifth day, the Lennons were starting to suffer from cabin fever. So Rock's invitation, although a little vague, was an opportunity at least to enjoy a little timeout. His very surname was enough to get Lennon's attention, too.

The young Canadian was staggered when the couple agreed to pack up their entourage, including a two-man film crew from Apple Films, and take a train east the next day. With his university sidekick, Hugh Segal, in tow, Rock picked the Lennons up at Ottawa's station to ferry them to the city's seat of learning. First, though, Lennon insisted on a whistle-stop tour of the country's capital, which was also home to Trudeau. Rock, who was already nurturing early ambitions of a political career, couldn't believe his luck. So much so that he thought nothing of driving past the prime minister's official residence in the city's New Edinburgh neighbourhood in the naïve hope that he could simply turn up with a Beatle in tow to talk about world peace.

In a memoir printed years later by Ottawa's *Globe and Mail*, Rock, who would go on to serve as Canada's federal health minister and for a time his country's ambassador to the United Nations, recalled the surreal events when he became a Beatle's unofficial Canadian tour guide for a day, including the moment when 'Get Back' came on the car's radio.

'I spent the day with Lennon, watching as he managed the incessant demands of mega fame, a star-struck twenty-one-year-old making dinner plans with an almost mythical figure who for five years had held my generation transfixed. He was calm at the centre of a constant, frantic happening, ignoring the kooks and crazies drawn by his raucous road show, and polite and patient with those of us trying to plan some sense into his schedule. In early evening, he told me that he wanted to see something of the city. He and Yoko Ono sat in the rear of my Volkswagen as I drove them around the capital, with John at one point singing along to The Beatles' "Get Back" on the radio. ("Turn it up!" he yelled from the back.) Disappointed that the prime minister had not joined us at the "Peace Conference", Lennon agreed when I suggested we visit 24 Sussex to see if Trudeau was home. In his absence, Lennon left a hand-written note, which led to a return visit in December of that year, when the two met on Parliament Hill.'

The 'peace' panel at Ottawa University, however, largely fell flat. Lennon was already tiring by the time he arrived and he was seriously irked as photographers took pictures of Yoko's daughter, Kyoko. Inside the hall, he offered only a few ambivalent soundbites. 'You've got to make people aware that there is an alternative, that war and violence aren't inevitable,' he declared wearily.

By now, the Lennons were seriously up against the Canadian immigration clock. Their temporary visa was due to expire on 5 June and the couple had no desire to outstay their welcome, despite the warmth directed at them by most Canadians during their stay. As far as Lennon was concerned, it was another peace box ticked. He said, 'Canada was great. I felt we really made a connection with the country's youth and it was such a positive vibe.'

That view was echoed by Anthony Fawcett, the art world specialist, who had become their personal assistant. He said, 'At times like this, I felt his peace campaign was working. The personal contacts and exchanges were worth so much more than any photo in a newspaper. More important, he was getting his message over to the kids who needed his advice and who really believed in him.'

There was still time for the Lennons to play the ordinary tourist before heading home. On 4 June, again with a film crew in tandem, they headed up to Niagara Falls to see the famous landmark in all its tumbling glory from the Canadian side. On the other side of the falls was America, its borders shut to the Beatle. It was, for now, as close as Lennon was going to get to the land of the free before heading back across the Atlantic.

In the can, at the very least, was a quirky new song that, unknown to him then, would become his breakout from the Beatle bubble and one of two recordings that would perhaps define his legacy as much as those songs he wrote with McCartney. Crucially, he felt vindicated about the choices he and Yoko had made to stand bravely alone in the face of all the cynics. Now the real test would be to see if he could carry forward the message that had become a mantra born in Montreal and prove it wasn't just simplistic and gullible sloganeering. And that meant testing it closer to home by rebuilding bridges with the other Beatles and, specifically, McCartney.

The thought occupied his mind as they flew back to Britain via Frankfurt and his new multi-roomed home in Ascot on 5 June. Was there still time for them to also give peace a chance? Or, when it came to his musical career, did those same words have a hollow meaning? More and more, Lennon was trapped between the world of The Beatles and the one he wanted to live in with Yoko.

*

Mainland Italy and about six hundred Mediterranean miles separated George Harrison and Paul McCartney for the first two weeks of June 1969. But the disconnect between them was more than just geographical, it was musical and philosophical. In Harrison's eyes, McCartney had behaved like a spoilt child over the past few months, spitting out his dummy because he couldn't get his own way. Their caught-on-camera flare-up during the filming for 'Get Back' still left a bitter taste. And now they found themselves similarly divided over Allen Klein, the future of Apple and everything they had put their nervous systems on the line for.

They were equally polarised over the future of The Beatles. McCartney couldn't bear the prospect of life without the band he had invested so much in. Harrison frankly no longer cared if he never played again with the man he blamed for stifling his musical creativity, although he was always willing to throw his lot in with Lennon and Starr. Having written a song with Dylan and collaborated most recently with Cream, he had already glimpsed an alternative musical future, one where all the musicians were part of a cooperative rather than being under the heel of an autocratic bandleader. Their estrangement, professional and personal, was all the more poignant since they had started off as friends 'growing up together playing guitar'. They were also on different pages domestically.

McCartney was settled with a by-now five months pregnant Linda and had formed his own little nuclear family with her daughter Heather as a bulwark against the pressures of the outside world.

Harrison, by contrast, was finding the walls of his four-year marriage to Pattie closing in. Temptation was a routine by-product of being a rock star and Harrison, a red-blooded man, as McCartney later testified, frequently indulged his own desires. Pattie, cuckolded in Kinfauns as a result of her husband's adulterous dalliances, felt an icy chill blowing through their relationship. Harrison, by June 1969, had become bitter, withdrawn and was pulling the drawbridge up on his world. Very few were allowed inside, and Pattie wasn't one of them any longer. More so since she simply could not match his obsession with meditation and Hinduism.

She noted: 'Things were not going well with The Beatles and he was bringing home bad vibes. We would argue and bicker, never reaching any conclusion so we were left feeling irritated with one another. He spent more and more time away from home – sometimes he wouldn't get back until four or five in the morning. At others, not at all. When he wasn't recording he would be at the Apple offices, which I knew was full of pretty girls. George was sexy, good-looking, witty and famous – an irresistible combination. He had never used aftershave in the past but since we had come back from India and the Maharishi, he had taken to wearing sandalwood oil, which I imagined was to attract other women. But if I accused him of anything he would deny it. He made me feel I was being unreasonable, nasty and suspicious . . . he didn't really confide in me, he was so angry and he would just keep it all in. He was just angry, and didn't want to talk about it.'

Pattie hoped that a good holiday in the sun would thaw the frigid chill from their lives. On 1 June, the couple flew from Heathrow Airport to the island of Sardinia where Harrison had rented a luxury villa in the secluded coastal town of Costa Smeralda for himself, Pattie and Terry Doran, as well as Klaus Voormann, the German musician/artist who had been a close friend of George's since the Hamburg Reeperbahn days.

They travelled light, although Harrison's guitar was rarely far from his sight. A committed sun worshipper, he was delighted to finally throw off the last vestiges of 'a long cold lonely winter' to feel the Mediterranean warmth on his back. And it provided the perfect setting for him to finish 'Here Comes The Sun', the song he had started a few weeks earlier while strolling in Clapton's garden. The holiday also gave him the privacy he craved. During their time on the island, Harrison's party remained pretty much free from media or fan intrusion. The only exception came when an Italian TV crew snatched some footage of George sitting lotus-like on a balcony while Pattie strolled round the grounds.

Isolation, meantime, was also fundamental to McCartney's month-long break on the Greek island of Corfu. The in-house fighting over Klein and the unyielding press speculation that The Beatles were finished had drained him of his sense of optimism. Nagging away was a feeling that he could no longer keep all the plates spinning. He had long stopped going to meetings at Savile Row, sending instead a lawyer to speak on his behalf. Apple, he felt, had become a prison, and Klein now had it in lockdown. He and Linda had never had a proper honeymoon but now the gap in all their schedules presented the right time for them to leave the pressures of Apple behind.

Initially, in order to throw the paparazzi off the scent, McCartney hinted that they were heading to France. Instead, they travelled to the tiny fishing village of Benitses, which had become a favourite of Hollywood's nouveau riche such as Warren Beatty, Gregory Peck, Audrey Hepburn and Paul Newman. For a month, until 16 June, the couple lived a low-key, almost frugal existence. Unlike Lennon, Harrison and Starr, who rarely went anywhere without an entourage in tow, McCartney only had Linda and Heather for company. And that was just enough.

At first, the inevitable whispers from locals followed their arrival, but within days the visitors were able to stroll anonymously round the few shops and tavernas as the townsfolk discreetly turned a blind eye to the Beatle in their midst.

Contact with Apple was non-existent. He didn't even leave a forwarding number. Of course, he couldn't escape his old life entirely. He continued his habit of buying British newspapers –

and there, one day, staring back at him from a Montreal hotel bedroom, smiling benignly and clutching a symbolic rose with his Japanese wife beside him, was John Winston Ono Lennon. You had to laugh.

Nevertheless, Benitses was, like the time he had spent at the Maharishi's Ashram, a time-lapse moment. A lull amid the lunacy – and one that, according to seasoned observers, had arrived at the right time.

Ray Connolly, a journalist on London's *Evening Standard*, had a foot in both the Lennon and McCartney camps. He was liked and trusted by both of them, a neutrality that gave him privileged access to the world's most exclusive showbiz club. Watching them close up, Connolly saw a friendship being torn asunder by circumstances that by now had spiralled out of control on either side.

He told me: 'Personally, I think they were all having a nervous breakdown at that point, round about June, especially John and Paul. They had always worked at a relentless pace and the need to come up with albums and singles so regularly was killing them. People today have simply no conception about the rate of the recording output up to *Abbey Road* in such a short space of time. It's frightening when you look back.

'It might have been a better idea for them to have taken, say, a year off after *Let It Be*, but of course they didn't. Paul was a workaholic and he wanted them to get back in the studio. But by that time John had already decided he didn't want to be a Beatle any more. He had made up his mind before they started work on *Abbey Road*. They were never out of the studio but the constant grind to come up with new albums and singles was killing them. I've long thought that. And I do think John and Paul were on the verge of nervous breakdowns, especially when you factor in all the business matters that were happening in the background. And then you have their own private lives, which were anything but private. John was with Yoko and Paul was with Linda and they were also an unwitting factor in pitting

John and Paul against each other.' Connolly's observations were right on the money. The ripple effects from the internecine warfare had naturally fallen on partisan lines where their wives were concerned. Both Yoko and Linda were strong, independent women – and neither held back when the gloves came off over their menfolk and Klein.

Linda said, 'It was weird times. Allen Klein was stirring it up something awful. Between Allen Klein in one ear and Yoko in the other ear, they had John so spinning about Paul it was really quite heartbreaking. So stupid. It reminded me of the [Sergei] Eisenstein [early 1940s] movie *Ivan the Terrible*; they were all whispering. It was like that with John; he was getting so bitter about Paul, and all Paul was saying was that he didn't want to sign a big management contract with Allen Klein. Nothing to do with anything else.'

Even outside their immediate circle, allies were being lost as Klein's cost-cutting putsch continued. Peter Asher, brother of McCartney's former fiancée Jane, was mourning the recent death of his father Richard when he got wind of Klein's Apple coup – and promptly fled on 5 June. With him he took James Taylor, arguably the brightest star in the Apple Records firmament outwith The Beatles themselves. Angry that Asher had pre-empted his dismissal, Klein resorted to the age-old management tactics of threatening to sue Taylor for breach of contract until McCartney interceded on the latter's behalf, arguing that Apple's aim was to give artists freedom, not tether them to a punishing contract system.

In an interview at the time Asher said, 'I had a great affection for the way Apple used to be rather than the way it has now become. I have no wish to knock Apple, but I am simply not happy there any more . . . and that is the reason why I am leaving.'

Years down the line, he expanded on his ill-feeling towards Klein. 'Allen Klein was a very bad idea . . . I had spent some time in New York and knew of his reputation. I'd heard a lot about him and knew people who'd worked for him. I just didn't think he was the right man for the job, that's all. The Rolling Stones were already wary of him, so I didn't think he'd work for The Beatles. The decision to leave wasn't that difficult, really. James Taylor had already decided that he wanted to go back to America, and since I was a firm believer in his talents and was going to be his manager, I decided to take the gamble and go to the States, as well. '

Thumbing through his own back pages, Taylor was less charitable when he laid bare his own thoughts in the pages of *Rolling Stone*: 'That old craperoo, the bullshit music biz thing, is creeping in. I think The Beatles have discovered the business trip isn't fun. You can't goof off. I get the feeling Apple is like a rich toy. I'm bitter, I guess. I feel they've let me down.'

Like Harrison and Lennon, McCartney had packed an acoustic guitar for his Corfu trip. One night he reached for it to complete a song that had been swirling inside his head for several months. He had already made a couple of half-hearted passes at 'Every Night' on 21 and 24 January at Twickenham Studios during the 'Get Back' sessions. He only had the first two lines and every word hinted at an aching, desperate plight. Four months down the line, though, and those pangs had been supplanted by the kind of domestic bliss he had long craved and found with Linda, a happiness that was reflected in the words that followed.

He recalled the period in an interview with *Mojo* magazine. 'It had been a heavy, difficult period, but meeting Linda and starting a family was the escape. I'd see there was life out there ... I said, "How the hell am I ever going to get out of these heavy meetings? And it was, well, don't go." Ching. Brilliant plan! Boycott them. That was like the Idea of the Century. We did that, so they had to ring us up. "Oh, we're going to have a meeting, what's your decision?" No or whatever. We just escaped, got out of Dodge, went and enjoyed life.' However, as his Benitses break wound down on 16 June, he had made his mind up over the future of The Beatles.

By the time McCartney set foot back in Cavendish Avenue, Harrison was the only Beatle still on holiday, having headed for a brief stopover in Rome. No studio sessions had been earmarked but McCartney was prepared to take the first step, carefully traversing the landmines he knew lay ahead. Lennon, despite his hyped-up public statements, was nevertheless right to be worried about money. No new music meant no new money. Those IOUs were still burning a hole in the Apple safe. And the taxman was waiting in the wings with reams of paper saying 'You Owe Us Millions'.

Swallowing hard on his misgivings, McCartney recognised Klein's plan to renegotiate royalty rates with EMI and Capitol was fundamentally important. But this left him exposed to accusations of hypocrisy. On the one hand he wanted nothing to do with Klein; on the other, he was happy to benefit financially from any deals Klein might make. The solution, as it always did, lay in the studio. If his songwriting partner could be persuaded to resuscitate the band, no matter how reluctantly, Harrison and Starr would surely follow. But there would have to be some ground rules. No one wanted to return to the dark days of Twickenham. He had by now heard an acetate of the Glyn Johns-produced 'Get Back' album – and he didn't hate it.

He told music journalist Paul Du Noyer: 'Listening to it one night in June, I thought, Jeez, this is brave, but it's a great album. It really is just The Beatles stripped back, nothing but four guys in a room. Or five with Billy Preston. I remember getting a thrill 'cos I was in this empty, very white room listening to this album – very minimalist – and thinking, "Great, very impressed. This is gonna be a great album."'

Deep down, however, reservations remained that the Great British Record-Buying Public was not yet ready to 'see The Beatles with their trousers down'. Tapping into that instinct, they ultimately baulked at releasing an album of unvarnished material showing the band at its self-indulgent worst.

Lennon had already been back home for several days when McCartney returned from Greece. When they made contact, Paul wasted no time in pitching his idea to further delay 'Get Back' and instead agree to make a real album. Like they used to.

'The idea was that we should put down the boxing gloves and make a really special album,' said McCartney in the *Beatles Anthology* twenty-six years later. Harrison chimed in: 'The feeling was that we should get back together and tidy the whole thing up.'

Starr, just back from the West Indies but planning to round off the month with a few days in France with Maureen, was a shoo-in. Notionally, all sides of the square had been carefully reassembled. Now only one other familiar piece was needed to turn it into a familiar pentagon . . .

*

Lennon had returned home drained but elated from the Montreal bed-in. 'Give Peace A Chance' had gone from being a throwaway line to becoming almost an incantation – and that was before the song of the same name would seep into the public's consciousness. Public exposure for the Lennons, however, had reached saturation point. At that moment, they were probably, for better or worse, the two most famous people on the planet.

So what now? Like his bandmates, he was still officially on sabbatical for the rest of June. And he had taken a genuine shine to Yoko's daughter Kyoko, who had innocently clambered over bedsheets in Montreal having become a mini-me celebrity in her own right. But his close attachment to the little girl had triggered an age-old guilt complex over the way he had neglected his own child, Julian. There he was playing happy families with another man's child while his own son languished thousands of miles away with Cynthia, a sad by-product of a broken marriage and a broken home. So he came up with a spur-of-the-moment plan to whisk six-year-old Julian away for a traditional British seaside holiday that would attempt to mend broken fences. The idea was to take a road trip to Wales and then head up to Liverpool for a whistlestop tour of his Merseyside relatives. He could kill two birds with one stone – do the right thing by Julian and gently introduce Yoko to his inner family circle for the first time.

Gripped by his customary impulsive eagerness, he then widened the circle to include a visit to his cousin, Stan Parkes, and aunt Mater in Edinburgh before heading up to Durness, the picturesque Highland village perched on the rugged coastline of Scotland's northernmost fringes, where he and Stan had roamed happy and free for several adolescent summers.

What's more, he would drive all four of them – him, Yoko and the two kids – every step of the way, a happy-go-lucky quartet crammed into his Mini Cooper. The fact that he had barely been behind the wheel of a car since passing his test in 1965 mattered not a bit. Nor was the fact that, even with his glasses on, he was a myopically poor driver.

Setting off on 23 June, the first part of the journey was uneventful. They pitched up at Tywyn, a seaside resort on Cardigan Bay on the west coast of Wales. They stayed the night in the Corbett Arms Hotel before starting on the next leg north to Liverpool. For all his good intentions, Lennon was aware he faced a frosty reception from the network of aunts, uncles and cousins who thought he had taken leave of his senses by ditching a homely, local lass for a weird Japanese artist. And, of course, there was no way to avoid the latest vainglorious stunt – John was on the front pages of every newspaper in the country almost every day. And was that really our nephew peering from beneath the shaggy, shoulder-length mane and thick beard, wondered his aunts.

Nervously, Lennon arrived outside his aunt Harriet's home – a property he had bought for her family in 1965 – in Gateacre Park Drive in the suburb of Woolton. A mile down the road lay St Peter's Church, where, almost twelve years ago to the day, he had first encountered the musically precocious Paul McCartney. Take the same road in the other direction and you would eventually arrive at 251 Menlove Avenue and Mendips, the Thirties-built semi-detached house where he had been brought up by Harriet's oldest sister Mimi.

Harriet was his mother Julia's youngest sibling, one of 'five, fantastic, strong, beautiful, and intelligent Stanley women', he later said. Those qualities, however, didn't include a filter when it came to speaking their mind and Harriet, having been put in the picture by Mimi during several fraught phone calls, wasted little time in berating Lennon over his lifestyle and peculiar new bride. Not to mention the embarrassment he was bringing to the family name. Then there was the small matter of him putting his privates on parade on the cover of *Two Virgins*. Not even the prospect of using Julian as a kind of human shield offered him any protection.

The temperature fell further when Yoko declined the offer of a roast dinner in favour of macrobiotic food they had brought with them from London. It was an inauspicious, though hardly surprising, start to his tour of the relatives.

The stay was punctuated by long, awkward silences and stony stares. The sub-zero welcome followed him when he visited his aunt Annie and her husband, Charles Cadwaller, across the water on the Wirral. Annie, known to the family as Nanny, was even more outspoken than her sister. Her son, Mike, reportedly recalled one of several testy exchanges between aunt and nephew. 'I remember Yoko commandeering the kitchen to prepare their meals, probably within earshot of my mother, who was unable to disguise her disapproval ... "he can't just eat beans ... he needs a proper meal ... he's fading away ... he's all skin and bones ..."'

There was, possibly, a hint of racism behind the kitchen whispers directed at Yoko. Hurt though he was, Lennon preferred to play the diplomat.

By now, even he had realised the impracticality of driving all the way to Edinburgh and then a further three hundred-odd miles, including hazardous single-track roads, to Durness in a tiny Mini. So he summoned his chauffeur Les Anthony to drive to Liverpool with a newly bought Austin Maxi, one of the first off the production line, which the Lennons would then use to hit the high road across the border to Scotland.

After loading up the Maxi with suitcases on 29 June, they made their strained farewells – no kisses or hugs for Yoko – and headed in the direction of Scotland's capital.

Edinburgh was a city full of fond memories for Lennon. Not least because it was where Stan lived. Both boys recalled lovingly how they would be taken to see the world-famous Edinburgh Tattoo, the skirl of the pipes leaving a lasting and nostalgic impression on the young Lennon. Also, it had always provided that brief stopover on his way to the Highland croft in Durness. Now Lennon was reliving that journey for the first time as an adult – and a driver.

The Parkes lived in Ormidale Terrace, a stone's throw from Murrayfield Stadium that reflected the ostentatious standing of his aunt Mater and her second husband, a dentist named Bertie Sutherland. When the Lennons arrived, Mater was, coincidentally, in Durness, so they were greeted by Stan, who was six years John's senior. Despite the age gap, the two men had always been close, more like brothers-in-arms than cousins as Stan helped Lennon navigate the tricky path of his fractured childhood. Yoko's arrival, however, tested the bonds of their friendship. Stan readily admitted he could find nothing likeable about her.

'I couldn't see what he saw in her at all and I told him,' recalled Stan, in a conversation we had before he passed away in 2016. 'She hardly spoke to me. I got the impression she just wanted John for herself and she wanted to keep him away from his family. It was always about control. I couldn't believe how he just seemed to do everything she said. I told him to stand up for himself more but he just laughed and said he knew what he was doing. But it was crazy to me. I didn't like her from the start.'

Sensing which way the wind was blowing, John must have been disappointed not to have Stan in his corner. He was already resigned to the fact that Mater, arguably the most volatile of all the Stanley sisters, was queuing up to give her potty nephew a piece of her mind. To shovel salt into deep family wounds, he was also finding it tough to reconnect with Julian, who now only saw him as an absent dad who had fled the family home for another woman who clearly had little time for him. The perils of parenthood had never been clearer to both him and Yoko.

As the Maxi made its way north and west to Durness, once his idea of heaven on earth, he couldn't escape the thought that the whole 'fookin' thing was turning into the fookin' holiday from hell'. Twenty-four hours later, he would find himself on a Highland road to perdition.

*

Late was the hour when the phone rang in George Martin's London home, an occurrence that was not unusual for a man used to unconventional working patterns. He picked up the receiver to hear a familiar Liverpool accent on the other end. Typically, Paul McCartney, after some brief social niceties, cut to the chase. 'We want to make another album, and we want to do it the way we used to do it. Will you produce it?'

Martin let the request hang in the air for a brief moment, torn between curious contemplation and self-righteous indignation. In the space of a few seconds, bittersweet memories flitted into his mind's eye. Memories of four streetwise but rough-hewn Liverpool lads giving him lip the first time they ventured into EMI Studios. Memories of the day he proudly told them they had just recorded their first number one single with 'Please Please Me'. Memories of the groundbreaking music, from their debut LP to the White Album, they shaped together over the following six years. Memories of the shared moments incarcerated inside EMI's Number Two studio until dawn that had turned them into an unlikely bond of brothers. Memories, now hurtful and sad, of how that bond had slowly splintered over the last eighteen months.

So it was by no means a straightforward case of yes or no. It meant stepping back onto a carousel that he firmly believed had come crashing off its moorings. It meant reconnecting fully with John Lennon, Paul McCartney, George Harrison and Ringo Starr to rediscover the alchemy that had transformed all their lives and redrawn the boundaries of popular music and culture.

Martin, moreover, still carried the scar tissue from being snubbed over 'Get Back'. Now, five months down the line, McCartney was on the phone trying to reforge links in a familiar chain, using all his natural charm to persuade Martin to help them create that old Beatle magic once again. 'An album like we used to . . .' McCartney, repeating the same sales pitch he had made to Lennon a few days previously, made it sound so tempting: 'We'll put down the boxing gloves.'

Before committing himself, Martin was anxious to scan the small print. And in this case, that ensured securing the cooperation of Lennon, a man who had already made clear his distaste for Martin's ability to turn The Beatles' base metal into gold.

'I didn't think we would work again together after *Let It Be* and frankly I didn't really want to. *Let It Be* was such an unhappy record and I thought that was the end of The Beatles and I thought I would never work with them again,' recalled Martin. 'And I thought it was such a shame to go out that way. So I was quite surprised when Paul rang me up and said, "We want to make another record, would you like to produce it?" And my immediate answer was, "Only if you let me produce it the way we used to do it."

'And he said "We do want to do that." I said, "John included?" And he said, "Honestly, yes." And I said, "Well, if you really want to do that, let's get together again."'

It spoke volumes for the trust he still had in McCartney's ability to rally his bandmates and drag them out of the acrimonious quagmire that was 'Get Back'. Perhaps he was influenced by the fact that a number of potential songs to form the spine of a new album were partly in the can, cold and unfinished leftovers from January and beyond. So he wasn't looking at an epic six-month production like *Pepper*, more like six weeks. And then there was that lingering but unrealised ambition he had to ease The Beatles into a more symphonic-based terrain, to weave all their disparate song fragments into one long suite. An interesting proposition but could it be done?

Surprisingly, Lennon, the incurable rock 'n' roller, had already given the project a green light. McCartney, always open to new pathways, was already on board. Harrison was prepared to tie up loose ends, and Starr, as always, just wanted to play with the boys.

All in, it looked like they would be doing one more for the road . . . *Abbey Road*.

© Trinity Mirror/Mirrorpix/Alamy

As The Beatles worked on *Abbey Road,* George Harrison became more immersed in the Hare Krishna movement. He oversaw a recording of the Hare Krishna mantra, which eventually reached Number Twelve in the UK single charts.

The first day of July saw McCartney back at work doing what he had always done in a way, shaping The Beatles' musical future for good or bad. In his mid-June conversations with Lennon he had notionally mentioned 1 July as a possible date to kickstart the sessions proper for a new album. McCartney, keen to dial back on the bossiness that had fractured the 'Get Back' sessions, made it clear that the plan was not laid down in stone. Which was just as well, because Lennon had no intention of pitching up at EMI Studios on that day. He was still enjoying taking time out with Yoko, Kyoko and trying to repair his relationship with Julian on their Highland holiday. Harrison, while cautiously committing to the sessions, wasn't yet ready to snap to attention when the headmaster clicked his fingers. Starr, flying back from France with Maureen after another vacation in the millionaires' playground of Cannes, made up the third truant.

The date was, nevertheless, important. Informally or otherwise, it drew a line under the ramshackle 'Get Back' project and initiated work on their next album and what McCartney and Martin hoped would be a period of proper focus to achieve their goal of finishing a new album, probably their last.

Some nine tracks, including 'Something', 'Golden Slumbers', 'Carry That Weight', 'She Came In Through The Bathroom Window', 'Mean Mr Mustard' and 'You Never Give Me Your Money', were already good works in progress, though none had yet acquired The Beatle quality kite mark. And then there was that intriguing notion, still being kicked around between McCartney, Lennon and Martin, of stitching together a medley from the patchwork quilt of musical cast-offs they both had lying around.

There was undoubtedly a lot riding on the project. Lennon, his cultural antenna always fixed to the winds of change blowing through music, was fearful that The Beatles were in danger of becoming relics. McCartney, though, was convinced that the band was still musically relevant.

Studio Two had been block-booked for the entire month and into August as well, if they needed it. Six weeks to find out whether to stick or twist. But the plans were thrown into immediate chaos when a call was put through to McCartney from a shaken Derek Taylor. Lennon, Yoko and their two kids were currently laid up in a remote Scottish hospital. Lennon, he reported, had driven his Maxi into a ditch on a road outside the small village of Tongue, almost ninety miles north of Inverness. The accident happened as the couple, having stopped off at a tearoom, were on their way back to Durness, taking in the scenic route round Loch Eriboll. The roads there are notoriously narrow and Lennon had already forgotten the sage advice of Stan Parkes when he set off from Edinburgh: 'Don't forget the Highland etiquette on single-track roads of letting another driver pass.' When Lennon saw another car, reportedly driven by a German tourist, on the road ahead, he panicked, knowing there wasn't room enough for both of them. Instead of pulling over to the side, he steered the car off the road where it came to rest at a 45-degree angle.

Luckily, no one was seriously injured. Lennon had a gash on his jawline, which would eventually require seventeen stitches while Yoko also needed stitches in her forehead. The two children were suffering from no more than shock. An ambulance took the injured party to the Lawson Memorial Hospital in Golspie, little more than a country clinic. Naturally, the staff were shocked to see a bleeding Beatle walking among them, looking somewhat sheepish but nevertheless displaying the good manners that Aunt Mimi had long ago instilled in him.

'He was not in the least demanding,' said Dr David Milne, who treated the couple's injuries. 'He was slightly embarrassed at the predicament he found himself in but apart from that he was a model patient. There was a bit of commotion when they were first brought in. They were quite shaken up.'

It was Lennon who put in the call to Apple, which was then relayed to Paul in North London. It was clear that he would be out of action for the foreseeable future. Still, McCartney reckoned, there was no point in cancelling the sessions already in the EMI diary.

The next day, he was joined by Harrison and Starr and for the next six days the 'Threetles' – an eerie portent of what was to come twenty-five years down the line – laid down tracks and overdubs for 'Golden Slumbers' and 'Carry That Weight', while Harrison finally took the wrappers off 'Here Comes The Sun', the second of what would become his major contributions to the next album.

Devoid of the preachy overtones that weighed down some of his more recent songs, 'Here Comes The Sun' was warm, exuberant and brimful of optimism with a chorus that was delightfully infectious. On hearing it for the first time, McCartney must have winced at its effortless-sounding melody, one that could just as easily have sprung from his own well.

As with 'Something', Harrison had a clearly defined vision for how the song – his song – should sound. Diplomatically, McCartney adopted the position of almost a session musician and retreated to the margins as Harrison taught him and Starr their parts for 'Here Comes The Sun'. Even at this early stage, the song presented tricky percussive challenges for a drummer. Heard inside the Studio Two echo chamber, it was already a subtle confluence of laidback Western folk music and complex Eastern ragas based mainly on an Indian polyrhythmic technique called a tihai. It consists of three equal repetitions of a rhythmic pattern, followed by two equal rests, adding up to the time signature that sounds weird to Western ears. The result was wonderfully exotic.

Harrison may not have known it himself, but the song's time signatures switched from 11/8, 4/4 and 7/8 on the bridge. Starr spotted it immediately and rose to the challenge as he, Harrison and McCartney laid down backing tracks on what was the drummer's twenty-ninth birthday.

Indeed, it was a happy harbinger of Starr's drumming, which over the next six weeks would scale impressive new heights. A contributing factor was his old drum-heads, relics from the far-off days of Beatlemania, finally being replaced.

He said, 'The drum sound on the record was the result of having new calf-heads. There's a lot of tom-tom work on that record. I got the new heads on the drum and I naturally used them a lot – they were so great. The magic of real records is that they showed the tom-toms were so good. I don't believe that magic is there now because there is so much manipulation.'

Starr also benefited hugely from the leap forward in recording techniques and the recent installation of a transistorised mixing console at the EMI Studios, notwithstanding the fact that every track was now being recorded in stereo, despite The Beatles' own belief that they always sounded better in mono. Studio engineer Geoff Emerick said, 'This was the first time I was able to record Ringo's kit in stereo because we were using 8-track instead of 4-track. Because of this, I had more mic inputs, so I could mic from underneath the toms, place more mics around the kit – the sound of his drums were finally captured in full. I think when he heard this, he kind of perked up and played more forcefully on the toms, and with more creativity.'

Starr was front and centre on 'Carry That Weight', the McCartney song that segued directly from 'Golden Slumbers'. Paul had always intended for the songs to be linked when they were first aired in Twickenham in January. Now, months later, they needed next to no reworking, but the drumming on 'Carry That Weight' gave the song a palpable sense of renewed energy. With Lennon absent, the vocal duties were shared between all three Beatles, but it was Starr's distinctive nasal baritone that gave 'Carry That Weight', an early comment on the growing meltdown at Apple even before Klein's arrival, its sullen forecast of a lifetime burden shared by four closely linked individuals.

McCartney said, 'I'm generally quite upbeat but at certain times things get to me so much that I just can't be upbeat any more and that was one of the times . . . "Carry that weight a long time" like forever! That's what I meant.'

'Golden Slumbers' also touched on the same melancholy that was evident in 'You Never Give Me Your Money', 'Let It Be', 'The Long

And Winding Road', 'Two Of Us' and 'Every Night', each song proof nevertheless that despondence can create great art even in an eternal optimist like McCartney. Written at the tail end of 1968, the lyrics to 'Golden Slumbers' were 'borrowed' from a ballad by the Elizabethan poet Thomas Dekker after Paul saw the ballad's sheet music propped up on the piano at his father's home in Heswall, Cheshire. Most of the words remained unaltered except the tell-tale intro that was pure McCartney.

McCartney recalled: 'I can't read music and I couldn't remember the old tune, so I just started playing my own tune to it. I liked the words so I kept them and it fitted with another bit of song that I had ["Carry That Weight"]. I remember trying to get a very strong vocal on it, because it was such a gentle theme, so I worked on the strength of the vocal on it, and ended up quite pleased with it.'

Away from the business entanglements, in the studio, things went better between McCartney, Harrison and Starr without Lennon and definitely without Yoko. The tension was palpably absent. It didn't necessarily guarantee a stress-free zone but it did mean by and large a smoother vibe. There were no unwelcome asides from the touchline or awkward silences as everyone – studio staff included – tiptoed round the double-strength tag team of John and Yoko.

Engineer John Kurlander told me: 'The mood was very good from what I can recall. I'm not saying they didn't occasionally disagree but there was no slamming doors or finger pointing. Right from the start of July they seemed to be very focused. John wasn't there at the start so that might have had something to do with it. But right from the start you could tell they had brought their A game to the studio. Musically, it was gelling very well and we could all hear that.'

Beneath the studio bonhomie, however, lurked the ever-present spectre of broken business alliances. Nems had been lost and the battle for Northern Songs with ATV seemed equally to be a lost cause. For McCartney, guilt could only be apportioned in one direction. But the future had still to be written and McCartney was convinced that Apple could yet be salvaged. Conditional on that was persuading Starr and Harrison that Klein would destroy them all. His first point of influence was Ringo.

The McCartneys invited the drummer and his wife Maureen to Cavendish Avenue for dinner. With Linda on cooking duty, the evening was going well until the host gingerly brought up the subject of Apple and, inevitably, Klein. Sensing a set-up, Starr shuffled uncomfortably and politely refused to shift allegiances, especially since it would mean going behind the backs of the other two. Suddenly, Linda burst into tears and declared: 'Oh, they've got you too.' It was a cack-handed attempt at emotional blackmail and Starr wasn't falling for it.

Meanwhile, Harrison took advantage of the pre-booked studio time at EMI to do a little moonlighting. By the summer of 1969, London had replaced San Francisco as the new epicentre of the Hare Krishna movement. Up and down Carnaby Street and the King's Road, shaven-headed Krishna devotees, draped in orange robes and carrying their prayer beads in a bag, mingled with ordinary shoppers, bowler-hatted bankers, mini-skirted secretaries and long-haired hippies. Harrison was a closet Krishna, happy to chant his mantra for hours on end but unwilling to commit to some of the religion's more disciplined tenets, such as no illicit sex and abstaining from alcohol and drugs. For a Beatle with strong appetites, that was a step too far. But no one was in any doubt about the sincerity of his support – financial and practical – for a movement that had set up its own HQ in London and to which he felt a clear spiritual affinity. And it wasn't long before the Krishnas zeroed in on Apple, treating the offices in Savile Row almost like a transcendental annexe. Lennon and McCartney were both known to take cover when the street-level chanting announced the devotees' arrival on their turf. Derek Taylor, bounding sharply from his chair, was more to the point: 'Christ, it's the bloody Krishnas! Lock the door.'

But the devotees knew that with Harrison's patronage they were Beatle-proof. Not only that, he could be the key that could bring others to join them at a time when millions of young people were turning away from orthodox religions and seeking some other inner light. The answer was obvious to all parties – turn the Hare Krishna mantra into a record and have the world's most famous adherent play on it.

Harrison bought into the idea right away. In fact, he was the prime mover behind the sessions at Apple and Abbey Road to turn the sixteen-word 'Great Mantra', the chant that underpinned the Hindu religious organisation, into a three-minute, radio-friendly pop song.

He corralled Ken Scott, a veteran of Beatles sessions, to act as engineer. Having sat through the dysfunctional White Album sessions from twelve months ago and having also witnessed the efforts by the Lennons to tip over the Beatle boat, Scott thought he had seen it all. But the sessions for the Hare Krishna mantra during that first week in July took matters to a new and surreal level.

'On the surface it all seemed pretty bizarre to see them there in the studio with the robes and the beads,' he recalled. 'But then again I had seen a lot of strange things over the years so it didn't faze me that much. The important thing was to help George get the job done and he knew where he was going with the session.' Indeed, Harrison acted as producer for the session as well as playing lead guitar and bass guitar. Elsewhere, other devotees were roped in to beat time with a pair of kartals and Indian drums, while someone was commandeered to strike the gong at the song's climax.

Among them was Joshua Greene, a young American student newly arrived in London from the Sorbonne in Paris. Greene had already tapped into his Krishna consciousness when he found himself at the Radha Krishna Temple in London. He said, 'I just found the nicest people on Earth. They were asking about me and I just happened to mention that I had been in a college band and they said, "Really? Come with us." We then piled into a Volkswagen mini-bus and pulled up outside this building with a big number three on the outside.

'We walked inside and there was this big green apple on the wall and then I found myself in a recording studio. And suddenly I'm standing next to George Harrison. He went over to hug some of the devotees and then he hands me a harmonium and says just play along. So I'm just jamming on the harmonium and I start thinking to myself, "If I stay with these people I get God *and* The Beatles. Okay, I'm in."'

When they reassembled at EMI Studios a few days later, having listened to playbacks, Harrison wanted a bigger chorus and so gathered an ad hoc group of backing singers from every nook and cranny inside the warren that was EMI Studios to help bring the track to a multi-layered crescendo. Chris O'Dell, the American who had drifted into the band's social circle, was also roped in to help. She later said singing the mantra had left her feeling 'physically and spiritually changed', adding that 'chanting the words over and over again was almost hypnotic . . . there was a point of freedom where there was no effort at all, no criticism or judgement, just the sound generated from deep inside, like a flame that warmed us from the inside out.'

Harrison was delighted with the track, which he saw as his gift to help the Krishnas spread the word of God to a cynical world. Speaking of the sessions years later, he said, 'Well, it's just all a part of service, isn't it? Spiritual service, in order to try to spread the mantra all over the world. Also, to try and give the devotees a wider base and a bigger foothold in England and everywhere else. There was less commercial potential in it, but it was much more satisfying to do, knowing the possibilities that it was going to create, the connotations it would have just by doing a three-and-a-half-minute mantra.

'That was more fun, really, than trying to make a pop hit record. It was the feeling of trying to utilise your skills or job to make it into some spiritual service to Krishna. It was just like a breath of fresh air. My strategy was to keep it to a three-and-a-half-minute version of the mantra so they'd play it on the radio, and it worked.'

He added: 'I did the guitar track for that record at Abbey Road Studios before one of The Beatles' sessions and then overdubbed a bass part. I remember Paul and Linda arrived at the studio and enjoyed the mantra.'

Karma, though, did not extend to another rock god. On 3 July, the morning after Paul, George and Ringo regrouped at Abbey Road, came the news that Brian Jones had been found dead at the bottom of his swimming pool. The founder of the Rolling Stones had tragically become the founder of the '27 Club', so named after the company of stars who would be cut down in their prime at the same age. Jones had gone from golden-haired deity to bloated junkie. His demise – the official verdict was death by misadventure – came after he had been fired by the Stones for no longer being able to function as a musician. Even so, Jones's death was still shocking.

Strangely, none of The Beatles commented directly on his death. Apple produced a perfunctory statement that was devoid of any genuine sentiment. Lennon, perhaps the Beatle who was closest to Brian, remained incommunicado to the dwindling group of journalists parked on the lawn outside the Lawson Memorial Hospital in Golspie.

Jones had even once joined in on a Beatles session, adding some ropey sax to the novelty number 'You Know My Name (Look Up The Number)'. Only seven months earlier, John had hung out with Jones on what would be his last public appearance as a Stone at the band's chaotic film, *The Rolling Stones Rock and Roll Circus*. Even then, Jones, his eyes glazed and sunken and his skin parchment-white, had the whiff of death about him.

Lennon recalled: 'He was one of them guys that disintegrated right in front of you. In the early days he was alright because he was young and confident. But in the end you dreaded he'd come on the phone – you knew it was trouble. He was in a lot of pain.' It was a reminder that even rock gods are not immortal.

*

After the media frenzy of the previous few months, the hospital stay provided the Lennons with some splendid isolation, a time of much needed introspection away from the self-induced narcissism that had permeated both their lives. News, though, travelled fast.

Within hours of being admitted to the Lawson, the news wires were chattering out bulletins from the Highlands to Fleet Street and on to television autocues.

Watching at home, no one was more surprised at the broadcasts than Cynthia Lennon, who knew nothing about her former husband's trip to northern Scotland with their young son. As far as she was concerned, they were still in Liverpool. She knew more than anyone that John was a bad driver and that, given the length of the journey, this was literally an accident waiting to happen.

Alarmed, she contacted Peter Brown at Apple and made hasty plans to retrieve the youngster, who was by now in the trusted care of Lennon's Aunt Mater in Durness. It was a long journey, not helped by the fact that she accidentally first boarded a plane for Ireland instead of Scotland.

En route to Durness, they stopped at the hospital but Lennon couldn't find a reason to speak to the woman who had been his college sweetheart and the mother of his son. A ward nurse was summarily dispatched to tell Cynthia that John and Yoko didn't want to be disturbed.

One person who did breach the NHS-fortified Maginot Line was the Reverend David Paterson, a minister in the ultra-conservative Free Church of Scotland. His position gave him unfettered access to the wards and the opportunity to lock horns with the man who once declared that The Beatles were 'bigger than Jesus'.

On the surface, the two men appeared to have little in common. But Lennon welcomed the chance to debate the issue with a man of the cloth away from the flashbulbs and scribblers. They quickly struck up a friendly rapport on a whole range of subjects encompassing religion, philosophy, war and peace while agreeing to disagree on the overall message of Christianity.

Overall, however, visitors from the outside world were discouraged. Persistent press requests for interviews, once a part of the couple's daily routine, were simply ignored. Even the UK release of 'Give Peace A Chance' on 3 July – the same day Brian Jones's death dominated the news headlines – passed without any hint of bedside self-promotion or even a pre-recorded statement. 'Give Peace A Chance' confused many Beatle fans, who initially thought it was the latest release from the Fabs, especially since the song was credited to Lennon and McCartney. Lennon would later say, 'I didn't write it with Paul, but again, out of guilt, we always had that thing that our names would go on songs even if we didn't write them. It was never a legal deal between Paul and me, just an agreement when we were fifteen or sixteen to put both our names on our songs. I'd put his name on "Give Peace A Chance" though he had nothing to do with it. It was a silly thing to do, actually. It should have been Lennon-Ono.'

The single, in retrospect the start of Lennon's solo career, saw the introduction of the Plastic Ono Band, a conceptual group which was more a nod to Yoko's idiosyncratic art than any notion of ground-breaking rock 'n' roll by Lennon.

With Lennon absent, Starr and Maureen stepped into the promotional breach to help officially launch the Great Peace Anthem at a press bash at Chelsea Town Hall. Lennon's silence seemed like an opportunity lost given the message contained in the song's grooves. But he was strangely happy to keep the media blindsided.

Dr Milne was impressed by his patient's lack of starry self-absorption, contrary to a public image that suggested a rampant conceit. He told me: 'I had long chats with John and he just seemed like an ordinary bloke. We covered a wide range of subjects. We spoke at length about the life he had been leading. He told me he had been through it all from religion to drugs. He was very honest. He didn't give the impression of being a pop star, he was extremely ordinary and down to earth.

'One night he went down to the kitchen and said, "Have you got any leftovers?" I remember another night a group from his Apple organisation had flown up to Inverness and then taken a taxi from Inverness up to Golspie. They arrived at 9.30 p.m., and I went to John and said, "Some of your mates are at the door." And he said, "I didn't ask them to come. Tell them to go away." He said, "Don't be fooled, I'm paying for all this." He seemed very intelligent to me, well read and very well up on world events. I thought he was quite an impressive figure.'

Dr Milne practically became the Lennons' unofficial press spokesman for the week, wheeled out before the cameras and print journalists to give regular condition updates. In truth, there was very little he could tell them that would spark the call to hold the front page. Today, there would be fifteen-minute updates on Sky News, CNN and BBC News 24. But almost fifty years ago, the column inches generated by the Lennons' hospital stay amounted to little of substance. A trawl through the archives of Scotland's *Daily Record*, the *Scottish Daily Express*, the *Mirror* and the *Scotsman* reveal few headlines and prove that Lennon succeeded in his bid to recharge his drained batteries away from the media spotlight. Even Cynthia's ill-fated arrival at the hospital after that turbulent flight to Glasgow to collect Julian failed to ignite any serious coverage.

Dr Milne added: 'I was actually quite impressed by the media. They had a rough time because they just had to sit out in the car park night and day. They were scared to leave in case they missed something. If their editor phoned and they couldn't answer right away they would be sacked. I used to go down at nine o' clock at night to tell them, "Look, they've gone to bed for the night, you'd be as well to go down to the pub." But they said they daren't do that.

'Part of their orders had been to get a photograph and apparently some painter or someone who was working at the hospital had got in and surreptitiously taken a photograph, which he then tried to sell to the newspapers.'

Nevertheless, Lennon didn't fully pull up the drawbridge on the outside world. He sent a typically witty postcard with deliberately misspelled words from his hospital bed to Derek Taylor. He began by declaring, in capital letters, 'THIS IS NOT A BEGGING LETTER.' Lennon, an inveterate postcard doodler, then went on: 'I am a crippled family who need som mony to git out of Scotcland [*sic*] a few hundred will do.' At the bottom of the card he signed off as 'Jack McCripple (ex seamen).' The card is addressed to 'Dirty

Tayler MBE at the Apple HQ in London'. The front of the card shows a castle and Lennon has drawn a line to one of the windows and written 'held prisner'.

But if Lennon liked to believe he was indeed a hostage to misfortune, his scheduled release date was coming up fast. Six days after being admitted to the Lawson bleeding and bruised, the couple prepared to face the world again. For the hospital, this would mean an end to the constant phone calls from worried fans that had almost caused the switchboard to go into meltdown. And for the staff, a sense of relief that business would go back to normal, even if the Lennons' stay had interfered little with the normal running of the hospital.

Joyce Everett was one of several young nurses who often attended Lennon and Yoko and, like her colleagues, remembers only a husband and wife who had been injured in a car accident and not the stellar couple of pop culture folklore. During the Lennons' recovery she was the only staff member to speak to not just one Beatle, but two.

'My outstanding memory is picking up the phone one night and it was Paul McCartney,' she said. 'He was my favourite Beatle, so that was nice. He was just asking how John was. It was a coincidence that I picked up the phone. But I just stayed quite cool about it and told him how he was. There was no facility in the hospital to pass Paul's call through to him or anything like that. But the message was passed on that Paul had phoned to ask how he was and I suppose he was quite pleased about that.

'This was at a time when they weren't supposed to be getting on so it's nice to know there was still a friendship there. During the time they were in the hospital they were fine . . . They kept themselves to themselves and there were never any problems. They also had a ward to themselves, so that kept them out of the way of the usual running of the hospital. And it meant that the other patients weren't disturbed in any way by what was going on. I mean, they knew that someone famous was in the hospital especially since so many journalists were camped outside the main entrance. You couldn't help but notice, but there were no paparazzi with mega lenses or anything like that.'

On Sunday, 6 July, twenty-four hours after the Rolling Stones played a free concert in London's Hyde Park to honour the memory of Jones (McCartney, heavily disguised, was rumoured to be among the crowd), the Lennons got ready to re-enter the public domain. On the morning they left, a helicopter landed on the hospital lawn to take John, Yoko and Kyoko to Inverness airport where they would fly by private jet back down to London.

Before departing, the couple went out of their way to thank all the staff who lined up outside the entrance to wave farewell to the most famous patients in the hospital's history. They handed out signed pictures and albums, one of which was given to Dr Milne as a token of goodwill for his discretion as much as his bedside manner. He recalled: 'I got an autographed record – I can't remember which one now – that I gave to one of my sons.' The waiting press finally got their picture. One group shot still hangs in the entrance to the hospital.

They also got their parting soundbite, a mere twenty-four words to sum up six restful but nevertheless long days: 'If you're going to have a car crash, try to arrange for it to happen in the Highlands. The hospital there was just great.'

John, wearing a large floppy black hat, shook everyone's hand and then, with one final flourish, they stepped aboard the chopper. As the helicopter banked south towards Inverness, Lennon could not have known he would never again visit his beloved Scottish Highlands, an affair that had begun when he was nine years old.

There remains, however, the perfectly legitimate question about why they were allowed to remain in hospital for six days. Under normal circumstances, they would have been discharged after being kept in overnight for observation. Yoko, though, was in the very early stages of pregnancy again, a fact unknown to all but a select few. And given her previous miscarriage, the hospital's medical staff decided to monitor her for longer. But that revelation still didn't kick into the long grass of history one theory that the Lennons used their surroundings to again try to purge their bodies of drugs, specifically the heroin they still used. What is beyond scrutiny is the fact that they couldn't be seen to be taking drugs in hospital. For one thing, it simply wouldn't be tolerated. And the breadcrumb trail of clues would be impossible to conceal from trained nursing staff, as Yoko herself confirmed. 'We wouldn't kick in a hospital because we wouldn't let anyone know.'

Waiting for them in London was an old life, one in which a drug-enforced siege mentality would quickly re-establish its hold and see them return to a state of opulent misery. McCartney, Harrison and Starr were also nervous about how Lennon's return would affect the relative harmony of the sessions. No one had to say it out loud but it was an obvious question: what was it going to be like in the studio again?

The next day, Wednesday, 9 July, the answer was quickly forthcoming. An ambulance pulled up outside Abbey Road and out popped Lennon alongside a slightly unsteady Yoko, all in black and wearing a bandana to conceal the forehead scar caused by the road accident. What happened next, though, left everyone – front-office staff, engineers, session men, roadie Mal Evans, George Martin and the other three Beatles – open-mouthed with astonishment. The doors to Studio Two flew open to reveal four men in brown overcoats wheeling in a massive double bed from Harrods, the luxury Knightsbridge department store that furnished the couple with a money-is-no-object pipeline of caviar and fine foods. Lennon instructed the bed to be arranged and made up in a corner facing outwards towards all the sound booths. Yoko climbed in between the sheets but not before asking for a mic to be hung overhead so she could take her place as a part of a Beatles collective, offering up unwanted suggestions and criticisms. Even by Lennon standards, it was an extraordinary turn of events. McCartney declared: 'What could we say? She was John's bird.' The awkward silence spoke volumes but everyone was thinking the same thing. None of the other Beatles dared protest.

'The three of them were a little bit scared of him,' recalled engineer Phil McDonald. 'John was a powerful figure, especially with Yoko – a double strength.' McCartney, though, set aside diplomacy and took his revenge in the only way he knew. 'Maxwell's Silver Hammer', another unpopular curiosity from Twickenham, was just the type of song to get under Lennon's skin. Bordering on vaudeville, it was a teeth-grating track about a psychotic murderer who pops off his victims by smashing their skulls with a silver hammer. The subject matter – and the song's music-hall structure – was as far removed from, say, 'I Am The Walrus' or 'Strawberry Fields' as you could get. Lennon loathed 'Maxwell' and refused to have anything to do with it. Starr and Harrison felt the same way but had already been press-ganged into action as McCartney forced them to endure take after excruciating take in a bid to pummel the song into a Beatles single, which, insisted Lennon, 'it never could be'.

It was a familiar stand-off. Lennon knew he was deliberately baiting the band by turning the studio into another bed-in; McCartney, in turn, could always rely on the kind of 'granny music' so despised by Lennon to infuriate his erstwhile songwriting partner. More worrying was Lennon's lack of new material. Nine weeks had passed since all four of them were last in the studio. Still under discussion was the idea, first mooted in April, to weave a long suite out of all the snatches of song fragments he and Lennon had tucked away. But they still needed standalone contributions from Lennon to at least give the impression that it wasn't all smoke and mirrors, that whatever it was they were working towards was, in fact, a bona fide Beatles project.

Over the next two weeks they maintained slow but steady progress in honing 'Here Comes The Sun', 'Something', and the universally hated 'Maxwell' while tackling McCartney's 'Oh! Darling'. That track was his homage to the Fifties rock 'n' roll of his teenage years and he was determined to make it sound as if it had just been pulled off the peg from the era that had done so much to shape his musical adolescence. He recalled: 'I came into the studios early every day for a week to sing it by myself because at first my voice was too clear. I wanted it to sound as though I'd been performing it on stage all week.'

Lennon later said he would have been a better choice to sing it, but by then egotism had replaced co-operation. He declared: 'I always thought I could have done it better – it was more my style than his. He wrote it, so what the hell, he's going to sing it.'

On 21 July, Lennon finally broke free from the creative ennui that had been holding him captive for weeks. He had long ago ditched Timothy Leary's pitch for him to write a political campaign song called 'Come Together, Join The Party'. But the idea of 'Come Together', with its double entendre, stimulated his sense of mischief. Playing it to the others for the first time, his excitement was palpable and suddenly all the bullshit went out the window. Visceral and crackling with energy, it was the best song he had produced since 'Don't Let Me Down', even though the 'gobbledygook' lyrics were still unfinished. But McCartney, a veritable jukebox of rock 'n' roll, quickly spotted an obvious problem. The tune was a virtual steal of Chuck Berry's 1956 single 'You Can't Catch Me', which also featured prominently in the 1958 movie *Rock, Rock, Rock*. And in case anyone was in any doubt about the provenance of the song, its lyrical reference to 'old flat-top' would be Exhibit A, m'lud, when the notoriously litigious Berry's publishers took them to court seeking damages for plagiarism. Lennon sheepishly copped a plea as McCartney suggested slowing down the song with an almost voodoo-like feel and masking its origins with a 'swampy' bassline. The result showed The Beatles at their unified best. Lennon always reacted well to constructive criticism from his songwriting partner. As McCartney later put it: 'John came into the studio one day with this song, he plays it for me, "Here come old flat top, He come groovin' up slowly . . ." And I go: "What? We can't do that! That [lyric] is Chuck Berry's 'You Can't Catch Me!'. Anyway, it became "Come Together". It shows *just* the influence.'

Lennon never shied away from the obvious similarities, which would later see the original song's publishers, Big Seven Corporation, now owned by American music mogul Morris Levy, sue for damages. In one of his last interviews, he admitted: ' "Come

Together" is *me* – writing obscurely around an old Chuck Berry thing. I left the line in "Here comes old flat-top." It is *nothing* like the Chuck Berry song, but they took me to court because I admitted the influence once years ago. I could have changed it to "Here comes old iron face", but the song remains independent of Chuck Berry or anybody else on earth.'

Over the next nine days, 'Come Together', showcasing again Starr's innovative tom-tom fills, gradually took shape to become a Beatle tour de force and one of Lennon's personal favourites. 'It's funky, it's bluesy, and I'm singing it pretty well. I like the sound of the record,' he said.

McCartney was delighted to see his old partner, bolstered by a good track, at last bringing something to the party. He decided to cash in on John's better mood by again trying to persuade him that one side of the new album should be a symphonically styled medley of short songs. Faced with a pincer movement – George Martin was as much a driving force as McCartney – Lennon reluctantly got on board. Over the next few days, they casually fused together 'Mean Mr Mustard', 'Polythene Pam' and 'Sun King', a song that unblushingly took as its jumping-off point Fleetwood Mac's mellifluous instrumental, 'Albatross'. 'Sun King', although beautifully melodic, consisted of one chorus containing only nine original words, making it lyrically the second shortest song in The Beatles canon next to 'Wild Honey Pie'. The rest was more Lennon-esque nonsense sung in pseudo Spanish, exposing John again to the suspicion that he was lyrically bankrupt.

The next day, 24 July, after a first pass at the song, McCartney spent an hour finessing a catchy new song called 'Come And Get It' without any help from his bandmates. He played every instrument himself before double-tracking his own vocal. It could have been another classic Beatle song but bizarrely would remain destined for another group altogether.

Despite the occasional niggle, all four musicians were largely on the same page, driven perhaps by the unspoken notion that the sun really was setting on the band. If this was to be the borderline – no one said it was, but it felt like it might be – they needed a grand, sweeping and memorable exit. McCartney already envisioned the medley as an epic climax to side two but it still needed a magical sign-off, something that would be remembered as a final Beatle bow to the world, something that summed up the whole of the parts.

The answer lay in a song that, in its title alone, was perfect. Recorded during seven takes on 23 July, 'The End' was a high watermark for each Beatle's individual musicianship and, in time, fulfilled McCartney's hope for an unforgettable swansong.

It began with a reluctant Starr being coaxed into performing his one and only drum solo, which in turn led into a ferocious 24-bar guitar duel between McCartney, Harrison and Lennon in that order. Unpretentious as he was, Starr never felt the urge to take the spotlight as a drummer. His job, he reckoned, was always to serve the song and not his own ego. But for 'The End', he was finally persuaded to show off the chops that proved his musicianship was on a par with that of any of his contemporaries.

In the *Beatles Anthology* he declared: 'I've always hated drum solos. That drum solo is still the only one I have ever done. I was opposed to it but George Martin convinced me.' McCartney added: 'Ringo would never do drum solos. He hated drummers who did lengthy drum solos. We all did. And when he joined The Beatles we said, "Ah, what about drum solos then?", thinking he might say, "Yeah, I'll have a five-hour one in the middle of your set," and he said, "I hate 'em!" We said, "Great! We love you!" And so he would never do them.

'But because of this medley I said, 'Well, a *token* solo?' and he really dug his heels in and didn't want to do it. But after a little bit of gentle persuasion I said, "Yeah, just do that, it wouldn't be Buddy Rich gone mad," because I think that's what he didn't want to do.'

Missing at this point, however, was a vital ingredient – the vocals – which would not be added for another three weeks. Among those who had a box seat at the instrument-only recording was Emerick, dovetailing his duties as the head of the new Apple studio with those of balance engineer on the new, still as yet untitled, album. And he watched in awe as the four musicians found themselves in perfect synch. In his memoir, he wrote: 'For the hour or so it took them to play those solos, all the bad blood was forgotten. John, Paul and George looked like they had gone back in time, like they were kids again, playing together for the sheer enjoyment of it.'

It was indeed a joyous, throwback moment and, as it turned out, one of the last times all four played with such unbridled joy on a specific track.

By the last day of the month, they had broken the back of the medley, which was now almost ready to be sequenced. In the can also was 'Octopus's Garden', the Starr-penned song, which relied heavily on unaccredited contributions from Harrison.

In a marathon session on 30 July, McCartney adopted a de facto producer's role to stitch the constituent parts of the medley into one seamless whole. Editing and crossfading began to weave together a rough uninterrupted mix of 'You Never Give Me Your Money', 'Sun King', 'Mean Mr Mustard', 'Her Majesty', 'Polythene Pam', 'She Came In Through The Bathroom Window', 'Golden Slumbers', 'Carry That Weight' – and 'The End', still minus vocals. The aim had been to suss out if the musical theory worked in practice and to give them the chance to iron out any kinks. Against all odds, they all liked it, even the reluctant Lennon who could be heard ad-libbing in broad Scouse: 'Fab . . . that's great . . . real good.'

The only discordant note came from McCartney, who felt that 'Her Majesty' was out of synch with the rest of the medley. He instructed engineer John Kurlander to 'throw it away', a request that in Kurlander's opinion ran counter to every EMI protocol he knew. He told me: 'We were not allowed to just dispose of bits of tape. That could get you into all sorts of trouble. So when everyone was gone I just tacked 'Her Majesty' onto the end of the master tape. I never thought any more about it but I only did because I didn't want to get into any trouble from George Martin or anybody else for that matter.'

The July sessions, while ultimately fruitful, had been underpinned by a fragile and occasionally forced camaraderie. No one was pretending that it was now no more than a job of work. They rarely hung out together socially and if they did it would only be two at a time. But Sunday, 20 July – the day before Lennon re-entered the fray with 'Come Together' – saw all four, and their wives, break into their weekend for a private film screening at Apple.

The movie of choice was not Dennis Hopper's recently released, hippie-rite-of-passage film, *Easy Rider*, but a rough cut of *Get Back*, the warts-and-all photoplay from January that graphically trapped them on celluloid, caught in the crosshairs of their own conflicts. Michael Lindsay-Hogg had spent the last few months stitching together over two hundred hours of film into some kind of pared-down, watchable whole. His last music-based project had been *The Rolling Stones Rock and Roll Circus* the previous December, but it had met with a withering response from a jealous Mick Jagger, who felt his own band had been upstaged by The Who. The upshot was the circus never came to town. (It lay unreleased for twenty years.) Now Lindsay-Hogg wondered if the same fate lay in store for *Get Back*, which, in its rough state, ran to just under three hours. It must have seemed like a Cecil B. De Mille epic, which in a way it was.

Photographs of the screening tell their own story of inter-Beatle relations. Even though it's a small room, Lennon, McCartney, Harrison and Starr are seated far apart. Accidental or deliberate, the informal seating spoke volumes. And the running time was too long to hold their attention, especially when the film was a harrowing depiction of a band – their band – self-destructing before their eyes. Watching it was painful for all of them and only brought an unspoken and uncomfortable truth horribly closer. Fearful of their reactions, Lindsay-Hogg was braced for the perfect storm of being berated by all four, but not one dissenting voice was raised as the credits rolled. Harrison left with his wife Pattie and his parents, Harry and Louise, to go back to Esher to watch Apollo 11 astronaut Neil Armstrong take his giant leap for mankind. Starr, naturally, headed to a club. Lindsay-Hogg joined the Lennons and the McCartneys for a 'chummy' dinner and went home with a feeling of job done. But if he thought his movie was on the brink of a four-signature sign-off, he was quickly disappointed. Early the next morning, he received a phone call from Peter Brown.

Lindsay-Hogg recalled the conversation as follows: 'Peter said, "There's a lot of footage of John with Yoko in there, and I think it ought to come out." And I said, "I think it's really interesting." And he said, "Let me put it another way, I've had three phone calls [from three Beatles] this morning saying it ought to come out."

'So there was much more in the original cut of John and Yoko relating. You saw that she and John – and I'm not saying she had anything to do with breaking up The Beatles – were like a separate camp in the group. And so we took that out.'

Also out was anything that could harm 'the Beatle brand', a state of affairs that, ever since, has clouded any prospect of Lindsay-Hogg's initial vision ever seeing the light of day. That meant shredding any material that could shine a light on the bust-up between Harrison and Lennon that saw George verbally quit.

The director told *Entertainment Weekly* in 2003: 'They were sort of falling apart at that time, and it was hard to get some of those moments into the movie because as well as being the stars, they were also the producers. They all had slightly different agendas. George didn't like it because it represented a time in his life when he was unhappy. He was a very sensitive – almost too sensitive – sort of sardonic guy when he was pushed. It was a time when he very much was trying to get out from under the thumb of Lennon/McCartney – I mean the songwriting team. If there were twelve cuts on the album, they'd get ten, Ringo would be thrown one, and George would get one.

'George was feeling his artistic oats, and he was writing some wonderful songs, and was looking for a chance to have more expression for himself. I was aware that they were beginning to get on each other's nerves. If you notice, there's a shot looking down on McCartney, and the shot of George talking is on a long, slightly fuzzy lens. That's because, knowing that this was coming, I didn't want them to feel the cameras were intrusive. I put one camera up in the gantry shooting down, so they didn't see it. I moved the other camera back to the end of the studio. So they didn't really know the cameras were there, which gave them the opportunity to get it off their chest. But I knew I wanted to show the disagreement between these two musicians.'

Of course Allen Klein had grand plans for the film. It had always been envisaged by The Beatles and Lindsay-Hogg as a TV film, but with so much footage having been shot, Klein spied dollar signs. Lots of them, in fact. The commercial potential of turning it into a major film to be shown in cinemas all over the world was self-evident. A low-budget film showing the band recording a new album would undoubtedly be a huge success – and he was in for twenty per cent of the proceeds under the terms of the deal he had cut with John, George and Ringo in May. The fact that it showed The Beatles in freefall didn't matter. The fans would have to buy their tickets first. Money in the bank.

He also had an opinion on Lindsay-Hogg's rough cut. The film, he said, should be all about The Beatles and nothing but The Beatles. All material that showed those circling the outer margins of the band's orbit – like those he had already identified as leeches – must be excised. That meant no Neil Aspinall, Mal Evans, George Martin, Glyn Johns, Terry Doran or Peter Brown. No Beatle wives, even. But there was so much footage of Lennon and Yoko joined at the hip that his request was beyond absurd.

Johns also remembered seeing Lindsay-Hogg's early edit. 'Klein saw a rough cut of it and said he didn't want anyone else in the film but The Beatles, so everyone else who was in any shot at any time was taken out, the net result being that it got a bit difficult to watch after a while. Also, some of the stuff that I know was in there originally was extremely interesting, conversations with other people, members of the film crew, people who were just around, people visiting, like Billy Preston but Klein said that only The Beatles could be in the film and that was it.

'There was some amazing stuff – their humour got to me as much as the music. John Lennon only had to walk in a room, and I'd just crack up. Their whole mood was wonderful, and that was the thing, and there was all this nonsense going on at the time about the problems surrounding the group, and the press being at them, and in fact, there they were, just doing it, having a wonderful time and being incredibly funny, and none of that's in the film.'

But Klein would not be swayed and he soon persuaded the entire band that the film should be blown up from 16mm film to 35mm – a task that threw up technical challenges – and marketed as a major Beatles cinematic event. Which, of course, meant virtually recutting it from scratch, a process that would take several months and push back any possible release into the next decade. In the meantime, there was no avoiding the images of broken light that Lindsay-Hogg had captured so well. Cinéma vérité masquerading as real life.

John Lennon invited his bandmates to his new estate at Tittenhurst Park, but there was little warmth in the housewarming as the forced smiles of each one betrayed the breakdown in relations. This was the last time all four Beatles were pictured together.

AUGUST 1969

As endings go, it was unremarkable and without fanfare. A normal turn of events, one that had been played out hundreds of times before. In the early hours of 21 August 1969, John Lennon, Paul McCartney, George Harrison and Ringo Starr walked out of the EMI Studios in London's Abbey Road and, following a few amicable farewells, made their weary way to their cars, parked nearby. It had been a long session – almost twelve hours – to apply the finishing touches to *Abbey Road* and find common ground, especially between Lennon and McCartney, over the album's final running order. The discussions had been difficult, sometimes fractious, but agreement had finally been reached.

And yet this mini tableau, so familiar to them, would put the seal on a black day for millions of Beatles fans around the world. This day would go down in history as the last time these four musicians would gather in a recording studio together at the same time. Coincidentally, it came only a few weeks short of the anniversary of their first arrival in London as a quartet for their debut EMI recording session in September 1962.

Never again would they find the collective joy in creating the magic that had come to define the Sixties. Never again would they share the kind of intimacy that had seen them conquer the world. Not that, at the time, they knew it. Yet August had arrived on such an encouraging note, thanks to a new Lennon song, 'Because', that had the potential to recall those early days when each of them was in perfect harmony inside the studio.

Lennon had a well-founded reputation as a brash and visceral rock 'n' roller, but his mellower side was frequently overlooked. This new song fitted easily into the same kind of tender category as 'This Boy', 'In My Life', 'Across The Universe' and even the lullaby lilt of 'Good Night', from the White Album. According to Lennon's famous retelling, the song had its roots in

Beethoven's Piano Sonata No. 14 (the Moonlight), which he had heard Yoko playing. He asked her to play the piece backwards and a light bulb went off in his head.

He presented 'Because' to the band on Friday, 1 August. It was the last new song that all four would work on from scratch. The song, like so many of Lennon's most recent offerings, was lyrically sparse, just twenty-four different words in two brief verses and an even briefer chorus. In fact, the serene imagery was partly filched from Yoko's book, *Grapefruit*. But that was to take nothing away from a ballad that gave The Beatles the opportunity to revisit the kind of three-part harmonies so evocative of their early years. They hadn't attempted that kind of vocal interaction for years, but George Martin, a specialist in this kind of discipline, was convinced that it would be worth the efforts of Lennon, McCartney and Harrison to rediscover their special synthesis.

In that eight-hour first session, their long-time producer patiently coaxed the band through twenty-three takes of the backing track, while doubling Lennon's guitar lines on a harpsichord to give it a slightly medieval tone. Starr was on this occasion a silent partner but contributed a gentle tap on the hi-hat to give his bandmates a percussive compass.

Further work on layering and refining the harmonies was carried out on the following Monday with McCartney, Harrison and Starr buoyed by Lennon's new-found zest for a track they all loved. Everyone knew, however, that serious work would be needed to get it right. Mood and atmosphere were everything so the lights inside Studio Two were dimmed, even though it was mid-afternoon. Harrison had brought incense along to help provide a chilled-out vibe. Then he, Lennon and McCartney positioned themselves in a semi-circle with the sparse backing track playing in their headphones and they sang harmony as if they had been doing it all their lives. Which, in many ways, they had. Repeated takes were required over the next five hours to get the phrasing right, a process that required self-control and no small measure of serenity from all involved.

Among those who witnessed the song slowly coming to life was Geoff Emerick, who would later recall the painstaking efforts that went in to creating what was one of Lennon's last significant contributions to the band.

He wrote: 'The problem was that George Martin had worked out nine harmony parts for The Beatles to sing, but we only had five tracks to record them on. That was resolved easily enough when it was decided to have John, Paul and George Harrison sing their three-part harmony together live, instead of overdubbing each part one at a time and then have to do two additional passes in order to add on the remaining six parts. It was as much an aesthetic as it was a technical decision because their voices had always meshed so well naturally . . . they knew they were doing something special and they were determined to get it right. There was no clowning around that day, no joking. Everyone was very serious, very focused.'

The next day, Lennon, McCartney and Harrison regrouped round a single microphone to graft similarly intricate vocals on to the vine of another song, one that would become the band's 'cosmic' valediction. 'The End', with its three-way guitar duel, proved that the band could still keep pace with the emerging school of heavy rock. Crucially, it added to the feeling that they were pooling their musical resources towards completing the album.

August also saw Harrison emerge as The Beatles' unlikely sonic scientist. In the first week he oversaw the installation at EMI Studios of a Moog synthesiser, the pioneering keyboard-based instrument that, starting in 1969, was to become every rock star's expensive new toy. In those days it was an elephantine piece of equipment, with banks of wires protruding in every direction. Primitive it might have been, but Harrison, the band's most technically adept musician, foresaw limitless opportunities to expand The Beatles' sound.

He had introduced it to Lennon and McCartney, who both immediately bought in to its seemingly infinite possibilities. Within days, they had recorded Moog overdubs on 'Here Comes The Sun', 'Maxwell's Silver Hammer' and 'Because'. The Moog seemed to lift each song into a new, almost symphonic zone, but Harrison later acknowledged the amateurism of his earliest efforts on the instrument. 'It was enormous, with hundreds of jack plugs and two keyboards. It was one thing having one, but it was another thing making it work. When you listen to the sounds on songs like "Here Comes The Sun", it does some good things but they are all kind of infant sounds.'

The synergy that infused them all by working on powerful material had provided a renewed focus. 'When we were working on a good track, all the bullshit went out the window,' said Starr. Equally, however, Paul, George and Ringo were painfully aware that the mood music could change in an instant, especially where Lennon was concerned. Yoko was still an unwanted presence in the studio, often sniping in stage whispers from the sidelines, ramping up her husband's easily stoked neurosis. Adding strength to Lennon's paranoia was his heroin habit. He was still able to mine brilliant tunes, such as 'Come Together', 'Because' and 'Sun King', but the words revealed a man who increasingly relied on nonsense prose. At the height of Flower Power, the lyrics to 'Strawberry Fields' and 'I Am The Walrus' scanned like a hippie avatar's Holy Writs. But the obscure lyrics in his newest material read more like vacuous doggerel.

By August, the Lennons were dangerously addicted again, a situation that was even more perilous for Yoko, who was pregnant. Occasional visitors to Tittenhurst Park that summer glimpsed the tell-tale signs of drug paraphernalia in various rooms, despite Lennon's later insistence that they 'never shot up'. His bandmates had known for months. The subject matter had infused White Album tracks such as 'Everybody's Got Something To Hide Except Me And My Monkey' and 'Happiness Is A Warm Gun', with their allusions to fixes. Generally, though, the topic remained off the table.

Among those watching from the sidelines was Barry Miles, former head of now-defunct Zapple and the joint pioneer behind the London underground newspaper, *International Times*. In an email interview for this book, he laid bare the impact of Lennon's addled state of mind during this period.

'John was strung out on heroin so he behaved like most junkies, manipulative, self-centred, in pain. He wasn't on a heavy dose but he was addicted. It doesn't matter whether you sniff it, shoot it or shove it up your ass, you're still a junkie. You could still have an intelligent conversation with him, when Yoko wasn't interrupting, and he seemed open to new ideas, but he had that passive-aggressive thing that junkies often have.'

This meant that those closest to Lennon had to walk on eggshells. As McCartney later said: 'He was getting into harder drugs than we'd been into and so his songs were taking on more references to heroin. Until that point we had made rather mild, oblique references to pot or LSD. But now John started talking about fixes and monkeys and it was harder terminology, which the rest of us weren't into. We were disappointed that he was getting into heroin because we didn't really know how we could help him. We just hoped it wouldn't go too far.'

In the post-Beatle years, Lennon refused to sugarcoat the reasons for his heroin addiction, pointing the finger of blame at The Beatles and the inner sanctum at Apple, whose anti-Yoko attitudes, he felt, bordered on racism. He declared: 'We took H because of what The Beatles and their pals were doing to us.'

Since June, the Lennons' retinue had grown to include Dan Richter, a thirty-year-old American actor and mime, who had known Yoko since 1964, and his wife Jill, whose ties with the London underground gradually gained them access to the couple's tight-knit circle.

Always quick to seize an opportunity, Yoko suggested the Richters move into Tittenhurst. The couple quickly became their de facto personal assistants. The fact that Dan was a heroin addict simply sealed the deal and by August he had become Lennon's 'dope buddy'. Few people outside Lennon's immediate circle knew of his dependence, but the clues were hiding in plain sight for anyone who cared to look. His skin was sallow, his eyes sunken and he displayed all the signs of junkie psychosis: unpredictable mood swings, lethargy, drowsiness and bouts of self-pity.

Richter, who had gained peculiar fame as the evolutionary man-ape at the start of Stanley Kubrick's 1968 film, *2001: A Space Odyssey*, witnessed their inexorable descent into the squalid mess of heroin. He told me: 'I wouldn't say he did a lot of drugs but John liked to get high. You have to put it into context. It was like they were going through a divorce. There was a lot of anger, a lot of passion. It was a very unsettling time for John. It was the end of The Beatles, you know, and that was a big, big deal. John wanted to move on. He was an immensely creative man and he felt that he was stuck in The Beatles, that he was being stifled creatively.'

Having been at the centre of a worldwide peace blitz for months, the couple finally recognised that their craving for another kind of fix – publicity – was draining away. The media circus had long ago left town but Lennon realised the need to retreat from the storm he and Yoko had created. Almost all interviews were cancelled. Only the likes of DJ Kenny Everett, a friend for years, were allowed past the Apple guards. Sanctuary lay behind the large walls of Tittenhurst, where they enjoyed an almost hermit-like existence. They officially moved in during the first week in August, but invitations for visits were rare. Not even Klein, the man in whom Lennon had invested so much faith to save The Beatles' fortunes, was encouraged to call in.

In other ways, Lennon and McCartney's lives were running on parallel lines. They had both chosen women born overseas as their brides. They had married within days of each other, and both their wives were now pregnant. Linda was due at the end of the month. Yoko, having already suffered at least one miscarriage with John, was not as far along. But those coincidences were rare points of common reference or even conversation topics between them. For now, all they could do was return to the songs they were singing.

Tantalisingly, by the first week in August, they almost had enough songs for an album, so their thoughts naturally turned to a title and a cover. Two years had passed since *Sgt. Pepper*'s Summer of Love grandiosity and a year since the frostiness of the White Album sessions. But they were still The Beatles and a new LP demanded a cover that reflected their noble status. On Friday, 8 August, the four emperors of EMI put the wheels in motion.

*

The clock had not long struck ten that morning when Lennon, McCartney, Harrison and Starr sat on the steps outside the EMI Studios in the upmarket London suburb of St John's Wood. Normally, it would be an ungodly hour in which to play Spot the Beatle. The foursome kept vampire hours, especially when working on an album, as they had been throughout July and August. It was a beautifully sunny day in the capital and, for once, even The Beatles' mood matched the weather. Linda McCartney snapped away on her camera, capturing some excellent portraits as they waited for Scottish photographer Iain MacMillan to arrive for the official photoshoot.

There had already been a loose discussion over what to call the new album. Geoff Emerick smoked a popular brand of cigarettes called 'Everest' and an idea was floated to combine the imagery of the world's highest mountain with the world's biggest band. Of course, it would mean travelling four and a half thousand miles to the Himalayas and back again for a couple of pictures, but these were days when extravagant dreams outweighed commonsense practicalities.

Everyone drifted back into their private thoughts until the silence was broken by Starr: 'Why don't we call it "Abbey Road", do the picture outside on the Zebra crossing and be done with it?' As usual, it took the most grounded Beatle to provide the most uncomplicated of solutions. Soon, McCartney had sketched out a plan. And now here they were, at the appointed hour, their eyes squinting in the bright summer sun – only Harrison had shades with him – waiting patiently for MacMillan to arrive.

Lennon was dressed all in white, as was his custom these days, his leonine hair now halfway down his back; Starr was sedate in a black suit; McCartney was almost as conservative in a similar Tommy

Nutter two-piece, only the sandals hinting at unconventionality; Harrison was dressed from head to toe in Levi's denim, the rock star's uniform of choice in 1969.

Parked in the foreground, like a happy accident, was a white Volkswagen Beetle. Tentative enquiries to see if it belonged to anyone in the studios or a local resident proved fruitless and it became an ironic – and iconic – part of the backdrop. MacMillan, a friend of Lennon and Yoko's, was only told about the assignment a few days before.

As he arrived in his van and unloaded a stepladder, McCartney quickly explained the script. Someone had a word with a friendly cop to hold up the traffic to allow MacMillan to mount his ladder and shoot off some quick frames on his Hasselblad camera.

In all, he took six shots of the band striding back and forth across the black-and-white crossing. In every one, the order was the same – Lennon impatiently telling them all to keep in step, led the way, followed by Starr, McCartney and Harrison. In three of the shots, McCartney nonchalantly cast off his sandals. He said: 'I kicked off the sandals and walked across barefoot for a few takes and it so happened in the shot he used I had no shoes on. It didn't seem a big deal.'

MacMillan was looking for a shot that captured The Beatles in symmetrical lockstep. Later, as he studied the negatives in his darkroom, it was evident only one would come close.

Naturally, the daylight appearance of all four Beatles attracted a number of curious bystanders, some of whom crept unintentionally into MacMillan's viewfinder. But there were no hordes of screaming fans; August '69 was light years from the bedlam of Beatlemania.

Watching the scene unfold from further down the street was Derek Seagrove, one of three painters and decorators who were working inside EMI Studios that day. They were part of a crew from Uxbridge-based company Fassnidge, Son & Morris, who had a regular contract with EMI to carry out work in the studios. And he just about stole into the shot that within six weeks would become part of Beatle folklore.

He said, 'I was actually working in the studios that day. I am the guy on the right, in the bottom left-hand corner of the picture. Most people when they look at the picture think we are outside somebody's house but in actual fact we were at the other entrance to EMI Studios as it was then.

'I was thirty-one at the time. There were two of us on the job that day and then another guy came and joined us outside the studios when the picture was being taken. It was just a coincidence that he was also a decorator working on some flats across the road. He saw what was happening and he actually joined us . . . I was with a colleague called Steve Millwood. On the day the picture was taken we were only at the studios by chance.

'I wasn't much older than The Beatles. I was born in 1938, so I was two years older than John Lennon. It wasn't unusual for me to be at Abbey Road. I had been there on numerous occasions. I used to see them having a cup of tea in the canteen. We used to sometimes be at the next table and they would come in. We used to just say a casual hello to them, that kind of thing.'

Seagrove went on: 'On this particular day we saw them all walking out the front door together around about ten or so, which was a bit unusual in itself. You rarely saw them at that time of day. We knew something was going on. I suppose curiosity got the better of us so we followed them. We stopped at the gate and they walked up the other end. We just stood there and watched what they were doing.

'The guy who was taking the photograph was up on a very tall pair of steps and he was actually waving to us to get out of the way. But we decided to just stand our ground. He was waving his arms and shouting at us but we refused to budge, being a bit young and a bit bolshie, I suppose. We had no idea about the significance of the picture. We didn't know what it was for. Of course, later on I wish I had been able to get them to sign a copy of the album but by the time the album came out they were never seen again in public and you certainly didn't see them at the EMI Studios. It would have been worth a fortune. If the picture had been taken today we would probably have been airbrushed out of it and airbrushed out of history as well.'

Another eyewitness was John Kosh, a highly rated young designer recently appointed at Lennon's behest as Apple's creative director – and someone whose arrival went against Klein's cost-cutting grain. He has his own recollections of the photograph that would come to provide a lasting image of The Beatles.

He said, 'The thing was, as far as I can recall, the pictures were only supposed to be publicity shots. They were never intended for an album cover, no matter what Paul McCartney says. It changed into an album cover when EMI saw the shots and decided they wanted an album cover by, say, Wednesday and this was Monday, something like that.

'That same evening we had the pictures rush-processed. We put them on the lightbox and went through them one by one. And it seemed to me that the one we chose was the most obvious one. They were all supposed to be in step but of course they're not. It took about twenty minutes for people to decide that it went from publicity shots to an album cover. We were poring over the pictures when we got a note from EMI saying they needed an album cover fast.

'I had been working on *Let It Be*, which of course was supposed to come out first. Then the lads had got together again and did such a fantastic job that everyone knew this record would have to come out before *Let It Be*. So that then was the trigger for everyone running about like blue-arsed flies.

'It was my decision not to have the word "Beatles" on the cover, which caused me all kinds of trouble. It occurred to me that anyone who didn't know who these four guys are must have been living in a cave or something. They were the four most famous musicians on the planet. They didn't need the name of the band on the album. So we did not put the name "Beatles" on the cover which, looking back, was pretty radical for a twenty-three-year-old.

'But in all honesty I was scared stiff. And then Sir Joseph Lockwood, who was the chairman of EMI, phoned me at 3 a.m. He said I would cost them thousands of sales by not having the name of the band on the cover.

'He was absolutely livid, furious. I was still half-asleep but when someone like that is raging down the phone at you, you wake up pretty quick. To be honest, I was shocked, not so much by the phone call as the language. He had this upper-class English accent and he was calling me a fucking prick. The reason he phoned me at three in the morning was he had just found out the cover had gone to press.

'So I went into Apple the next day scared stiff and the first person I saw was George Harrison and I told him about the phone call and that Sir Joseph Lockwood was after my blood. He just said, "Fuck it, man, we're The Beatles."

'In the end, the album has sold something like twenty-six million copies or something ridiculous like that, so I feel fairly vindicated. But at the time I was very nervous and very worried. You really did have to hold on to your sphincter. Sir Joseph Lockwood was a very powerful force in the music industry and had been for a long time. He was a man used to getting his own way.'

While Kosh fretted about appeasing music-industry aristocracy, Kevin Harrington was at the beck and call of rock 'n' roll royalty. As an assistant to Mal Evans, The Beatles' faithful gofer-in-chief, Harrington had already enjoyed a box-office seat at the rooftop concert back in January. Now here he was witnessing another epochal moment. But Harrington is adamant that the photo session was not as spontaneous as history has depicted it.

He recalled: 'The actual picture was taken on a Friday but the previous Sunday I was asked to go to EMI Studios. I didn't know what it was until I turned up with Steve Brendell [another assistant] and saw Iain MacMillan the photographer. We normally had Sundays off but I was happy to do anything for the band.

'Iain said he needed four people to walk across the Zebra crossing. So we went into the studios and grabbed a couple of porters. And we then spent twenty minutes or so walking back and forwards across the Zebra crossing. Iain seemed to have a drawing in his hand about how it was supposed to look, at least that's what I remember. The drill was that Iain wanted four guys just to act out how it would look in the picture. It was really just a mock-up for

Iain to show the band how it would look. I know a photo exists of the four of us but I am not in a position to publish it.

'When you worked for The Beatles anything could happen. Nothing was strange. We might have guessed it was for an album picture but I'm not one hundred per cent sure, but I was there on the Friday when they shot the picture for real. The thing was that the London traffic in those days was virtually non-existent. There was hardly any traffic going down Abbey Road except for the occasional bus or taxi. A policeman came along and he stopped whatever traffic there was. The whole thing lasted about twenty minutes. I think Iain was happy with what he had but The Beatles didn't like to hang around much. They always wanted things done pretty quickly.'

MacMillan himself remained largely tight-lipped about the picture that, in many ways, became the defining image of The Beatles in their final days as a band. He rarely talked about it, breaking cover only a few times to reference his famous shot. He was quoted in the *Guardian* in August 1989 as saying: 'That photo's been called an icon of the Sixties. I suppose it is. I think the reason it became so popular is its simplicity. It's a very simple, stylised shot. Also it's a shot people can relate to. It's a place where people can still walk.

'The whole idea, I must say, was Paul McCartney's. A few days before the shoot, he drew a sketch of how he imagined the cover, which we executed almost exactly that day. I took a couple of shots of The Beatles crossing Abbey Road one way. We let some of the traffic go by and then they walked across the road the other way, and I took a few more shots. The one eventually chosen for the cover was number five of six. It was the only one that had their legs in a perfect 'V' formation, which is what I wanted stylistically.'

By 10.30 a.m., the shoot was over. The Beatles had time to kill for a few hours before they were due back at the session to continue work on 'The End', 'I Want You' and 'Oh! Darling'. Harrison and Evans headed off to London Zoo, Starr went shopping, while Lennon and McCartney, along with Linda, headed back to Paul's nearby house for lunch.

Almost at the same time, four members of a notorious Los Angeles hippie family, led by a charismatic drifter named Charles Manson, were making plans to invade the home of American actress Sharon Tate, the wife of Hollywood film director Roman Polanski. Some eighteen hours later, Tate, who was eight months pregnant, lay dead in a pool of blood alongside her former lover Jay Sebring, friend Stephen Parent, screenwriter Wojciech Frykowski and Frykowski's girlfriend Abigail Folger, heiress to the Folger coffee fortune.

Worldwide revulsion greeted the murderous rampage, which Manson claimed had been carried out under the flag of a race war he'd named 'Helter Skelter', one of the tracks on the White Album. By the time he and his followers were hauled before the courts, The Beatles would be further linked to one of the most heinous crimes of the decade.

*

As the days ticked down, all the jigsaw pieces were slotting together. Agreement had been reached on a decision to call the album *Abbey Road*, and a potential cover picture was in the can. Now all they needed was to maintain their fragile unity – eyewitnesses still talked about tightrope tensions and occasional walkouts – to finish the work in the studio that had been launched on 1 July.

Throughout the next week, they continued to pick up the pace. Playbacks revealed that most of the songs were in good order, requiring only overdubs and additional instrumental tweaks to bring them up to scratch. Over the next twelve days they all answered the call of duty to finesse the tracks, each of them privately aware that the songs – most of them, at least – were better than they had any reason to expect. Checking the list of tracks that had already been recorded, Lennon, fearing that McCartney was again the dominant voice on the album, was keen to re-animate 'I Want You', his searing love song to Yoko.

He had first aired the track at Twickenham in February and had made another pass at it in April. Up to now, he had used the newly commandeered Moog synthesiser sparingly, only employing its distinctive textures to give 'Because' a gossamer tinge. Normally, he much preferred to compose on the piano or guitar. He was, nevertheless intrigued by the instrument's potential to create soundscapes which went against the musical grain. As such, it opened up the possibility of blending rock structures with his new Yoko-inspired passion for all things avant-garde. 'I Want You' was the obvious choice for an intermarriage between two contrasting musical styles.

On 8 August, hours after waving MacMillan off to develop his photographs, Lennon enlisted Harrison's help to twiddle the Moog sufficiently to generate the wall of white noise that would eventually dominate the song's marathon fadeout. Later in the month, Starr, of all people, would liberate a wind machine from an EMI cupboard to distort the background even more.

On 11 August, together with McCartney and Harrison, Lennon added harmony vocals by repeating the one line, 'she's so heavy', to the track recorded on 18 April at Trident Studios, leaving him with two distinct versions and, typically, unsure as to which one he liked better. It was at this session that he decided to officially add 'She's So Heavy', in parenthesis, to the title. ('Heavy' was the buzzword of the times and was also McCartney's favourite adjective to describe the miserable vibe that he believed Klein had brought to Apple.)

Lennon would continue to wrestle with the dilemma over the two versions for another nine days. The fourteenth of August saw a marathon session aimed largely at fusing together all the dissonant fragments of the medley into one collective whole, using crossfades and loop effects to give the impression of a single, cohesive track. The medley was mainly a Lennon-McCartney production, but Harrison played a huge part with some of his most inspired and understated guitar work.

He said, 'During the album things got a bit more positive and, although it had some overdubs, we got to play the whole medley. We put them in order, played the backing track and recorded it all in one take, going from one arrangement to the next. We did actually perform more like musicians again.

'Likewise with the vocal tracks: we had to rehearse a lot of harmonies and learn all the back-up parts. Some songs are good with just one voice and then harmonies coming in at different places and sometimes three-part work. It's just embellishment, really, and I suppose we made up parts where we thought it fitted because we were all trying to be singers then.'

George Martin's return to the fold also meant reinstating the production values which had always been so important in helping to burnish their raw material into high-end merchandise. A (silent) musical collaborator, Martin, with his intuitive grasp for what worked, was equally comfortable working with single musicians as he was conducting a huge orchestra to add a grand and sweeping backdrop to even the most mundane material.

Several songs were obvious candidates for orchestration – the fusion of 'Golden Slumbers/Carry That Weight', 'The End' and the two Harrison songs - 'Something' and 'Here Comes The Sun' – that already stood out. This was the first time that any of Harrison's work had been given any symphonic treatment by Martin.

On Friday, 15 August, Harrison finally took centre stage amid a line-up that, according to Mark Lewisohn's *The Complete Beatles Recording Sessions*, included twelve violins, four violas, four cellos, a string bass, four horns, three trumpets, one trombone and one bass trombone. All the hired musicians were on a very expensive clock but Sir Joseph Lockwood had long ago decided that The Beatles should be given a wide economic latitude because of their importance to his company's bottom line.

A problem, however, quickly arose with 'Something'; Harrison was unhappy with the lead guitar line he had laid down during an earlier session. But even allowing for the fact that The Beatles were now using eight tracks for the first time, there wasn't enough space to redo it separately as an overdub. So he took the plucky decision to re-record his lead part live with the orchestra.

It said much for his newly emboldened state of mind that he felt confident enough to pull it off alongside the cream of London's top classically trained musicians. He betrayed no sign of nerves as he effortlessly nailed the solo, one of the most elegant he ever committed to record.

Watching through the cracks in their fingers upstairs were Martin and Emerick, neither of whom was confident that Harrison could do it without several expensive – and embarrassing – retakes. But their concerns were quickly set aside.

'He actually did it live with the orchestra,' recalled Emerick. 'It was almost the same solo [as before] – note for note. The only reason I feel he wanted to redo it was emotion.'

During two more sessions, on 18 and 19 August, the finishing touches were added to 'Golden Slumbers/Carry That Weight', and a piano track was tacked on to 'The End', while Harrison added the distinctive Moog track that gave 'Here Comes The Sun' a bit more sonic punch.

By now, the finishing line seemed near. Only two serious outstanding issues remained. The first one was the nagging puzzle that was 'I Want You (She's So Heavy)'; the second one was accommodating Lennon's reservations over the running order. Both matters were resolved once and for all at the session on Wednesday, 20 August.

The first four hours were spent revisiting 'I Want You (She's So Heavy)', which by now had become the most convoluted recording in the band's career, having undergone a number of reworkings since its first public airing in February. By mid-August there were two distinct versions. The first three minutes of the version recorded at Trident contained all the vocals and also included a beautiful, swirling organ track played by Billy Preston; the second part done at Abbey Road included the recently added three-part harmonies overlaid on a monstrous blues riff repeated over and over. The solution was obvious: remix both versions and then edit them together to create one master track. It clocked in at seven minutes and forty-seven seconds, outpacing 'Hey Jude' as the longest track they ever committed to tape.

The song fused elements of hard rock, blues, bossa nova and even jazz to form a piece of music that proved The Beatles could create anarchic rock just as efficiently as any of their late Sixties contemporaries. It was the sound of a post-apocalyptic nightmare set to music and was the most radical rock track they ever recorded.

Happy at last with the new mix, Lennon had nevertheless one further, unorthodox demand to make of Emerick as they listened to the newly edited playback. With the tape almost running out, and Lennon demanding the swirling climax sound louder and louder in the fadeout, he told Emerick to suddenly splice the tape with scissors to create a jarring, slashing ending.

Gut instinct told the engineer this was crazy, but he nevertheless complied and the song came crashing to a cliff-edge, full stop. 'I thought the song was going to have a fadeout,' he recalled. 'But suddenly John told me, "Cut the tape." I was apprehensive at first – we'd never done anything like that. "Cut the tape?" But he was insistent, and he wound up being right.'

It was the last song that all four collectively worked on under The Beatles' banner, and irony was not hard to find. The track was an undisguised love song to Yoko, the woman who history would unfairly blame most for driving a wedge between Lennon and his bandmates and ultimately causing the group to split.

The rest of the session was devoted to agreeing a running order for the album and finding common ground over the sequencing of the tracks. After the first listen, 'Oh! Darling' and 'Octopus's Garden' were transposed.

Up to then, Lennon believed he had won the argument with McCartney especially for 'I Want You (She's So Heavy)' to be the last track on the album, and possibly, just possibly, the final song on any Beatle album, giving Lennon what he was always used to getting – the last word.

Even at this late hour – it was almost midnight – he was still lobbying for all his songs to be on one side and all McCartney's on the other. He still remained unconvinced over the merits of the medley, which at this point was earmarked for side one. But the truth was they had come too far down the road to start backtracking now.

Boxed into a corner, and with McCartney and Martin blocking all the exits, Lennon reluctantly gave way and the running order was flipped, leaving 'I Want You (She's So Heavy)' as the final track on side one and 'The End' appropriately bringing the curtain down on side two (apart from one, final secret surprise).

But despite the last-minute bickering, they all agreed on one thing. Heard from start to finish, *Abbey Road* sounded like a genuine Beatles album. It was an aural sleight of hand where any friction lay undetected between the grooves of what would become their last will and testament.

By 1.15 a.m. all four Beatles headed out of EMI Studios into the light rain, each of them naturally unaware they were crossing a borderline. This was the last time all four would each be together at the same time inside a recording studio. Musically speaking, 20 August was the day when The Beatles as a band faded out of time but not out of memory.

*

On 22 August, Lennon at last threw open the doors of his new estate in Ascot to his three bandmates. Tittenhurst, with its Georgian entrance, sweeping grounds, its lawns, stately trees and great walls of rhododendrons, camellias and azaleas, its avenues of Weeping Blue Atlas Cedars and lush meadows, was a pile fit for a millionaire rock star. But even in that short time, the house had become more like a rehab facility than a home.

In the weeks leading up to *Abbey Road*'s final sessions he had tried unsuccessfully to wean himself off heroin again. Gradual withdrawal and even methadone hadn't worked. So he gave in to his own impulses – the only solution was to go cold turkey. It meant 'thirty six hours rolling in pain' wrestling with the fallout of self-cure rather than self-harm. But on the day he played host to Paul, George and Ringo at Tittenhurst, there was very little evidence on the outside that his demeanour had changed. The housewarming was decidedly chilly.

The visit had been organised by Derek Taylor, who recognised that the release of their new album would require new promotional pictures. The band was adamant they wouldn't do any live appearances or interviews – anything to avoid the sheer banality of repeated questions about their future.

Initially, the idea was to shoot some pictures at Apple but then the location was suddenly switched to Ascot. Two photographers were trusted with the assignment: Monty Fresco of the *Daily Mail* and Ethan Russell, the American who had already documented the grim images from the 'Get Back' sessions at Twickenham in January.

Unfortunately for both men, the pictures they captured at Tittenhurst were, by and large, as joyless and morose as the Twickenham images. The Beatles were photographed at various locations in the sprawling grounds. The session began in front of the main house, the musicians standing among the pillars supporting the terrace canopy. They then trudged down the main garden path, past the statue of Diana, goddess of the hunt, to a paddock of high grass, an old cricket pitch, where they stood, being photographed and filmed from all sides.

Lennon and Harrison hid their features under wide-brimmed, black hats and thick beards (Lennon's hadn't been trimmed since the Abbey Road photo shoot) but there was no way to disguise their jaded attitude. Starr looked more hangdog than usual, as if the whole thing was a huge effort. Even McCartney, normally the consummate PR man, struggled to raise a smile in most of the images. With them, but mostly out of shot, were Yoko and a heavily pregnant Linda.

Linda had brought along a small cine camera and casually shot some silent footage of all four Beatles smiling awkwardly while stroking some donkeys from nearby stables. Only her husband manages a half-hearted salute for the camera.

And with that gesture, The Beatles waved a hushed goodbye to the world. (There was an odd synchronicity to the occasion given that it fell seven years to the day they had first been filmed for television, by Granada TV, during a lunchtime gig at the Cavern.) More importantly, from a historical perspective, it was the final time John Lennon, Paul McCartney, George Harrison and Ringo Starr would be pictured together.

In the years that followed until the tragedy that unfolded in New York on 8 December 1980, there were plenty of two-way and occasional three-way assemblies of ex-Beatles. But as they went their separate ways that afternoon, all that remained was an unspoken truth. The game was up.

Forgotten in the mists of time is the fact that this was perhaps their most photographed session ever. The two photographers shot numerous pictures, some staged, others much more spontaneous. One photograph amid the dozens he shot stood out for Russell. It shows the morose-looking group in front of a tree with its branches bent over and touching the ground.

Russell said: 'There are better pictures from the session, and by that I mean more interesting, but none are so quite so aggressively sad. I love this one because it's wide and particularly dramatic. Even the tree looks sad and defeated. I call the picture "Weep".'

George Harrison, though, was not one to shed any tears for The Beatles. 'I can't honestly say what I felt after that record was finished,' said the band's lead guitarist, who at that time was already glimpsing an open road ahead to a possible solo career. 'But I don't recall thinking that was it because there was so much going on all the time. There were plenty of other activities to fill the gaps. I was certainly not missing being in the band.' He demonstrated this by ploughing ahead with various engagements. First up was a reunion with the one musician who ranked higher in his esteem than any other – Bob Dylan, rock music's most mercurial talent. Dylan had been absent from the concert stage for more than two years following a motorcycle accident. During that time, the musical landscape had shifted out of previous recognition. Nineteen-sixty-nine was the year rock music embraced a new grown-up congregation.

Blazing a trail across Europe and America were the likes of Led Zeppelin, with a cocksure frontman who made Mick Jagger look like a cuddly uncle, a virtuoso lead guitarist who was in the process of reinventing the genre with his epic riffs, a drummer renowned for his thunderous fills and a bass guitarist whose sheer multi-instrumentalism made him an indispensable part of the equation. Zeppelin may have represented rock's new wave but the old guard had no intention of disappearing. This month Elvis Presley, buoyed by his electrifying 1968 Comeback Special, was preparing for a month-long residency at the Las Vegas Hilton. The Who had already unveiled *Tommy*, Pete Townshend's ground-breaking rock opera, and the Rolling Stones were in the process of ending a three-year-long performance hiatus to plant their flag on stage as 'the greatest rock 'n' roll band in the world'.

This was also the year of big outdoor events: the aforementioned Stones' Hyde Park tribute to Brian Jones and the free concert at the same venue on 5 June by the Blind Faith quartet of Eric Clapton, Steve Winwood, Ginger Baker and Ric Grech. Change was in the air. So, too, was the intoxicating scent of new money. Rock was suddenly bigger and grander, its presentation leaping in scale with every new tour that was announced. Woodstock, staged on a sprawling farm site in rural upstate New York between 15 and 18 August, drew an astonishing 400,000 fans to see the biggest gathering of groups since the Monterey Festival two years earlier.

Promoters on both sides of the Atlantic scrambled to get a slice of this lucrative new opportunity. Among them were two young Englishmen, Ray Foulk and his brother Ronnie, who the previous year had staged a festival on the Isle of Wight, a beautiful island, rich in poetic history, off England's southern coast. It had been a moderate success but in 1969 both men had set their sights on raising the bar considerably. Three names sat atop their wish list: Elvis, Bob Dylan and The Beatles. Presley was not a typical festival act and had sold his rock 'n' roll soul for his residency in Sin City; Dylan, having shunned invites to perform at Woodstock despite the venue being almost within a stone's throw of his home, remained in concert exile; The Beatles, though, were possibly within reach. The Foulk brothers had been encouraged by the band's January rooftop gig to believe they could pull off the showbusiness coup of the decade. Combining youthful bravado with a sense of audacity, they put the call into Apple.

Ray Foulk told me: 'It was a shot to nothing really but they were already falling apart. We put the call in but we got a very negative response. We didn't have high expectations anyway because they weren't really a functioning band. So we then turned to Bob Dylan, who said yes, and it was like winning the Lottery.'

Dylan, along with his wife Sara and their kids, flew into the UK on Tuesday, 26 August, where among the first to meet and greet him were Harrison and Mal Evans. The two musicians hadn't seen each other since the previous November when Dylan had allowed Harrison into his inner circle, an overture that was the beginning of a lifetime friendship between them. On this day, however, it was only the briefest of reunions; Harrison had to go back to London while Dylan was keen to check into Forelands, the farmhouse that would be his home on the Isle of Wight for the next five days ahead of the actual gig on Saturday, 30 August.

Two days later, Harrison and Pattie joined the Dylans at Forelands, and they would come and go until the night of the show. Foulk, who tended to stay out of the way, nevertheless couldn't fail to spot the empathy that existed between Harrison and Dylan. Harrison even gifted Dylan one of his Gibson guitars to play at the concert.

Foulk said, 'It wasn't my style to go hobnobbing with the stars but I had to go there to deal with management problems. I wandered into the sitting room one day and there's George Harrison and Dylan strumming their guitars and singing the Everly Brothers song, "All I Want To Do Is Dream", which was spellbinding in a way. I also saw George starting to write a new song ["From Behind That Locked Door"] about Dylan actually, just asking him to loosen up a little.'

Meanwhile, Paul McCartney's world had completely shifted on its axis. In the early hours of 28 August, Linda had given birth in the Avenue Clinic in St John's Wood to a baby girl they named

Mary after the cherished mother McCartney had lost to breast cancer when he was just fourteen. Like any new father, it was a life-changing moment, the day he 'saw magic' unfold before his eyes. The baby's arrival left McCartney, a man who had grown up in a warm and extended family unit, ecstatic. He said, 'It was great for me because it was a very good balance set against the tension of The Beatles at that time.'

When they returned home to Cavendish, Paul and Linda drew the curtains, literally and metaphorically, on their public persona. Linda took one or two pictures of the proud father that made their way into newspapers. But they just wanted to spend precious time together as a new family. So as far as Apple was concerned, McCartney was off the grid, even more than he had been lately. Even the knot of Apple Scruffs permanently on standby outside his home gave him some space. One said, 'We still didn't like Linda but we all agreed to back off a bit. Put it this way, we were told in no uncertain terms to back off.'

McCartney, so good with other people's children (Lennon's son Julian being a particular case in point) took to parenthood right away, 'glowing with the whole joy of it all'. But it meant that everything else took a back seat, including any possibility of joining his bandmates and their respective wives for Dylan's set at the Isle of Wight on the last day of the month.

Lennon and Yoko arrived at Forelands in a helicopter that landed not in a nearby field that had been set aside for such purposes, but in the gardens, destroying in the process dozens of flowers in the downdraught from the rotor blades. Harrison and Starr arrived in a separate chopper. It was the first time the three Beatles and Dylan had been in the same room since May 1965 when they all had ringside seats for the American's Royal Albert Hall gig.

Foulk witnessed the handshakes and warm greetings. He said, 'You could tell they were happy to see each other. I think everyone knew that The Beatles were breaking up but I didn't see any tension between them during the time I saw them. There was only one moment, not long after they arrived, when Lennon said something like, "Excuse me, we have to talk shop for a moment." And then they went off in a huddle for a couple of minutes but that was it really.'

Dylan was naturally apprehensive at the prospect of appearing in front of an audience of 150,000 festivalgoers, who, as Lennon later said, were expecting to see some kind of divine musical presence. So, to lighten the load and ease any pre-gig boredom, he invited all three Beatles to a game of tennis in the grounds of the farm. It's hard to imagine a more incongruous scene. Grainy pictures, taken on Pattie Harrison's camera, have emerged showing Harrison, his long hair blowing in the wind, and Dylan both swinging tennis racquets.

Over the years, stories about the three Beatles and Dylan on the Isle of Wight have taken on a mythic quality. They rocked out together in a superstar jam at the massive barn that had been turned into a huge rehearsal area; they drew up plans to appear on stage for the encore, but Yoko canned the idea because she was not invited to take part. Ray Foulk was quick to dismiss the gossip as the products of someone's fevered imagination.

'There was a lot of newspaper talk,' he says. 'Dylan himself actually encouraged it by saying something at a press conference like he'd love to do it, so the suggestion was in the public domain, which meant some fans left somewhat disappointed. But here's the thing; The Beatles didn't arrive with any instruments. If you are professional musicians like The Beatles at the top of your game you don't arrive without instruments or not having rehearsed. That would have been completely unprofessional. There was no chance whatsoever.

'Dylan's manager, Albert Grossman, was asked, "Wouldn't it be nice?", and he said, "Wouldn't it be nice to go to the moon?" They knew the whole world was watching and they wouldn't have wanted to make fools of themselves. The stories are nonsense.'

A couple of hours later, all three Beatles, along with Yoko, Pattie and Maureen, took their seats in the roped-off press section just yards from the front of the stage. Sitting beside Lennon was

Tom Paxton, the acclaimed American folk singer who in the afternoon had also witnessed the 'collegiate' atmosphere among The Beatles and Dylan. 'I didn't sense any antagonism with The Beatles', Paxton told me. 'I saw three guys who were interacting normally and seemed very relaxed in each other's company.' But in the minutes before Dylan finally took to the stage at around II p.m., Paxton got a glimpse of what public life was like for a Beatle.

He said, 'Bob introduced me to John Lennon. That night I sat with John and Yoko and something happened that I have never forgotten. Security was intense so there wasn't anyone there who wasn't in some way connected with the music business. Even so, a fellow leaned over from behind and asked John for his autograph. John, very polite and very quietly, said, "No, if I start I'll never get to stop," and the guy burst out with a profanity, spewing hate all over John's head. He called him every name you could think of. Throughout this entire barrage John sat with his head bowed looking at the ground. When it was all over, I said, "Does this happen a lot?" and John said, "Every time I leave the house." I thought, "My God, what a price to pay."'

Lennon was not even a comfortable concertgoer, preferring instead to stick with the studio experience. Dylan's performance left him firmly underwhelmed. Despite Ray Foulk's observations, Lennon later held out one intriguing possibility. He declared: 'If there had been a jam, we would have got up. It was killed before it happened. It was so late by the time he got on. The crowd was dying on their feet.'

He, Harrison and Starr then headed back to Forelands for the traditional after-show party. And it was Harrison who, in a moment of one-upmanship, furtively placed on the turntable a record that had then not even rolled off the EMI presses. Seconds later, the room was filled with the sound of a pulsing bassline and the unmistakable voice of John Lennon singing 'Come Together'. Harrison's test pressing was the first time anyone had ever heard the finished version of *Abbey Road*.

Paxton recalled: 'It sounded fantastic. We had quite a party. Bob loved it and so did everyone else. Looking back, it was an incredible moment to be among the first people in the world to hear that record. It's still my favourite Beatles album.'

For the three Beatles, however, the moment was bittersweet. The songs emanating through the speakers suggested business as usual. In truth, the business had hit the buffers and had been emphatically derailed in the dog days of the summer of 1969.

Lennon, McCartney, Starr and Yoko Ono sat down with Allen Klein to sign the new deal with Capitol Records, but minutes later the meeting ended in shock as John suddenly announced he was leaving The Beatles.

SEPTEMBER 1969

So far as The Beatles were concerned, September kicked in with a feeling of sombre finality. The sense of camaraderie – brittle though it was at times – that had carried *Abbey Road* over the finish line had turned out to be a mirage. The band was now staring at a future that promised nothing but pain. The *Abbey Road* sessions, coming after the lassitude that had marked the sessions for 'Get Back' and the White Album, had left them all mentally and creatively drained. 'It's torture whenever we make an album,' John Lennon had complained. This time it felt different, as if a watershed had been reached

The twenty-sixth of the month had been pencilled in as the UK release date for the first proper Beatles LP in ten months. It meant, of course, a series of promotional interviews, an exercise in tedium that none of The Beatles could face, particularly as the media was so fixated on the band's future. Paul McCartney, for his part, was revelling in his role as a new father. George Harrison was plunging deeper into Krishna consciousness on a metaphysical quest to find his Eternal Self, while continuing a musical exploration with the likes of Billy Preston, Doris Troy and others on the Apple label. (He had, moreover, just learned that his mother, Louise, was suffering from cancer). Lennon and Yoko occasionally broke cover, notably on 10 September, when they hosted a screening at the Institute of Contemporary Arts in London of a new film they had made. It was called *Smile*, a fifteen-minute slow-motion study of Lennon's penis becoming erect. John wittily predicted the critics wouldn't touch it.

On the same day as the Lennons were indulging in celluloid silliness, Ringo Starr was lying in a bed in Middlesex Hospital. The drummer, the one the others fretted most about in the event of a split, was the first to pay a physical price for the collective stress that had built up during the past nine months. He had been admitted with severe stomach pains, a sure sign of the latest strains placed on a nervous system already weakened by almost fatal childhood illnesses. He was allowed home after three days, and went back to playing the only role he ever knew – waiting patiently by the phone for a summons to come into the studio for a session.

Lennon was especially conflicted over his place in the universe. Dylan's Isle of Wight performance may have left him unmoved, but it also spoke to his internal struggle. One half of him loved the idea of going back on stage, the natural home for any performer; the other half was frightened to death by the immense expectations that accompanied talk of a Beatles gig. 'They would be expecting God or something,' he observed. Of course, if he were to go it alone or with Yoko, as they had done at Cambridge in March . . . the thought would remain parked for the moment.

On 1 September, as thousands of festivalgoers began the long homeward trek from the Isle of Wight, Dylan himself arrived at Tittenhurst, seventy-five miles away. He and Sara stepped out of an Apple-chartered helicopter to be greeted by Lennon and Harrison. Lennon was keen to repay the Bard of Hibbing for his hospitality at Forelands. Prior to that occasion, the last time the two men had spent any meaningful time together had, of course, been in May 1966, when, monitored by the camera of film-maker D.A. Pennebaker, they sat in the back of a limo, both of them either stoned or drunk. As included later in the rarely seen film, *Eat the Document*, it was far from their finest moment. 'The camera captured the incoherent ramblings of two impossibly stoned rock stars riding around London in the back of a chauffeured limousine,' sniffed *Rolling Stone* magazine fifty years later, in May 2016.

Lennon often appeared unsettled in Dylan's presence, as if intimidated by the American's mercurial personality. Now, though, he was on home turf, happy to show off his rock-star mansion. It should have been an easygoing visit; three hero-worshipped, influential and wealthy rock stars, comfortable in each other's presence. But the conversations turned out to be laboured and awkward. Harrison and Dylan clearly had a rapport, but Lennon felt like an outsider, an ironic role reversal of his teenage relationship with Harrison. In a bid to cut through the unease, he suggested he and Dylan join forces on a new song he had been working on. 'Cold Turkey', he hoped, might appeal to the non-conformist in Dylan. But Dylan declined the invitation to jam in Lennon's newly built home studio. Perhaps he was still weary from his show the night before. Perhaps he was simply bored in Lennon's company. Perhaps – and this seems more likely – he simply didn't like the song, with its harrowing lyrics about heroin withdrawal.

The truth may never be known, given that the visit still remains largely shrouded in intrigue five decades later. Dylan, typically, has never publicly referred to it; Lennon did, briefly, but only in passing during his soul-baring interview in *Rolling Stone* the following year.

'He came over to our house with George after the Isle of Wight and when I had written "Cold Turkey",' Lennon told the magazine's editor Jann Wenner. 'I was trying to get him to record. We had just put him on piano for "Cold Turkey" to make a rough tape but his wife was pregnant or something and they left.'

Soon, Dylan's helicopter was ferrying him and Sara back to London before they headed across the Atlantic the next day. They were driven to Heathrow by Harrison, whose friendship with Bob continued for the rest of his life. Lennon and Dylan met again only rarely. Bob was the first but not the last to pass on the latest musical diary entry in the ongoing real-life ballad of John and Yoko.

Convinced that 'Cold Turkey' had Number One written all over it, Lennon breezily pitched it as The Beatles' next single during a band meeting early in the month. 'I said, "Hey, lads, I think I've written a new single,"' he recalled. His cheeky optimism echoed new evidence uncovered by Beatles historian Mark Lewisohn of a previously unknown taped band conversation suggesting Lennon, perversely, still clung to a belief that The Beatles could continue. Unsurprisingly, McCartney and Harrison, who had already heard the track, decided a song that graphically choreographed the pain of heroin withdrawal was unsuitable for the band. It wasn't a question of not liking the song – Starr would play drums on the sessions when it was recorded by Lennon on his own, later in the month – the decision was solely down to image. The lyrical content alone was a guarantee of it being shunned by radio programmers, thus depriving it of valuable airplay. Lennon viewed the snub as simply more evidence of his growing musical detachment from the band he had founded. The fact was, he simply didn't need them any longer. Especially now that he had another musical outlet for the music the other Beatles considered too outlandish – The Plastic Ono Band. He later said, 'I thought: "Bugger you, I'll put it out myself."'

This latest example of musical disengagement between Lennon, McCartney and Harrison was brought into sharp focus during a conversation captured by Anthony Fawcett, the Lennons' assistant, round about the time of Starr's hospitalisation. He let a tape run during several fraught and revealing chats and reproduced them in his own book of that period, *One Day at a Time*.

Mostly, they bring into the open the simmering undercurrent of hurt feelings, guilt and introspection that was rapidly nearing boiling point, especially over Lennon and McCartney's carve-up of the band's singles. One exchange went as follows:

Lennon [to McCartney]: We have the singles market, they [George and Ringo] don't get anything. We've never offered George B-sides, but because we were two people, you had the A-side and I had the B side.

McCartney: Well, the thing is, I think that until now, until this year, our songs have been better than George's. Now this year his songs are at least as good as ours.

Harrison: Now that's a myth, because most of the songs this year I wrote about last year or the year before. Maybe now I just don't care whether you are going to like them or not, I just do 'em . . . most of my songs, I never had The Beatles backing me.

Lennon: Oh, come on, George. We put a lot of work into your songs, even down to 'Don't Bother Me'. [But] in the last two years you went Indian and we weren't needed.

Harrison: That was only one tune. On the last album [the White Album], I don't think you appeared on any of my songs.

Lennon: Well, you had Eric [Clapton] or somebody like that . . .
McCartney: When we get in the studio, even on the worst day, I'm still playing bass, Ringo's still drumming and we're still there, you know . . .

Except they weren't. There was a reluctance to admit the truth that was clear to each of them individually. Then came the phone call that arguably set in motion a chain of events from which there would be no way back.

*

John Brower was a hipster dabbling in music promotion in Toronto, the Canadian metropolis with a bar on every corner and a band in every bar. Kim Fowley was a music scenester already basking in a reputation as a record producer, songwriter and Sunset Strip Svengali. Fate brought the men together when rock journalist Ritchie Yorke suggested to Brower that Fowley would be the ideal person to bring on board for a major music event he was planning in the city.

Nostalgia was back in vogue for the simple three-chord chug that had sparked rock 'n' roll into life a decade earlier. Fowley and Brower, like millions of others, felt its electrifying charge. Brower had already helped stage a Toronto festival in June. Buoyed by its moderate success, he and his business partner, Kenny Walker, set their sights higher by announcing plans for a one-day-only rock 'n' roll revival festival, which would see the founding fathers of the genre share a bill with those new artists seeking to carry the torch for the next generation. Brower moved quickly to secure the likes of Jerry Lee Lewis, Gene Vincent, Little Richard and Chuck Berry alongside contemporary bands such as Junior Walker and The All Stars, the up-and-coming Alice Cooper, Tony Joe White, and The Doors, who were given top billing for the show that was planned for Saturday, 13 September, at the University of Toronto's 20,000-seater Varsity Stadium.

216 AND IN THE END

It was an ambitious undertaking and one, which, unfortunately, quickly showed signs of unravelling. Ticket sales failed to catch fire. With less than two days to go, fewer than two thousand briefs had been sold, leaving Brower and Fowley, whose primary role was to anchor the evening from the stage, staring into a financial abyss.

Desperate times called for desperate measures. In a moment when ambition seemed to overtake reality, Fowley, who had once met The Beatles in 1965 in London, suggested Brower cold-call Apple in London to try to get John Lennon involved. Perhaps the appearance of a Beatle appearing from music's Mount Olympus introducing the heroes who had fired his own rock 'n' roll dreams would be enough to rescue the event. As Fowley told Brower: 'He loves Chuck Berry and Little Richard, and The Beatles have done songs by both of them and they opened for Gene Vincent at the Star Club in Hamburg back in the early days.'

By any yardstick, it was still a long shot but Brower, nevertheless, put in the call at around 5 p.m. Toronto time (10 p.m. UK time) the night before the gig was due to take place. 'What do you have to lose?' Fowley challenged Brower as he summoned the necessary chutzpah to try and chisel Lennon into flying three and a half thousand miles at twelve hours' notice for what amounted really to twenty minutes' work. It seemed like mission impossible, but it turned out to be a carpe diem moment.

In London, despite the late hour, the Apple switchboard was still manned. An operator listened as Brower said it was a matter of extreme urgency that he speak to Lennon. It was like a Bible salesman dialling the Vatican and hoping to get through to the Pope, but the pleading in Brower's voice paid off. He was initially put through to Fawcett, the Lennons' human shield/call screener, who listened intently while scribbling down notes on a piece of paper . . . rock 'n' roll festival . . . Toronto . . . Gene Vincent . . . Bo Diddley . . . Chuck Berry . . . Little Richard . . . John Lennon . . . emceee. Sitting opposite and seeing the names of his heroes on the pad, Lennon suddenly became animated, and grabbed the phone.

The next part of the conversation blew Brower away. 'Suddenly I hear John saying, "Well, we wouldn't want to come unless we could play,"' Brewer would remember. For a nanosecond that could easily have been an eternity, he held his breath – he thought Lennon was offering him one of the biggest showbusiness coups in history.

'The phone in our office was on speaker so everyone could hear. There was a collective gasp before I stammered, "You mean The Beatles?" John replied, "No, just me and Yoko and we'll put a little band together."

"'Okay, we'll squeeze you in," I blurted, immediately realising how dumb that must have sounded. "We can't pay you but we'll get airline tickets for everyone and put you up somewhere nice. Is that okay?" Lennon agreed on one condition – that he be allowed to film it and record it for a possible live album.

Coincidentally, Yorke was at that same moment at Apple interviewing Harrison in Taylor's office and he immediately vouched for both men. All the stars were suddenly in cosmic alignment. Brower said he would sort out all the visas; Fawcett and Evans were dispatched to put in calls to various musicians on Lennon's wishlist for his pick-up band.

The first name that came to mind was Harrison's. But the guitarist no longer felt compelled to follow him blindly into some madcap scheme that, on the surface at least, seemed preposterous. Furthermore, he was in no mood to go on a long-haul flight with Yoko to play the kind of music he had no feel for. He said, 'John asked me to be in the band, but I didn't do it. I didn't really want to be in an avant-garde band, and I knew that was what it was going to be.'

Instead, Lennon narrowed his search down to Eric Clapton, Klaus Voormann, a long-time friend from Hamburg who now played bass for Manfred Mann and who had also designed the cover for *Revolver*, and Alan White, a twenty-year-old drummer who had impressed Lennon the night before as part of the resident band at a London club.

White, who would go on to have a stellar drumming career with Yes, was convinced he was being pranked when he took Lennon's call asking him to be in his garage band. Oh, and by the way, they would be flying from Heathrow the next morning to Toronto to play at an outdoor festival.

White told me: 'The first thing I did was hang up because I was sure someone was playing a joke. I just couldn't believe John Lennon was on the phone. And then he rang back and assured me it was him. He said, "Do you want to do a gig in Toronto?" and I said, "Yeah, sure" . . . as you do. He said, "Okay, I'll send a limo for you in the morning." The band I was playing with at the time were all pee'd off because I was supposed to do a gig that night with them . . . make some money for them, and I said, "Don't you realise I've got to go play with John Lennon?" We had to cancel the gig.'

Unlike White, however, Voormann was not ready to dive headlong into John's latest musical fantasy without first getting the lowdown. The two had been friends since Klaus had first wandered into Hamburg's famous Kaiserkeller Club, having been drawn there by the rowdy stomp of young guys playing a unique brand of rock 'n' roll. He was long considered part of The Beatles' inner circle but even that didn't give Lennon a free pass over his services.

He recalled: 'John asked me if I would do it, and I paused because I couldn't believe what he was saying. He would always get very uptight when you were not immediately like, "Yeah, that's great! Sure I'll do it!" I paused a little and said, "You'll have to explain this a little to me. I have no idea what The Plastic Ono Band is. Is that Yoko's band? Do we have to go naked onstage or what?" I had no idea in my mind. Suddenly it was not John Lennon; it was The Plastic Ono Band, so I knew it had something to do with Yoko. And he explained to me, "I want to go in the studio and record together, and I want the band to play. Eric said yes already. How about you?" I said, "Okay, I'll do it."'

Clapton's participation was key. Lennon and Yoko, at that point still committed to keeping their promise to Brower, then decided to hit the sack, leaving the job of rounding up Eric to Apple flunkey Terry Doran. In Toronto, Fowley and Brower carried out a pre-emptive media blitz announcing that Lennon and his band – they cleverly didn't say what band – would be appearing at the Toronto

Rock 'n' Roll Revival Concert the next day. Inevitably, ticket sales soared on the back of this unexpected coup, especially after Brower was clever enough to persuade Lennon to tape his confirmation for cynical and disbelieving radio station execs in a separate phone call.

By the next morning, however, the enterprise looked doomed. Lennon had woken up to the reality of what he had got himself in to, and was scared to death. He called their assistant, Anthony Fawcett, still bleary-eyed from making all the travel arrangements, and told him to apologise to Brower and send flowers instead.

In the meantime, Clapton had been roused from his slumbers at home and, guitar in hand, was already at the airport with Voormann and White. At that point, chaos ensued. Fawcett called Brower in Toronto from a payphone at Heathrow to deliver the bad, but not wholly unexpected, news that the Lennons had reneged on their promise. Standing beside him was an irate Clapton with whom, by a fortuitous quirk of fate, Brower already had a relationship. Just eight weeks earlier, the promoter had taken a massive financial hit over a gig in the city by Blind Faith, the supergroup Clapton had raised from the ashes of Cream. Now, history was in serious danger of repeating itself.

Desperate, he pleaded with Fawcett to let him speak to Clapton as a matter of urgency. Brower recalled the conversation as follows: 'Eric, you may not remember me, but I'm the promoter who lost $20,000 on your Blind Faith show last month. Please call John Lennon, and tell him he must do this or I will get on a plane, come to his house, and live with him, because I will be ruined.' On hearing this, Clapton rang Lennon from the same payphone and, according to Fawcett's account, ripped into him, accusing him of rock-star grandstanding and told him in no uncertain terms what he felt and virtually ordered him to get his backside in gear.

At the same time, Fawcett was involved in his own salvage operation. He said, 'Knowing their moods, I took a chance, decided not to send the flowers and asked everyone to stand by at the airport. I rushed over to Tittenhurst hoping that with a little encouragement they would change their minds and go through with the concert. When I arrived they seemed more relaxed and in much better spirits, having just finished breakfast. John appeared to be getting his confidence back about performing. I suggested we could still catch a later flight and there was a glimmer of enthusiasm. The clincher came when Eric called to tell John that he was really keen to play. Without a second thought about his earlier cancellation, everything was on again.'

Three hours later, the first incarnation of The Plastic Ono Band was seated, guitars in hand, in the back of a Toronto-bound Boeing 707, scrabbling their way through a rehearsal for an acoustic set of rock 'n' roll oldies that they should all know so well: 'Blue Suede Shoes', 'Money' and 'Dizzy Miss Lizzy'. Huddled alongside them were members of the Tittenhurst Mafia that now included Fawcett, Mal Evans, Terry Doran, and Dan and Jill Richter.

Lennon's decision to form a new band, in retrospect, was his first unilateral declaration of independence from The Beatles, but no one recognised it then as such. Certainly not McCartney, Harrison or Starr. As the plane soared high over the Atlantic, reality began to dawn on Lennon. Clapton had just come off a disastrous European and American tour with Blind Faith but was nevertheless gig-ready. Voormann was a veteran of live shows and White was too young and too gung-ho to bother about nerves, despite the stellar company. Lennon hadn't fronted a proper rock band before a paying audience since Candlestick Park more than three years earlier. Now here he was, busking at the back of a Boeing for an audience that expected to hear every note. He recalled: 'We tried to rehearse on the plane but we couldn't hear a thing.'

In terms of live, one-take-only musicianship, he was out of his league, especially alongside an artisan like Clapton. Ritchie Yorke, who had hitched along for the ride, remembers Lennon being sick with nerves throughout the flight, partly through fear of playing live and partly through heroin withdrawal.

'I haven't performed before a large audience for years,' said John. 'I did the Rolling Stones *Circus* film with a small audience and I did the Cambridge '69 gig, but they didn't even know I was coming.'

On the ground, meanwhile, Toronto was experiencing a form of born-again Beatlemania. When the plane landed at Toronto International, the Lennon entourage swept unchecked through Customs and was driven to the stadium flanked by members of the Vagabonds Motorcycle Club, who had volunteered to provide their own pop star-specific brand of security. After being greeted by Brower and Fowley amid a battery of flashbulbs, the musicians were taken to a cramped dressing room beneath the stands that reeked of sweat. Clapton recalled the Lennons especially being less than impressed. 'John just stood there in the dressing room, which was admittedly rather tatty, saying: "What am I doing here? I could have gone to Brighton." It was a long way to go for one concert.' Yoko also made a few salient observations. She said, 'We arrived in this dressing room, and it is a concrete locker room, it's dirty, it's ugly. I looked at John and he laughed and said, "Welcome to rock 'n' roll."' Joining in the melee was Allen Klein, newly arrived from New York, and D.A. Pennebaker, who had been hired by Apple to film the event and turn it into a 'happening'. The word then went out that Lennon needed some traditional rock-star stimulant to help him get through the occasion. When someone mentioned that coke would be just the pick-up required, another person returned with cans of fizzy drink before they found the rock star's idea of the real thing.

It had been agreed that The Plastic Ono Band would be the penultimate act, leaving The Doors to close the show. Kim Fowley, though, was already worried that even at this late hour a clearly strung-out Lennon might back out. He said, 'I was standing beside him and I said, "Are you all right?", and then he throws up. And he started to cry. He said, "I'm terrified." Imagine if you were in The Beatles as the only band you've ever been in in your life. The first time you are to step onstage with people that weren't in The Beatles. You're about to go on stage before twenty thousand with your wife, a friend, another friend and a complete stranger with songs you had learned acoustically on a plane from England suffering from jet lag and sleep deprivation. You would be terrified.'

But Fowley then hit on a masterstroke. Minutes before the band were due on stage, he addressed the audience and asked them to hold up matches and lighters to welcome The Plastic Ono Band. When Lennon, dressed in a white suit similar to the one he had worn for the *Abbey Road* cover photoshoot, walked on to the tiny stage, staring back at him was a raucous crowd and a sea of blinding lights; the effect was as mesmerising as it was reassuring. 'We're just gonna do numbers that we know because we've never played together before,' he said by way of an introduction before the conceptual band that he and Yoko imagined would push back musical boundaries, launched their live career on the back of a vintage rock 'n' roll standard.

The Carl Perkins-tinged slower version of 'Blue Suede Shoes' was followed by Lennon's old Cavern stomper 'Money', then 'Dizzy Miss Lizzy', before he made his one and only concession to The Beatles. He had already teamed up with Clapton once before when he sang 'Yer Blues' at the Stones' *Circus* the previous December, so at least Clapton had some idea of the chords.

By the time it got to the still unrecorded 'Cold Turkey', the band had found a fourth gear and Lennon sounded like the Beatles-liberated musician he now longed to be, freed from the shackles of other people's whims. It didn't matter that he could barely remember the words, relying heavily on a cheat-sheet of lyrics held up by Yoko.

The only discordant note was struck by Mrs Lennon herself, who began the performance writhing onstage inside a large white bag before emerging to take her place on John's left hand-side. But it was her screeching that reportedly brought some jeers from the audience, who, after all, had come for kickass rock 'n' roll. The last song sung by Lennon was a ramshackle performance of 'Give Peace A Chance' – 'the reason why we're here' – complete with made-up-on-the-spot lyrics that ushered in a twenty thousand-strong singalong. It sounded chaotic and it bordered on self-parody, but no one seemed to care. Besides, the band had achieved a sleight-of-hand no one expected them to, least of all themselves.

If they had left it there, the debut performance by The Plastic Ono Band might have garnered the kind of kudos it deserved, but Yoko was determined to have the last word. She took centre stage to shriek her way through freeform versions of 'Don't Worry Kyoko (Mummy's Only Looking For Her Hand In The Snow)' and 'John John (Let's Hope For Peace)', a track from the couple's as yet unreleased *Wedding Album*, the third experimental LP they had recorded for Zapple. It was a tough sell.

Alan White told me: 'We're playing pretty good considering the circumstances when suddenly Yoko crawls inside a bag and proceeds to lie down on the stage. That's when it started getting weird. She had a microphone in the bag and noises were coming out. I thought there might be something wrong with her. I'm looking across at Eric and Klaus, and they're like, "Keep playing! Keep playing!"'

The band finally exited the stage with screaming feedback issuing from the speakers, Lennon with his arm draped comfortably over his wife's shoulder in an apparent gesture of solidarity to shield her from the scattered catcalls. Overall, though, Lennon felt thrilled and elated, having conquered his demons with a little pharmaceutical help. He later said, 'I can't remember the last time I had so much fun. From now on I'm going back to playing rock 'n' roll on stage.'

Three thousand miles away, those words struck an optimistic chord with Paul McCartney, who was still nurturing a spectacular return to live performance for The Beatles. That prospect, though, as far as Lennon was concerned, lay further away than ever.

The Plastic Ono Band and its itinerant gang of hangers-on spent the next two days chilling out at the estate of Thor Eaton, one of the Toronto event's principal financial backers, and joint heir to Canada's largest department store empire. Reviews of the group's live debut were largely favourable despite its improvised nature and the inevitable flak that Yoko drew. And for Lennon they only served to reinforce an ineluctable truth as well as reconciling him to an inevitable decision.

On the flight back to London, he casually confided in Clapton, Voormann and Klein, the one person who had arguably more to lose from the end of The Beatles than he had, that he wanted out. The only problem was this: where exactly was out?

*

Throughout most of the summer, while The Beatles remained in *Abbey Road* lockdown, Klein was immersed in his own salvage operation. Already he had presided over the busted flush that had followed his own boast to buy out Nems 'for nothing'. On the line, now, was something more important – the future ownership of the lucrative Northern Songs catalogue, and talks with EMI and Capitol over increasing the royalty rates.

At stake were two helix-linked fortunes – The Beatles, and the Paul McCartney-disputed twenty per cent commission he was entitled to under his contract, provided he could deliver an improved deal on these two fronts. But this was meat and drink to a balance sheet barracuda like Klein. And in that sense he held the upper hand in talks this month with Sir Joseph Lockwood at EMI, safe in the knowledge that the band had already fulfilled the terms of their 1967 agreement, which was due to run until 1976. The negotiation tactic was simple: no deal meant no new Beatles music for the next seven years. And no new music meant cutting off the pipeline that had ploughed millions into the company coffers for six years, making EMI the most profitable record company in the world.

Klein only needed to point out the staggering worldwide sales of the White Album to back up his threats. This was the sword of Damocles he held over the record company suits when they began round-table talks at the start of the month.

But he kept one vital piece of intelligence firmly in the closet; he knew that Lennon was on the verge of quitting The Beatles and close to breaking point. He had spent weeks lobbying hard with EMI and Capitol in America to improve the band's royalty rates. Now here was Lennon complicating an already fragile situation. That information alone would have been enough to torpedo the talks and capsize Klein's eye-watering commission. Deploying his trademark bravado, he went into the discussions using the language of a New York punk as he went to war with his mild-mannered English opposite numbers and their Capitol counterparts.

During conversations with the Americans, Klein adopted a familiar gambit by threatening to sue Capitol for unpaid royalties amounting to approximately $2m. And with EMI he bluntly warned that the band could easily turn in a full album of different versions of 'God Save The Queen' if the company refused to budge on his demand for improved terms.

Klein knew that, financially, he held the high ground. Sales from the White Album had pushed EMI's share of the UK record market up from twenty-eight per cent to around forty per cent, and had accounted for more than £900,000 in retail sales. Browbeaten by Klein's abrasiveness, and fearful over the possibility of a financial black hole in their respective accounts, Lockwood and Capitol president Bob Gortikov ran for cover.

By 10 September, they had thrashed out a royalties agreement with Klein that would become a benchmark in the history of popular music. The deal saw The Beatles receive an unprecedented twenty-five per cent of the wholesale price of an album in America – a significant hike from the previous seventeen and a half per cent. In three years' time, that rate would increase further as long as a minimum of two Beatle-related albums (crucially, not necessarily group albums) were released in a calendar year up to 1976.

Klein also secured the rights for Apple Corps to manufacture and sell Beatles records in America. EMI would retain the recordings, but Capitol would manufacture the releases on Apple's behalf. Apple would then profit further from the difference between manufacturing and retail costs.

In the end, despite the labyrinthine outcome, it was a no-brainer for Lockwood, who feared an incredible backlash from EMI shareholders should the company's most prized assets be allowed to walk out the door. Gortikov later hinted that both companies had always been looking to find an even-handed compromise while lamenting Klein's unyielding negotiating stance. 'Did he have to be so nasty about it?' he would complain. Nevertheless, it was a monumental coup for Klein and one he hoped would finally woo McCartney over to his side.

Lennon, Harrison and Starr had given Klein the authority to negotiate on The Beatles' behalf, but McCartney and John Eastman continued to operate behind enemy lines.

Correspondence between Eastman and the compatriot he loathed continued to descend to an ever more embittered level. On 3 September, Klein replied to one Eastman missive by saying, 'Dear John, I am on a diet so stop putting words in my mouth. Your misuse and abuse of the truth is almost without parallel.' Trust remained a bridge too far as long as Klein held the reins of power at Apple. A notional accord by both men to share key documents was shredded when Klein repeatedly redacted key passages to keep Eastman out of the loop. But Klein was savvy enough to know that, in talks with EMI at least, he needed Eastman inside the tent to ensure that McCartney's interests were, in some shape or form, properly represented.

Meanwhile, an uneasy truce had settled between ATV and Lew Grade and the consortium that held the balance of shareholding power over the future ownership of Northern Songs. ATV already believed they had effective control of the company after persuading members of the consortium to throw their weight behind Grade's bid for overall control, though nothing was yet legally binding. By early September, however, weeks of jittery dissent within some members of the consortium had hardened into a full-blown retreat. Unnerved by constant rumours of The Beatles splitting and veiled threats about Lennon and McCartney not renewing their Northern Songs contract on its expiry in 1973, some worried that the value of their shares would soon tank, leaving them hugely out of pocket. Which way to jump – The Beatles or ATV?

Klein, on the other hand, had every right to fear they could yet be driven into Grade's arms and tip the balance of power finally in ATV's favour. Such a situation would see Lennon and McCartney losing the fruitful publishing rights to the songs that had formed their reputation and were key to their financial future.

Throughout September, Klein kept up an assiduous back channel with all the relevant parties while hoping still to bring Northern Songs on board. It was classic Klein, trying to play both ends against the middle, invoking a sense of project fear among the weakest links in the consortium chain. He proposed an advance agreement for The Beatles to buy back the consortium's shares in Northern Songs. At the same time, he was making private overtures to Grade to deliver The Beatles' shareholding in return for key concessions that would keep everyone happy. As both sides manoeuvred their pieces round the chessboard, Grade stealthily went in for the kill.

Quietly, ATV picked off the consortium's pawns before announcing on Friday, 19 September, that they now owned just over fifty per cent of Northern's shares. Checkmate. The battle was finally over and The Beatles had lost. The news was relayed to Apple where yet another fractious meeting was taking place between Klein, Lennon, McCartney, Starr and John Eastman. At one point, Eastman suggested, astonishingly, that McCartney should have the same voting power as the other three combined – a suggestion that tipped the normally even-tempered drummer into a rage. But the latest news about Northern was like a dagger to the heart of Lennon and McCartney. With no more cards left to play, Klein had no choice but to fold and try to come to an arrangement with his nemesis, Grade, over The Beatles' shareholding in Northern Songs.

An initial pact was agreed in which ATV would buy The Beatles' shareholding in the company in return for loan stock and cash. Separately, the band would tear up outstanding writs against Northern Songs, while Lennon and McCartney would re-sign as songwriters until 1976. In their book, *Apple to the Core*, authors Peter McCabe and Robert D. Schonfeld quote ATV's financial director Jack Gill as hailing the accord, worth about £9m to Lennon and McCartney, as a 'good deal for both sides'.

This, though, was the moment that McCartney, John Eastman and his father Lee, still operating in the shadows, had been waiting for: another Klein screw-up. Acting on the basis of 'two strikes and you're out', Eastman junior point-blank refused to align McCartney with any Klein-negotiated pact.

Gill said, 'John and Lee Eastman stopped the deal. They wouldn't let Paul be a party to an agreement negotiated by Klein on behalf of all The Beatles. There was no way the two Beatle factions could agree.'

Naturally, Klein laid the blame squarely on the shoulders of the Eastmans and insisted that McCartney had been eager for the deal to go ahead. He told *Playboy* in 1971: 'Paul knew about it and was happy with it. He'd been talking directly to Grade and he liked the deal. Everybody was happy. The board of ATV was going to meet to approve it and Grade was going to call a press conference.

'Then, on the morning of the ATV board meeting, Grade got a letter from John Eastman saying "Klein has no right to deal for Paul McCartney". It was bullshit. Paul didn't know anything about the letter. Paul told him, "I'm going to do what Allen says." We called Grade but it was too late.'

When the acrid smell of corporate gunsmoke cleared, the whys and wherefores counted for nothing. Yes, the loss of Northern Songs had been offset by the sweet black gold the new EMI/Capitol deal would bring into the Apple pipeline. But this was a balance sheet debit that not even Klein could easily explain away.

It was there in black and white. Klein knew the McCartney/ Eastman axis had been handed enormous leverage in the continuing battle for The Beatles. What troubled him more was how Lennon, already struggling to keep a lid on his anxiety about the future of the band, would react to the news that he now really would be 'fucked around by men sitting on their fat arses in the City' when it came to control over the songs he had written with McCartney. Twenty-four hours later, the answer was swift in arriving with devastating consequences.

*

The twentieth of September was high noon for Paul McCartney. Apple had long turned into a high-security prison from which there seemed no escape – and Klein was the leering, pipe-smoking jailer who haunted his waking moments. Grade's corporate ambush the day before ensured another sleepless night, increasing McCartney's loathing for all things Klein. But today promised better things on the business front when he walked into Apple to join Klein, Lennon, Starr and sundry others, including Yoko and Linda, for what would be a momentous event.

On the agenda were their collective signatures on the lucrative deal Klein had agreed with Capitol and EMI. Biting back on his hatred, even McCartney was forced to admit that Klein had indeed pulled a huge rabbit out of the hat. 'If you're screwing us I can't see how' was his less-than-gracious verdict on the deal. But he couldn't help thinking that, while the new deal signposted a better financial tomorrow, what if there was no tomorrow for the band? Perhaps naïvely trusting in the instincts that normally served him so well, he hoped to use the occasion to again try to persuade Lennon that The Beatles needed to get back to where they once belonged – on the road, playing live and rediscovering the joyous fellowship that turned them into a band of brothers in the first place.

It was, he reckoned, an easy sell, especially given the traction of Lennon's recent live show in Toronto. He also hoped to tap into Lennon's rivalry with Mick Jagger as the Stones were preparing for their first American tour in three years. But McCartney, more than anyone, knew that the future of The Beatles, as it almost always had been, was in Lennon's hands.

The previous day, in between business meetings, he had broken his self-imposed media blackout to give an interview to journalist David Wigg for the BBC Radio One programme *Scene and Heard*, ostensibly to promote *Abbey Road*, the album that was now less than a week away from being in the shops.

In a wide-ranging conversation, McCartney wistfully discussed the changes that time had inevitably wrought on the band. He touched on his new role as a father, the business differences with Klein and the great unknown that represented the future.

He told Wigg: 'I don't like doing the business bit that much. But you can't avoid it. See, the thing is, like, we were once a band, just a band. But then, because we were successful, you can't help it being successful. Money comes in. You can't help that, again. When money comes in, income tax is to be paid. So you can't really help just turning into a businessman because someone says to you, "Where's your income tax, mate?" You say, "Well, I better go on to someone," you know. "I hope I've got a bit to pay you" and stuff. So you got to get all that together, you know. So it's just force of circumstance. You can't help it.'

Wigg asks: 'Paul, what about the future of The Beatles? I happen to know that the organisers of the Isle of Wight pop festival are going to ask you and the rest of The Beatles if you will top the bill next year at the Isle of Wight. Now, what's your reaction to a thing like that? Are you likely to go back on stage and perhaps do a show like that?'

Paul: 'I don't know, you know.'

Wigg: 'Does it appeal?'

Paul: 'I've never known. I didn't know when we were playing the Cavern that we'd be on the Royal Variety Performance. And after that all the papers said, "Well, what's left for them?" So then we went to America. They said, "What's left for 'em?" then, you know. And we got into making better albums and stuff. I mean, I just don't know what's gonna happen. It'll be all right, though.'

Heard on tape rather than read in black and white, it sounds more like he was trying to convince himself, his normal optimism buried beneath the shifting sands of uncertainty that continued to threaten The Beatles. Timing, he felt, was everything as he headed into Apple to sit down with Lennon, Starr and Klein. (Harrison swerved the meeting, having decided to head to Cheshire to visit his parents.) Inevitably, Yoko was in tow.

To begin with, the atmosphere was cordial but the mood of forced jollity was impossible to ignore, especially between Lennon and

McCartney, who also had Linda and John Eastman in his corner. Peter Brown also fulfilled his diminishing role as a Beatle consigliere.

The first order of the day was to sign the paper that would bind The Beatles to EMI and Capitol for the next seven years in what both parties hoped would be a mutually beneficial partnership. Everyone recognised that it was an important moment, and one that should be properly recorded. Coincidentally visiting Apple that day was David Nutter, the photographer who had been corralled into taking John and Yoko's wedding pictures on Gibraltar back in March. Soon, he found himself standing in front of John, Paul, Ringo, Yoko and Klein shooting off several frames as they hunched over a desk pretending to sign the paper. His contact sheet shows all five mugging for the camera. In a couple, McCartney is shown holding up a giant magnifying glass to the paperwork as if poring over the small print for any tell-tale signs of Klein crookedness.

Nutter told me: 'I happened to be in the building and they said, would you take a picture? And I did. It was all very haphazard. I didn't know what it was for. To be honest, I thought they were signing a napkin or something. But I got the feeling there was a very bad atmosphere in the room. You could tell it wasn't a happy place to be.'

Job done and with a promise to deliver the prints later, Nutter was quietly ushered out of the room, unaware of the drama that was about to unfold. Conversation then shifted uncomfortably from the present to the future as McCartney made his pitch to Lennon for The Beatles to rekindle their lost magic by becoming a touring band again. In his book, *Many Years From Now*, he recalled the exchange as follows: 'It got a little bit, "Well, why are we doing this? Are we sure the group is going to continue? Well, how's it going to continue? What are we going to do? Massive big shows?"

'Then I propounded the theory, "I think we should get back to our basics. I think we've got out of hand, we've overwhelmed ourselves and I think what we need to do is re-establish our musical identity and find out who we are again and so we should get back to little gigs."'

Starr, no fan of touring, said nothing. Neither did Klein, though he could sense the tempest building inside Lennon as McCartney's words hung in the air. When he could hold back no longer, his reaction left them all reeling. Lennon fixed McCartney with his most intense stare, a glare that brooked no argument.

As he recalled it: 'Paul was saying to do something, and I kept saying, "No, no, no," to everything he said. So it came to a point that I had to say something. So I said, "I think you're daft. I wasn't going to tell you until after we'd signed the Capitol deal but the group's over, I'm leaving."'

It was the moment when dry tinder exploded into flame. Lennon had been waiting for weeks, if not months, to let these words flow out. Now they poured forth in an adrenaline-fuelled torrent – and there was no way to stem the tide. Also nagging away at his psyche was the confirmation of twenty-four hours earlier that The Beatles had lost the battle with ATV for control of Northern Songs. And now it was all over, everything. For John Lennon, The Beatles were finished. And he meant it.

More than any other, this was the moment when the twentieth century's greatest romance – a prosaic phrase memorably coined by Derek Taylor – turned to dust.

Visibly shaken, McCartney could feel the colour drain from his face: 'We paled and our jaws slackened a bit,' he later said. 'I didn't really know what to say. He had control of the situation. There's not a lot you can say to "I'm leaving the group" from a key member. I remember him saying it was weird and exciting. It was like when he told Cynthia he wanted a divorce. He was quite buoyed up by it. It was later, as the reality set in, that it got quite upsetting.'

Klein, for his part, insisted he had never seen it coming. In the recollection he presented to London's High Court months later, he said: 'Everyone was in a very cheerful frame of mind and regarded this as a good deal and a great occasion in the life of The Beatles.'

The meeting broke up minutes later to the sound of doors slamming. Among those who heard the commotion was *Evening*

Standard journalist Ray Connolly, who, despite being a friend of the band, nevertheless knew better than to pry too closely under the bonnet at that time. But he used it to pen a piece under the headline 'The Day The Beatles Died'. (Expecting a Beatle backlash, Connolly instead found himself the recipient of a single white rose from a not-so-secret admirer – Lennon – a sign that his story was right on the mark.)

Mal Evans reputedly found Paul in tears. Lennon stormed red-faced into his own office inside Apple before heading out the door with Klein and Yoko to a nearby restaurant called the Peppermill. Yoko recalled him saying: 'Now it's only you and me.' Behind them, Starr was left to come to terms with the fact that, suddenly, he had become an ex-Beatle. But he felt only relief over Lennon's bombshell declaration. He said: 'I just felt that John was being honest. We all knew it was coming.'

A sense of frustration and foreboding quickly fell over Klein, for whom the optics were disastrous. He had just witnessed his one moment of triumph ruthlessly snatched away, his Svengali-like hold over Lennon temporarily broken by his client's sheer impulsiveness. Ever since Toronto, he had been trying to keep Lennon on a tight leash, imploring him not to do anything that would torpedo the deal with the band's record companies and leave him looking like a fool. For once, though, his persuasive tongue failed him. If word got out that The Beatles were being scattered to the four winds, no amount of fast-talking would alter the reality. John Lennon was leaving The Beatles.

The only card Klein had left to play was to appeal to Lennon's loyalty to his bandmates – and his financial instincts – and beg him to keep silent until something could be worked out. They were all aware that if Lennon resorted to a scorched-earth policy, he could take them all down. Klein knew how this news would play out in the boardrooms of EMI, Capitol and the City. He had lost Nems, he had lost Northern Songs and now he had lost The Beatles, the biggest prize in showbiz. And it left him exposed to allegations of insider dealing. EMI and Capitol could easily claim that Klein had illegally coerced them into new deals while all the time knowing The Beatles had broken up – a move that would inevitably affect their stock market position and influence the bottom line. And, having had advance warning of Lennon's intentions, he would not be able to use plausible deniability as an excuse. It had been a dreadful forty-eight hours.

Lennon later told *Rolling Stone*: 'Allen was there, and he was saying, "Don't tell." He didn't want me to tell Paul even. But I couldn't help it, I couldn't stop it, it came out. And Paul and Allen said they were glad that I wasn't going to announce it, like I was going to make an event out of it. I don't know whether Paul said, "Don't tell anybody," but he was damn pleased that I wasn't. He said, "Oh, well, that means nothing really happened if you're not going to say anything." So that's what happened.'

In later years Lennon, whose honesty veered close to masochism, seemed to harbour slight feelings of guilt over his eruption. He admitted: 'When I finally had the guts to tell the other three that, quote, I wanted a divorce, unquote, they knew it was for real, unlike Ringo and George's previous threats to leave. I must say I felt guilty for springing it on them at such short notice. After all, I had Yoko, they only had each other.'

The next day the Lennons headed to Harrison's home in Surrey to explain the rationale behind his decision. According to George's wife Pattie, Lennon was furious, venting over McCartney and Klein for the Northern Songs debacle. Years later, though, Harrison suffered a bout of Beatle amnesia, claiming he couldn't remember when Lennon had handed in his resignation: 'Everybody had tried to leave so it was nothing new,' he said.

In the meantime, of course, EMI record manufacturing plants all over the world were being cranked up to deliver another new Beatles record into the world. Six days after Lennon privately declared The Beatles were dead, *Abbey Road*, the album that would become their unofficial eulogy, was released. The album flooded into UK shops on 26 September, though American fans would have to wait another five days for their turn.

Iain MacMillan's show-stopping cover picture underscored the changes that time had wrought on the four individuals who had become world famous. Bestowing an accidental immortality on the Zebra crossing outside EMI Studios (soon they would be renamed Abbey Road Studios) it caught The Beatles seemingly stepping off the page, an image that would prove all too prescient.

To some critics, The Beatles were now considered passé, a broken-down institution. And initial reviews of *Abbey Road* by the rock press, including their most loyal placemen in the likes of *NME*, seemed to confirm the notion that musically the group was a spent force, content to live off former glories.

Some of the notices were savage, accusing The Beatles of music by numbers, shorn of the dazzling invention that had reinvented the genre and touched millions. Writing in the *Guardian*, Geoffrey Cannon lamented what he saw as *Abbey Road*'s staleness. It offered little, he complained, that was new.

'*Abbey Road* contains talent comparable with any other Beatles album, but nevertheless is a slight matter,' he wrote. 'Perhaps to their own relief, The Beatles have lost the desire to touch us. You will enjoy *Abbey Road*. But it won't move you.'

In America, advance copies exposed the band to some of the most coruscating expositions of their recording career. In *The New York Times*, Nik Cohn lavished praise on the medley 'tour de force' that dominated side two, but he leavened that opinion by saying he could barely listen to the 'unmitigated disaster' that was side one. And he wasn't fooled by The Beatles' attempt to disguise their Chuck Berry rip-off on 'Come Together', the album's opener.

He wrote: 'The six tracks on the first side and the opening two tracks on the flip are all write-offs: there's a Ringo Starr nursery rhyme; a quick burst of sub-Brian Wilson; two songs by George Harrison, mediocrity incarnate; yet another slice of Paul McCartney Twenties nostalgia, and an endless slow blues. The badness ranges from mere gentle tedium to cringing embarrassment. The blues, for instance, is horribly out of tune, and Ringo's ditty is purest Mickey Mouse. The only interesting failures are two numbers by John

Lennon, "Come Together" and "Oh! Darling" [The latter song was actually sung by Paul].

'"Come Together",' Cohn added, 'is a slowed-down reworking of Chuck Berry's "You Can't Catch Me" and is intriguing only as a sign of just how low Lennon can sink these days. "You Can't Catch Me" is a very great song, after all, and lumbering it with the kind of "Look Ma, I'm Jesus" lyrics that Lennon unloads here is not a crime that I'd like to have on my conscience.'

Rolling Stone handed the task of reviewing the album to a twenty-year-old staffer, Ed Ward, whose words turned out to be so poisonous that his editor, Jann Wenner, spiked them before giving the assignment to writer John Mendelsohn instead. Encouraged by his Beatle-obsessed boss to adopt a less acerbic approach, Mendelsohn performed the ultimate sycophantic about-turn, hailing *Abbey Road* as a masterpiece: 'That The Beatles can unify seemingly countless musical fragments and lyrical doodlings into a uniformly wonderful suite, as they've done on side two, seems potent testimony that no, they've far from lost it, and no, they haven't stopped trying. No, on the contrary, they've achieved here the closest thing yet to Beatles freeform, fusing more diverse intriguing musical and lyrical ideas into a piece that amounts to far more than the sum of those ideas.'

Closer to home, *NME*'s long-time Beatle loyalist, Chris Welch, played it safe by declaring: 'It's strange that we have now reached the point where nobody worries TOO much about what The Beatles are doing on record. There are no cries of "We demand a new *Sgt. Pepper*!" for example, or yells of "Whatever happened to their 'Mr Moonlight' period?" Now we can just sit back, relax and enjoy Beatle offerings and appreciate them on their own level.

'Too much has passed under the bridge to start getting uptight, and the truth is, their latest LP is just a natural-born gas, entirely free of pretension, deep meanings or symbolism . . . while production is simple compared to past intricacies, it is still extremely sophisticated and inventive.'

Despite the album being pilloried by some critics, the verdict that really mattered would emerge from the court of public opinion. And first-week sales proved the band's enduring appeal among a fan base that had largely been on the same journey as them. Lennon and McCartney were reluctantly wheeled out for limited promotional duties and both praised 'Something' as the best track on the album: it was a belated appreciation from the two chief Beatles for a song that both had initially derided as a lightweight piece of confectionery.

In a track-by-track interview with Australian DJ Tony McArthur, John happily hinted that he had managed to body-swerve the album's weakest track, 'Maxwell's Silver Hammer': 'It's a typical McCartney singalong or whatever you call them. I was ill after the [car] accident [in Scotland] but he really ground George and Ringo into recording it.'

He was still nursing a grievance over the gagging order imposed by Klein. On 28 September, he reconvened The Plastic Ono Band at Trident Studios to record a proper version of 'Cold Turkey' – the track rejected by McCartney and Harrison – with Starr sitting in for the unavailable Alan White, while Clapton and Voormann were again on board. Everyone in that room that night knew The Beatles were dead.

Meanwhile, death was about to haunt McCartney in the most macabre way possible. A spurious article had appeared in the 17 September edition of the *Northern Star*, the newspaper of Illinois University, purportedly detailing the grisly demise of the Beatle. Poring over song lyrics and pictures of the band, a nineteen-year-old sophomore, Tim Harper, speculated that McCartney had been killed in a car crash in 1966. Outlandish as it seemed, Harper began to believe he had stumbled onto the biggest conspiracy of the decade. It swiftly took on a life of its own as his imagination soared on a flight of fancy. A spark that began as American campus kids shooting the breeze slowly caught fire and spread rapidly throughout the country's Midwest. In truth, they were the embers of an old, long forgotten rumour.

But, with the US release of *Abbey Road*, the cinders smouldered gently back into life thanks to Iain MacMillan's cover image.

And there, in all its hidden symbolism, was, it seemed, irrefutable proof of a morbid tableau. Harrison was the gravedigger, Starr all in black dressed as the undertaker, Lennon, in contrasting white, was the clergyman. And the image of McCartney offered up the most compelling testimony of all. The left-handed bass player was holding a cigarette in his right hand and walking barefoot – a grisly sign of death in several European traditions. What other evidence did the world need? The flames began to catch as the wind took the story higher with every breathless retelling. The conclusion was unavoidable, wasn't it? James Paul McCartney was literally a dead man walking.

As the world's youth reeled from claims that Paul McCartney was dead, Dr Oscar Tosi, assistant professor of audiology at Michigan State University, was called in to compare voice recordings to prove that McCartney was, in fact, still among the land of the living.

OCTOBER 1969

The tectonic plates that had once bound The Beatles together had shifted following Lennon's 'divorce' bombshell. In the weeks that followed, an awkward silence descended on the band. Cast adrift, McCartney and Starr were left clinging to their little piece of driftwood – a hope that this was just another typical Lennon outburst. McCartney said, 'Nobody quite knew if it was one of John's little flings and that maybe in a week's time he would feel the pinch and say "I was only kidding, lads."'

This time felt different, though, as if a Rubicon had been crossed. Being a Beatle now was, for Lennon, just a matter of legal semantics. Klein was coming to terms with a massive reversal of fortune. Every day he offered up a silent prayer that Lennon would stick to his vow of omertà and not give in to his instincts to tell the world The Beatles were finished.

Only Harrison was confident and savvy enough to glimpse the opportunities afforded by the sight of a new door opening as the old one creaked shut. Not least because nestling in his back pocket was a growing collection of songs that were tailor-made for a solo album. Huge advance UK orders ensured that *Abbey Road*, which was released in America on the first day of the month, quickly found its way to the top of the UK album charts, replacing Blind Faith's self-titled debut. Brilliant in its ragged genius, it seemed to kill stone dead the long-standing speculation over the future of The Beatles. From the outside, it seemed as if they were still very much a fully functioning band.

Abbey Road had also revealed its own secret star; outwith the voodoo pulse of 'Come Together' and the primordial heavy rock of 'I Want You', distinct from McCartney gems such as 'Golden Slumbers' and 'You Never Give Me Your Money', the album shone a light on Harrison as a musician whose star was most clearly on the rise. 'Here Comes The Sun' and 'Something', arguably the standout tracks on *Abbey Road*, had placed him centre stage – the one place, of course, he hated to be. Klein had forcibly pushed for 'Something', with 'Come Together' on the flip-side, to be the lead single from the album to give Harrison a share of the lucrative royalties pie which had for so long been sliced up by Lennon and McCartney.

But he felt uncomfortable at accepting compliments for the two songs that arguably outshone Lennon and McCartney's contributions. He bristled at suggestions he was 'a late developer', insisting that his 'new' songs were just as good as those he had done before. 'Late, early, you know. What's late and what's early?' he told the BBC's David Wigg this month: 'The last album we did [the White Album] had four songs of mine on it. I thought they were all right. So I thought these, "Something" and "Here Comes The Sun", were OK . . . maybe a bit more commercial but as songs not much better than the songs on the last album.

'But I've been writing for a couple of years now. And there's been lots of songs I've written which I haven't got round to recording. So, you know, in my own mind I don't see what the fuss is, because I've heard these songs before and I wrote them quite a while back . . . I wasn't Lennon or I wasn't McCartney. I was me. And the only reason I started to write songs was because I thought, well, if they can write them, I can write them. Some of them are catchy songs like "Here Comes The Sun" and some of them aren't, you know. But to me they're just songs, things that are there that have to be got out.'

In the same interview, he hinted at relishing the chance to one day being able to shed his Beatle baggage, describing his celebrity persona as only a temporary part. He was already looking further down the road at a different kind of life. Tellingly, he declared: 'I mean, even if it's being a Beatle for the rest of my life, it's still only a temporary thing. I got born seemingly to become Beatle George. But it doesn't really matter who you are or what you are, because that's only a temporary sort of tag for a limited sort of period of years.'

As it turned out, Harrison had also just discovered a new diversion. On 5 October, a comedy programme called *Monty Python's Flying Circus* debuted on BBC television. The show contained a series of anarchic and surreal sketches put together by the Pythons – Eric Idle, Terry Jones, John Cleese, Michael Palin, Graham Chapman and Terry Gilliam. Harrison watched the pioneering first episode with Derek Taylor and got the humour right away. It would be the start of a lifelong love affair with the groundbreaking troupe.

Harrison said, 'Derek and I were so thrilled by seeing this wacky show that we sent them a telegram saying "Love the show, keep on doing it." I couldn't understand how normal television could continue after that.'

At least two other Beatles, however, were unable to tune in. On the same night, Lennon was applying the finishing touches to 'Cold Turkey' at Abbey Road. Two nights earlier, with Starr on drums alongside Clapton and Voormann, he had taped the flipside, Yoko's 'Don't Worry Kyoko'. The song, with its chainsaw-effect guitar and sparse, minimal feel, was a shout-out to Yoko's estranged daughter during the Lennons' prolonged battle to gain custody of the child from Tony Cox. All of which made the events of the next few days even harder to bear.

On 9 October, Lennon's twenty-ninth birthday, Yoko was rushed to London's King's College Hospital amid growing fears that she was about to lose another baby. Lennon stayed by her side throughout, sleeping on the hospital floor rather than taking up an NHS bed. Four days later, Yoko miscarried again, leaving both of them traumatised and utterly bereft.

In the meantime, Apple continued to prep the UK and US releases of 'Cold Turkey', the first single he would release without the Lennon and McCartney imprimatur. 'Give Peace A Chance' carried McCartney's name as co-composer as a quid pro quo for him being the only other Beatle to play on 'The Ballad Of John And Yoko'. But anyone listening to 'Cold Turkey' for the first time knew it was unvarnished Lennon. Chartwise, he naturally wanted the song to do well even though he knew it was commercially a tough sell. As always, he was convinced that his art should mirror his life.

The sleeve, with a picture taken by David Nutter, carried the instruction 'play loud' in case anyone missed the message. Voormann had loved the song the first time he heard its composer run through it on the back of a Boeing jet flying across the Atlantic. But he knew then it was far from becoming the kind of record Lennon wanted. 'I was very frustrated on the plane from London to Toronto because I knew we couldn't do justice to the song with no real rehearsal,' Voormann said. 'I thought, "What a great song. We really have to rehearse this properly and make something of it." But when we went onstage, we just played the chords. It was silly. It was just spur of the moment.'

Now, however, Lennon, Clapton, Voormann and Starr honed the arrangement over the course of twenty-six takes of the studio version. 'We tried several things,' Voormann explained. 'And when I came up with that bass line that you hear on the record, and the guitar answered, that was it. Suddenly it was haunting. It somehow had this cold atmosphere.'

The song was slated for a late October release. Naturally, it would require some promotion and a little Fab Four fairy dust to help it on its way. That meant running the risk of Lennon being tempted to put a little wind in the song's sails by confessing that he had left The Beatles. What better way to generate publicity by presenting the showbiz scoop of the decade? As it turned out, he played it pretty low-key. Interviews were restricted to a chosen few, those he could trust not to ask the penetrating and straightforward questions that would cause his mask to slip. Even then, for anyone reading between the lines, the clues were still there.

He told David Wigg: 'Whatever happens to The Beatles, so-called, we'll always be sort of friends, you know. So all I want for The Beatles is their individual happiness. And whether that's in a collective form or not remains to be seen.'

Reviewers given an early pressing of the new single were stunned by the lyrics. It felt that once again Lennon was showing his chin to the showbiz establishment and inviting them to come and have a go. Inevitably, some radio stations immediately banned it, thus placing it alongside other Lennon songs that ran counter to executive norms of the period: 'A Day In The Life', 'With A Little Help From My Friends', 'Lucy In The Sky With Diamonds' and 'I Am The Walrus'.

Indignant and fed up at being banned, Lennon again felt the media had badly misrepresented his thoughts. He repeated his initial insistence that 'Cold Turkey' was seriously misunderstood. 'It's neither anti-drugs nor anti-alcohol. It does not have any connection with drugs any more than it has with the experience you have with thirty-six hours of rolling in pain. That's what miscarriage is, let's face it; thirty-six hours rolling in pain.

'I caught a chill in hospital while Yoko was having a miscarriage and I had what I would term "Cold Turkey" after it. That is, a fever of a hundred degrees. I was hot and cold for about two days . . . Everybody goes through a bit of agony some time in their lives. "Cold Turkey" is just an expression that I would have thought is suitable to explain the other side of life.'

Though few bought his explanation, Lennon carried on with a handful of media interviews while Apple insiders braced themselves for him to casually announce the Death of The Beatles. Instead, he found himself forced to deny not that The Beatles as a group were dead . . . only one of them.

*

The twelfth of October was a typically slowburn Sunday afternoon for Russ Gibb inside the DJ booth at Detroit radio station WKNR-FM. Apart from being a very able broadcaster, Gibb was also a big noise in the Michigan city, home to the 'Big Three' motor manufacturers, General Motors, Ford and Chrysler. As a concert promoter and founder of the city's Grande Ballroom, he was music royalty. His stint on the city's premier radio station also allowed him to tap directly into the city's youth culture.

Even at the age of thirty-eight, – the kids gave him the soubriquet 'uncle' – he was considered a prime point of contact for up-and-coming bands and later credited with giving the likes of MC5, Ted Nugent and Iggy Pop their first leg-up on the rock ladder. He was also on first-name terms with Eric Clapton and Mick Jagger.

On this particular afternoon, the clock seemed to be ticking slower than normal. 'It could be pretty boring for the jock,' he said. 'I liked to include phone calls from the audience and tried to find an issue to spark conversation.' So Gibb opened up the phonelines, as he often did, to chat directly to his constituency to learn what was happening on the campus grapevines and in the dorms.

Among the first callers was a student who gave his name as Tom and posed what, on the surface, seemed an outlandish question. He asked Gibb: 'So what do think about this story that Paul McCartney is dead?' Experienced pro that he was, Gibb knew a wind-up when he heard one. Experience also told him that rock stars often patrolled the border between life and death in the foggy minds of students toked up at late-night parties. After all, hadn't Bob Dylan been killed in a motorcycle accident in 1967 – yet strangely lived not to tell the tale?

'I laughed,' explained Gibb. 'I said, "I heard every rock star is either dead, a dope-dealer, beats his children, beats his wife, or something." Then the kid asked me if I ever played The Beatles' "Revolution Number 9" from the White Album backwards? Then I played it backwards, Number 9, Number 9, where a very pronounced English accent says "Number 9, Number 9", and it very clearly said, "Turn me on, dead man. Turn me on, dead man. Turn me on, dead man."

'I couldn't believe what I was hearing. That floored me. It was very distinct. I put that on and within three to four minutes, the phone lines were jammed in my studio.'

Amazed by the reaction, the station's managers suddenly glimpsed a ratings bonanza. The show was extended long into the night as other people called in with clues to support the bizarre theory. Gibb, while remaining open-minded, had a trump card to play. 'I had been in London and I had spent some time with Eric

Clapton who was a good friend, so I called Eric in London and I said, "Eric, have you heard there's a rumour going on in the United States that Paul McCartney is dead?" And he said, "No, what are you talking about? What, Paul is dead?"

'I said, "Yeah, they've got it in a record, and they've got it on so forth . . ." He said, "No, that's not –" and then he said, "Wait a minute, you know, come to think of it, I haven't seen Paul in about a month and a half." And that did it. After he said that, all hell broke loose.'

The breadcrumb trail of clues led all the way back to 'Strawberry Fields Forever', in which fans thought they could detect Lennon in the fadeout intoning, with funereal precision, 'I buried Paul'. The entire *Sgt. Pepper's Lonely Hearts Club Band* album was awash with clues. But the real giveaway, in the minds of the newest theorists, was hiding in plain sight in Iain MacMillan's *Abbey Road* picture. For the Paul-is-dead believers, the sleeve of their latest album was a treasure trove of signs that proved beyond any measurable doubt that McCartney, the co-composer of some of the twentieth century's most enduring pop songs, was dead – and the whole thing had been hushed up to an extraordinary degree.

Laid out in startling detail and kooky symbolism was MacMillan's eerie mise-en-scene. Most observers seeking confirmation of McCartney's demise convinced themselves they were indeed looking at a Fab Four funeral procession. And, crucially, the barefoot McCartney was the only Beatle out of step with the others, an accidental truism that captured better than anything the real behind-the-scenes carnage.

Elsewhere, there was the parked Volkswagen Beetle with its number plate of LMW28IF, another 'clue' that pointed to Paul's age. (The fact that he was twenty-seven at the time was irrelevant.)

Flip the sleeve over and you find a huge crack running through the tiles spelling out 'Beatles'. Joining all the dots, it pointed to the band being complicit in the decade's biggest cover-up.

Listening to Gibb's show was Fred LaBour, an arts reviewer for student newspaper, the *Michigan Daily*. LaBour used clues from the programme along with others he had invented himself – including the name of William Campbell, the alleged replacement for McCartney – as the basis for his own tangential take on the story. The *Michigan Daily* published it on 14 October, under the title 'McCartney Dead: New Evidence Brought to Light'. Although clearly intended as a spoof, it had an impact far wider than the writer and his editor expected. Soon it was picked up by American wire services, which clattered it out on telex machines to a dumbstruck world. Hoax or fake news? It didn't matter, though LaBour later admitted much of his story was the product of a febrile imagination.

He said, 'I invented a lot of the clues. I just imagined this whole scenario and wrote it as sort of a quasi-news story with a lot of facts, and enough facts that were true to sort of keep pulling you along and enough facts that weren't true that hopefully would let you know that this was a joke. This was a satire.'

In another interview he disclosed that he made up the William Campbell character: 'It was originally going to be Glenn Campbell, with two Ns, and then I said, "That's too close, nobody will buy that." So I made it William Campbell.'

The Paul-is-dead story swiftly became the biggest and fastest circulating sensation since the 1963 assassination of JFK. The Apple switchboard came under siege from overwrought fans and news organisations. Huddled outside 3 Savile Row, the Apple Scruffs buttonholed Beatle insiders for any scrap of information that would either confirm or deny the story. Others hopped on the tube or took a 159 bus to Abbey Road studios or set up a vigil outside McCartney's house on Cavendish Avenue.

'What fascinated me most was how they got their information,' said press officer Derek Taylor. 'Often they knew more about where the boys were than we did. It was often a process of abstraction and deduction with them. Sherlock Scruffs they were.'

Naturally Taylor was handed the task of delivering a firm rebuttal, while cloaking the words with his stock-in-trade ambiguity. This had the desired effect of sounding like a denial without actually offering up any real evidence that McCartney was still with us. No, McCartney was unavailable for comment. And, no, he wouldn't be giving any interviews. An irritated Lennon called the story 'garbage' while Starr's sole comment on the subject was: 'I'm saying nothing because no one believes anything I say.'

Like all conspiracy theories, the claims simply didn't stack up. But in the absence of irrefutable proof, the story refused to abate over the rest of the month. There was, though, method in Taylor's vagueness. The immediate upshot of McCartney's supposed demise was to propel sales of The Beatles' back catalogue up alongside *Abbey Road* into the upper reaches of the charts. Within days, *Abbey Road* had shifted huge amounts of new units all over the world, proving once again that nothing makes an artist more commercially viable than death. Meanwhile, the subject of this latest drama was largely living under a self-imposed house arrest. Normally the man about town of the London showbiz circuit, McCartney was suffering the first pangs of what would become almost a nervous breakdown. He was always the group's consummate PR man, who could schmooze the capital's high society and mix effortlessly with the youthful radicals of the London underground.

He was equally comfortable among the theatre luvvies as he was helping to publish *International Times*, the counterculture publication.

With a new family to look after, Linda's unquestioning love and a new album sitting at the top of the charts, it should have been the happiest time of his life. But Lennon's shock revelation had created a paradigm shift, the moment when McCartney's world came loose on its comfortable spindle. Ironically, especially given the circumstances, it felt like more like bereavement than a divorce. The Beatle bubble had finally burst, although he was still bound by contract to the band and controlled by Klein. He was estranged from his closest friend. And now he was the reluctant focus of the decade's most absurd showbiz intrigue. It's easy to understand his despair. Barry Miles told me: 'Paul's identity was wrapped up in being a Beatle and it was very hard for him to see himself separate from the band; it wasn't just a job, it was who he was.'

Dead or alive, McCartney was going through hell. As the Paul-is-dead story continued to pick up speed, he ventured out only once, he and Linda joining Ringo and Maureen for a cabaret performance by former Apple ingénue Mary Hopkin at the Savoy Hotel. Even that appearance refused to kill the rumours. Eventually, McCartney chose an escape route he thought would finally render him invisible from scrutiny. It may even have been Linda's idea.

On 22 October, fed up and emotionally spent, he bundled Linda, six-year-old Heather, baby Mary and their sheepdog Martha into the back of a Land Rover, making sure they had enough provisions for the journey, and set off on the arduous six hundred miles from London to High Farm, the broken-down homestead he had bought in 1966 on the Kintyre peninsula on Scotland's rugged Argyll coast.

It was, at that time, at least a ten-hour drive, which included navigating some pretty bleak terrain once they hit the high road north past Glasgow. But he hoped that the sheer remoteness of Kintyre, with its windswept beaches and open fields, would provide the sanctuary he desperately needed. Also, by putting so many miles between them while still remaining in Britain, McCartney was also symbolically properly cutting ties with Apple, the company in which he had invested so many hopes and dreams.

He later reflected: 'We decided the only thing to do was to boycott Apple, just get out of there. The meetings were just such a headache so we just came to Scotland. We took the kids, we took the dog, took everything we had, put a guitar on the top and took a potty for the baby and that was it.'

Ironically, another music superstar had just offered him a different kind of escape. The day before he left London, a telegram from Jimi Hendrix had landed at Apple inviting him to take part in a session alongside Miles Davis and jazz drummer Tony Williams. Hendrix, a fully paid-up member of the McCartney fan club, always regarded him as a bass guitar pioneer. Now he hoped to recruit a Beatle for an album that would fuse together rock with jazz, an innovative idea for the time.

The note said: 'We are recording and [sic] LP together this weekend in New York. How about coming in to play bass? Peace, Jimi Hendrix, Miles Davis, Tony Williams.' Of course, the likelihood is McCartney never saw it so the intriguing possibilities offered up by Hendrix remain open to conjecture. But it's feasible to imagine that the invite might have appealed. After all, he had watched largely from the sidelines as Lennon and Harrison took their first steps into another world with a variety of experimental solo work. Lennon especially had made it clear that the alternative universe provided by The Plastic Ono Band offered up a whole world of possibilities.

McCartney had worked with Badfinger and occasionally sat in on sessions for the likes of Jackie Lomax, James Taylor and Steve Miller. In general, though, resentment over Apple and Klein in particular and life in general was building to an uncharacteristic crescendo. He later admitted to natural feelings of pent-up anger during this period as he did a bunk with his family.

'I was going through a hard period,' he acknowledged in *Many Years From Now*. 'I exhibited all the classic symptoms of the unemployed, the redundant man. First, you don't shave, and it's not to grow a groovy beard, it's because you cannot be fucking bothered. Anger, deep anger, set in, with everything, with yourself number one, and with everything in the world number two.'

McCartney left London in a hurry, telling only a few select people at Apple of his plans, notably Taylor and Brown. He didn't utter a word to any of his bandmates or, specifically, Klein. All he wanted was a little solitude to save his sanity away from the media's constant gaze. But privacy for a Beatle, even a 'dead' one, was a hard-to-find commodity. In general, the press were unaware of his whereabouts, which only added more machinations over his mortality. And for those who did know, newspaper expenses didn't extend to covering the cost of an onerous hike to Campbeltown, the closest town to McCartney's rural retreat.

There is, however, always one who is willing to make the effort, especially when the biggest story of the year is on the schedules. Aware that the BBC was on his trail, Paul reluctantly agreed to a one-off interview. Scruffily dressed and looking every inch the welly-booted farmer, he tried to put his current life in context against the tidal wave of newsprint claiming he was dead. The explanation was simple; since getting married and becoming a father he had just decided to adopt a lower public profile rather than do 'an interview every week'.

He was, he assured everyone, still very much alive, declaring: 'If the conclusion you reach is that I'm dead, then you're wrong, because I'm alive and living in Scotland.' Linda said their holiday was being ruined by the press speculation, adding pointedly that 'everybody knows he's alive'. The story, however, wasn't going away anytime soon.

There may have been another reason behind McCartney's decision to skip his Apple bail on 22 October. A few days before, Klein had convinced all four Beatles – and Lennon and McCartney in particular – that it was finally time to hoist the white flag in their long-running and bitter battle over Northern Songs. Covert attempts by Klein to reach a last-minute deal with ATV and Grade had failed. All that remained was to agree a settlement for The Beatles' thirty-five per cent stake in the company that owned the publishing rights to the Lennon and McCartney songbook. For both of them it felt like a dagger to the heart. The question was: what to do next? Keep the shareholding and become songbirds locked inside Grade's golden menagerie or take the shilling?

On the table from Grade, under instruction from the City Takeover Panel, was an offer of 200p a share – the same price ATV had paid for the decisive block of shares held by Howard & Wyndham which had swung control of the company in Grade's favour. That would have given the two Beatles a cash windfall of something like £3.5m in ATV loan stock – a far cry from the eye-watering £9m Klein had rejected months earlier for the entire holding.

The Great American Hustler had been outdone by a sixty-three-year-old, cigar-chomping, old-school British boardroom bruiser, a truth even Klein acknowledged. He said, 'We made a lot of money, but it wasn't the best we could have done.'

It was almost the final act in a soap opera that had gripped the City for months. Indeed, it had become an allegory for the breakdown in relations between Lennon and McCartney and the various factions in their corners. But it had made Klein, previously a twisting target, much easier to hit for McCartney and the Eastmans. Loyalty to Klein was one thing, but even Lennon could see vast chunks of their fortune sailing down the river. And it awoke the deep-rooted fear he had of becoming a lifelong prisoner of the taxman.

During one interview in October, he declared: 'When all the Associated Television dealing was going on with Northern Songs, one day I was a millionaire and the next day I was broke. I can still afford to live well. Nobody has taken my home off me and I've still got a car and all the cigarettes I need, so I must be all right.

'I'm always worried about the taxes because they are such a big thing and I don't want to end up like Mickey Rooney, having to work just to pay the taxes off. I don't want to end up doing TV ads to keep myself going. I wouldn't be ashamed of doing it but I wouldn't want to write crummy commercial songs that I don't like because I've got to earn a bit of bread.'

Harrison, largely a bystander during the negotiations over Northern Songs, was equally vexed at the prospect of ending up broke. Days before Klein admitted all options over Lennon and McCartney's shareholding had finally been exhausted, he spelt out his own fiscal unease to David Wigg: 'It's very ironic in a way because we've all got, maybe, a big house and a car and an office, but to actually get the money that you've earned is virtually impossible. It's like illegal to keep the money you earn.

'"You never give me your money, you only give me your funny paper." You know, that's what we get. Bits of paper saying how much is earned. But you never actually get it in . . . uhh . . . It's the same thing [with] showbiz . . . and all they think of is, "Oh, all that money you've got and you've got a big house and car," and all that sort of thing. But the problems that come along with that are incredible. And I can tell you, everything material that we have, every hundred pounds we've earned, we've got a hundred pounds' worth of problems to balance it.'

Setting his spiritual beliefs aside, Harrison clearly had his mind on the material world. If this was to be the end, he was already seeking out a new beginning. He continued to earn his musical stripes by producing sessions for Apple stablemate Doris Troy while jamming with former Blind Faith bassist Ric Grech and Denny Laine, who years later would be taking flight as a mainstay of Wings, McCartney's post-Beatles group. Loosely mapped out in Harrison's mind was a road to a future without The Fabs, as he drily called them. Lennon had already signposted his intentions with 'Cold Turkey'. Now, in October's final days, a third Beatle was about to declare his hand.

Starr had spent the previous three weeks, by his own account, sitting morosely in his garden, and staring into the great black hole that now seemed to be his future. He said: 'I wondered, what shall I do with my life now that it's over.' Not even a brief holiday in Los Angeles with Maureen had lifted the blues. The solution, as it always did, turned out to be better than the puzzle. Salvation and opportunity lay in music so on 27 October he ventured back into Abbey Road's Studio Two to record the first track for what would become, figuratively and literally, a sentimental journey set to music.

Like his three bandmates, his early musical education had been a composite of vaudeville, country music, the Big Band sound of Duke Ellington and the first shoots of rock 'n' roll. Starr absorbed them all like a sponge from an early age, especially during family parties. Still, it was a surprise to many when he opted to record a whole album of pre-rock 'n' roll standards for his first solo project. In doing so, he would be the first pop star to cherry-pick his way through the Great American Songbook. In fact, his choice of songs was payback to the devoted mother and stepfather who had nursed him through the childhood illnesses that had wrecked his education but formed his happy-go-lucky personality.

He said: 'It came from my stepdad. He taught me all about the big bands – Billy Daniels, Billy Eckstine . . . all the Billys we used to laugh about. He was a really good singer. At parties in Liverpool everybody has to sing. He did one incredible thing that I have also passed on to my children. When I was playing the music I was playing he would never say, "Oh, that crap!" He'd always say, "Oh, that's fine but have you heard this?" And it would be Sarah Vaughan or Ella Fitzgerald or whoever, but he did it in such an incredible way. I did it because of Harry. He loved Glenn Miller, just all the big band stuff and great singers. I was brought up with all those songs. They were my first musical influences.'

Starr was now quite prepared to step out on to the highwire without a Beatle safety net, but he still needed a familiar face to hold his hand. He asked George Martin to man the production board and explained his idea to record separate tracks featuring arrangers such as Count Basie and Quincy Jones. Martin, a veteran of such music, immediately bought into the idea.

The first session laid down was a cover of Cole Porter's 1932 song, 'Night And Day', exactly the kind of singalong that was a staple during boisterous Starkey family parties. Martin, delighted to be able to step outside his customary circle, pulled out all the stops and hired a seventeen-piece orchestra featuring saxophone, trumpet, trombone, bass guitar, piano and drums to give Starr the kind of big band sound he was striving for. 'Night And Day' became the first track for the album, which, initially, was to be called *Ringo Stardust* before it morphed naturally into *Sentimental Journey*. 'It got me off my horse and back into recording,' said Starr, as firm plans were made to record more tracks in November.

The month ended with a break in Beatle tradition. There was a long-standing convention that the group never released singles that had already appeared on albums. But Klein, one eye forever on the bottom line, tore up that arrangement with the release of 'Something' and 'Come Together' (this time the broadcasting censors remained oblivious to Lennon's smutty wordplay) as a double A-side UK 45 on Friday, 31 October. Klein said, 'I suggested strongly that this single be released from the *Abbey Road* album. I thought that it was important for George to show himself. I thought "Something" was the best song on the album.' Lennon also insisted he had pushed for Harrison to be given top billing for once.

Commercially, the decision was a no-brainer. The radio-friendly single would give *Abbey Road* its second significant sales spike inside the space of a month and maintain the album's trajectory, a path that eventually would see it sell 4m copies in two months. It also ensured that by the end of the month the illusion of harmony remained, albeit one held in place by nothing more than smoke and mirrors.

Heartbroken over Yoko's miscarriage in October, a month later the Lennons headed for the Greek island of Spetses to help her recuperate and to escape the turmoil of their lives in London.

NOVEMBER 1969

It began as a single voice, just one man singing while gently strumming his acoustic guitar. Before long, however, it had grown into an incredible choir of some half a million people, all of them united under one protest banner and each of them chanting the simple nine-word refrain that crystallised all their thoughts. Young and old, black and white, it was an extraordinary display of solidarity.

Pete Seeger's impromptu rendition of 'Give Peace A Chance' at the Vietnam Moratorium Day march in Washington on 15 November inadvertently brought Lennon's anti-war campaign right into the heart of the American capital and straight to Richard Nixon's front door. 'Are you listening, Nixon?' taunted Seeger, the acclaimed American folk singer, who was sharing a platform with fellow activists Arlo Guthrie, the folk trio Peter, Paul and Mary, and four different touring casts of the musical, *Hair*. In front of them, a sea of faces stretched as far as the eye could see along both sides of the Mall across from the White House, the largest anti-war demonstration in American history.

It was held forty-eight hours after 40,000 protesters had walked silently down Pennsylvania Avenue to the White House in the so-called March of Death bearing placards carrying either the name of a dead US soldier or the name of a Vietnamese village bombed out of existence.

The song had reached a creditable Number Fourteen in the American single charts after it was released on 7 July but it was already fading into memory, despite the napalm-laden payloads carried by F-4 jets and the increasing numbers of American servicemen being brought home in body bags. This, though, was the day that the anti-war campaign finally found the anthem it was seeking, a song that would replace 'We Shall Overcome' and bring the peace movement into proper alignment with the counterculture. Seeger later admitted, astonishingly, that he had never heard Lennon's original recording, a strange admission for someone so closely linked to anti-war activism. But, as he stood on that stage, he suddenly felt himself being directed by some inner force to perform it before the biggest live congregation he had ever faced, not to mention a TV audience of millions.

'I'd only heard the song myself a few days before,' Seeger recalled, 'and I confess when I first heard it I didn't think much of it. I thought, "That's kind of a nothing of a song, it doesn't go any place." I heard a young woman sing it at a peace rally. I never heard Lennon's record. I didn't know if the people there had ever heard it before. But I decided to try singing it over and over again, until they did know it. Well, we started singing, and after a minute or so I realised it was still growing. Peter, Paul and Mary jumped up onstage and started joining in. I realised it was getting better and better. The people started swaying their bodies and banners and flags in time, several hundred thousand people, parents with their small children on their shoulders. It was a tremendously moving thing.'

In the eyes of most Americans, Lennon and Yoko Ono were dismissed as what would today be termed snowflakes, their activism naïve and self-serving. But in 1969, in that one instant, their credibility suddenly benefited from the power of Seeger's spontaneous and passionate performance that caught the mood of millions. From then on, 'Give Peace A Chance' would serve as the centrepiece for sing-ins at shopping centres planned throughout America and join the list of carols to be sung in nationwide Christmas Eve demonstrations. It became the song of the people.

Behind the twitching curtains of the Oval Office, Nixon remained implacably defiant. He delivered his own two-fingered salute to the protesters by watching a game of American football on TV in an attempt to turn a deaf ear to the chorus of disapproval on his own front lawn. The probability is he never heard the people singing 'Give Peace A Chance'. But when he was later briefed by White House aides on the events at the Mall, he put a call into J. Edgar Hoover at the FBI and asked him to update the file that was already opened on John Winston (Ono) Lennon. The fact that Lennon was then five thousand miles away and had no direct involvement in the protests didn't matter a damn.

Blissfully unaware of the events in Washington, Lennon and Yoko had just started a ten-day holiday in Greece to help her recover from the trauma of her latest miscarriage. But Lennon was an inveterate news addict and wasn't slow in getting up to speed over an occurrence that easily crossed international datelines. He watched transfixed as images of the march in Washington flashed up on the TV screen in his Athens hotel. Surprise quickly morphed into pride for a man who, by his own admission, was rarely impressed by anything. The next day he told a local newspaper reporter: 'It was one of the biggest moments of my life.'

He later expanded on his feelings to *Rolling Stone* editor Jann Wenner. 'I wanted to write something that would take over "We Shall Overcome". I thought, "Why doesn't somebody write one for the people now? That's what my job is, our job."'

The couple were joined by Magic Alex Mardas and his wife of just over a year. Mardas, who had retained his membership of Lennon's own magic circle despite being banished from Apple by Klein, delighted in showing his celebrity chums round his home city. Later, they chartered a yacht for a cruise round the Aegean islands, which included a stopover on Spetses, a picture-postcard bolthole popular with the rich and famous.

The break served a three-fold purpose: it helped them both draw a line under Yoko's miscarriage; it stiffened John's resolve over his decision to leave The Beatles; and it persuaded him to reset and widen the bandwidth of their peace campaign. There was, he believed, simply no going back. Only Paul McCartney remained a puzzle Lennon couldn't fully solve. The ties that had bound them so close for so long were not easily broken. But the differences between them – musical, business and personal – were now just too great to overcome. Lennon hadn't spoken to his erstwhile songwriting partner in weeks, their friendship having been replaced by a sense of Schadenfreude on his part. While McCartney was wallowing in self-pity in Scotland, Lennon was ploughing forward, and ready to further strip away the veneer of his Beatle past. His talent for shock had never waned – The Beatles are bigger than Jesus; the drugs; ditching his Liverpool wife and their young son for a weird artist; posing in the buff for an album cover; and the bed-ins that surely laid bare his eccentricity to a public that reckoned he'd lost his mind. The only thing he hadn't done was to expand his net of notoriety to include the Royal Family.

He put that right on 25 November, the day after returning from Greece. For four years, the MBE he'd been awarded had been given pride of place in his Aunt Mimi's seaside bungalow in Poole, Dorset, a symbol of royal patronage. It was a small payback for the woman who more than anyone had tried to steer him through a difficult childhood and even trickier adolescence. In Lennon's mind, however, the medal was a symbol of the sickening hypocrisy he had been forced to endure as a Beatle, bowing and scraping to an empirical class system he detested. But while sunning himself in the Aegean, he had hit upon a novel way to extricate himself from the phoniness of his decision in accepting it in the first place – Brian Epstein and Paul had made sure he did – and wringing out every last drop of self-publicity for him and Yoko. He would send his royal bauble back to the Palace and use it as another platform to highlight the insanity of war.

He had already mulled over the possibility in September with Derek Taylor. Of course, he couldn't face wrenching the medal off the top of Mimi's TV set himself, so his chauffeur Les Anthony was summarily dispatched to carry out the deed and deliver the medal back to Buckingham Palace, accompanied by a cheeky message from Lennon. Mimi was outraged, but she had no say in the matter. Nor did she know why her nephew wanted it back. She found out the next day when Lennon's letter to the Queen was splashed across every newspaper in Britain alongside several frosty editorials.

In his note to Her Majesty, a far cry from McCartney's charming little love song to the sovereign that was tacked on to the end of

Abbey Road, he said he was 'returning my MBE as a protest against Britain's involvement in the Nigeria-Biafra thing, against our support of America in Vietnam and against "Cold Turkey" slipping down the charts'. The flippant reference to his latest single was archetypal Lennon and guaranteed the stunt would generate just as much controversy as when he accepted it four years earlier.

Indignant old colonels queued up to berate him, but Lennon's remonstration over Britain's role in Biafra was well founded. Harold Wilson's Labour government was under fire for supporting the Nigerian junta which was engaged in a form of ethnic cleansing against its African neighbours, sparking a humanitarian crisis. Britain's support for Nigeria was rooted in a vital commodity – the country's untapped reserves of crude oil.

Explaining his decision, Lennon pointed to the absurdity behind the initial decision to give them the MBE. 'Lots of people who complained about us getting the MBE received theirs for heroism in the war. They got them for killing people. We deserved ours for not killing people. In a way it was hypocritical of me to accept it, but I'm glad I did, really, because it meant that four years later I was able to use it to make a gesture.'

He went on to accuse the British of covering up the atrocities carried out among the Biafran population in Her Majesty's name, saying it tore at his patriotic heart. 'All the press, TV and radio slant all the news from Biafra. All the stuff I learned about Biafra from journalists was a different story and I began to feel ashamed at being British and I'm a patriotic nationalist.'

He bristled at suggestions that his latest attempt at gesture politics insulted the Queen. 'It won't spoil her corn flakes,' he said flatly.

None of the other Beatles were told in advance of Lennon's intentions for the simple reason that he didn't have to tell them. Approached by one persistent reporter, Starr said, 'Look, he's not crazy, he's just being John . . . I don't mind him sending his MBE back. The MBE was awarded to John for peaceful efforts and it was returned as a peaceful effort. That seems to be the full circle.'

Amazingly, despite the slew of interviews, Lennon still held back from spilling the beans on the biggest story of them all. Which might suggest that he hadn't fully decided to withdraw life support from The Beatles. He couldn't announce the break-up of the world's biggest band and then days later go back on his word and open himself up to further ridicule.

Yet, incredibly, the Big Reveal was already in the public domain, delivered by McCartney to a reporter and photographer from *Life* magazine anxious to lay to rest once and for all the ongoing froth over his mortality.

Writer Dorothy Bacon and photographer Robert Graham were dispatched from London to brave the harshness of a wintry Scottish terrain to track down the 'dead' Beatle. Tramping through bogs and clambering over fences at High Farm, their cover was quickly blown. McCartney and Linda were alerted to their intrusive presence by the barking of their sheepdog, Martha. There was no turning back now, though. They eventually came face to face with their quarry only to find, unsurprisingly, an irate Beatle on the warpath. Seeing them approach, McCartney reached for the first thing that came to hand – a bucket of filthy rainwater – and duly hurled it at Bacon and Graham, who photographed the whole thing. Right away, McCartney realised it was a public relations disaster, which could put him at risk of further media encroachment.

Chasing after them in his Land Rover, he struck a deal. In return for a two-minute interview and family snaps, Graham would agree not to publish the offensive images and everyone could go home happy. The subsequent account appeared in the issue of *Life* that came out on 7 November under the small heading: 'The case of the missing Beatle – Paul is still with us'. The cover shot was a black-and-white image of the McCartneys huddled together, smiling awkwardly – Paul, Linda, baby Mary and Heather, holding a walking stick – with the rolling hills of Argyll in the background.

Turning on the charm honed by hundreds of press conferences, McCartney patiently explained the reasons for swapping the bright lights of London for the solitude of Scotland and called the Paul-is-dead farrago 'bloody stupid'. He said, 'On *Abbey Road* we were wearing our ordinary clothes. I was walking barefoot because it was a hot day. The Volkswagen just happened to be parked there. Perhaps the rumour started because I haven't been much in the press lately. I have done enough press for a lifetime, and I don't have anything to say these days. I am happy to be with my family and I will work when I work. I was switched on for ten years and I never switched off. Now I am switching off whenever I can. I would rather be a little less famous these days . . . the people who are making up these rumours should look to themselves a little more. There is not enough time in life. They should worry about themselves instead of worrying whether I am dead or not.'

But it was his next sentence that carried the real story: 'I would rather do what I began doing, which is making music. We make good music and we want to go on making good music. But the Beatle thing is over. It has been exploded, partly by what we have done, and partly by other people. We are individuals – all different. John married Yoko, I married Linda. We didn't marry the same girl.'

'The Beatle thing is over.' Buried in the text they may have been, but McCartney's remarks, the last interview he gave during the Sixties, should not have been open to casual misinterpretation. Yet they went unnoticed by the world's Beatle-hungry media. This was perhaps due to the fact that *Life* was a weekly general interest magazine tailored to a specific audience, valued more for the quality of its photography than its words. It didn't enjoy the mass circulation that newspapers carried, but here was a story the whole world was clamouring for – and its revelation stayed below the radar. When asked about The Beatles splitting up, Lennon was still keeping quiet about his intentions and would continue to do so for months to come. But here was McCartney delivering the news.

One man who couldn't fail to miss the shocking message inside the article was Derek Taylor. Sitting in his wicker-backed chair at Savile Row, Taylor's razor-sharp journalistic instincts quickly kicked into gear the moment he became aware of the *Life* article. The rest of the press office was put on high alert to start fielding what he felt would be an avalanche of phone calls ... but they never came. Relieved yet puzzled, Taylor nevertheless felt duty-bound to inform Klein that McCartney may have kicked over the Apple cart on The Beatles' future. It was the last thing the American, also then embroiled in legal warfare with the Rolling Stones, needed to hear. His relationship with McCartney remained Arctic cold. The bitter aftermath of the Northern Songs debacle and the battle with Grade continued to ripple into November, the only thing that now kept Lennon and McCartney on the same page, artistically and financially.

On 20 November, the two Beatles, through Maclen Music, issued a High Court writ against Northern Songs – now owned by ATV – demanding an audit of the books, the underlying message being that they still felt screwed by the deal. The claim centred on payments due to Northern by sub-publishers all over the world. It was an accountant's worst nightmare, a multi-layered paper trail across three continents, Europe, America and Australia.

Insulated from all this animus – since neither was a shareholder in Northern – were Starr and Harrison, who were both striding hopefully into the future. On 6 November, Starr pitched up at Wessex Sound Studios in London to record, irony notwithstanding, his version of the 1933 torch song, 'Stormy Weather', the second track he would commit to tape for his first solo offering. The surroundings were strange but George Martin was again on hand to lend an air of familiarity and authority to the session. Backed by an eighteen-piece ensemble that included trombones, trumpets, saxophones, Starr again received the big-band treatment. But not even this budget-busting ensemble could rescue his lacklustre vocal, which was lost anyway amid the brass orchestration. (The song would be left off the finished album.)

Three weeks later, he finally found his voice at Abbey Road with a much improved rendition of the Hoagy Carmichael/Mitchell Parish classic, 'Stardust'. Sticking with the sweeping orchestral textures, and using an arrangement he later credited to McCartney, Starr upped his game to deliver a performance that at least didn't expose him to public mockery from his rock contemporaries and those Beatle fans hoping to hear something resembling 'With A Little Help From My Friends'. His choice of material seemed bizarre. Just who was it aimed at in an era when heavy rock was in serious vogue and nostalgia for big-band music had long left the building?

In contrast, Harrison had no such worries about musical missteps. Apple's original mission statement was to help new acts gain a foothold on the ladder. Mary Hopkin, James Taylor and Badfinger had already benefited from McCartney's sure-footed mentoring skills before the rot set in. Edgier artistes, however, gravitated towards Harrison, who was already developing impressive skills in the role filled for The Beatles by George Martin.

Earlier in the year, he had produced and played on acclaimed albums by Jackie Lomax and Billy Preston. Then there was Doris Troy, an American R&B singer who had moved to London in 1968 and who quickly found her vocal and songwriting talents in big demand. In the summer, she had sung back-up on a Preston session for his album, and was surprised to find a Beatle in the producer's chair.

Knocked out by her performance, Harrison, with one swish of a Savile Row pen, quickly got her signature on an Apple contract. Their paths had briefly crossed once before when she had appeared on an episode of *Ready, Steady, Go!* alongside him and John in 1965. Troy, who was also being courted by the Rolling Stones, couldn't believe her luck. Not only had she landed a rock-star mentor who seemed to eschew rock-star behaviour, they were also in tune spiritually.

Troy, the daughter of a Baptist preacher, recalled: 'He was into this spiritual life – that was who he was. He wasn't a partying person. He always appeared to be really cool and really calm, he never cursed anybody. He was just a good guy – the child was serious.'

By late November, Harrison was patiently steering Troy through the choppy waters of her first proper album. They even wrote one track together, the soul-tinged 'Ain't That Cute', which would be released as the album's lead single and for which Harrison recruited the likes of twenty-year-old guitar whizz Peter Frampton, Klaus Voormann, Preston and, reportedly, Starr. Co-written it may have been, but the song's lyrics were pure Harrison, echoing the same, slightly world-weary theme as 'I Me Mine', which had been slated for *Let It Be*, and 'Isn't It A Pity', rejected in January by The Beatles, though it differed from these songs thanks to an uplifting slice of Memphis soul and a rollicking good tune.

But for all his earnest dedication to production duties, Harrison couldn't pull off a commercial hit the way McCartney had with Hopkin and would do again with Badfinger. For all its quality, 'Ain't That Cute' would fail to trouble the charts on either side of the Atlantic on its release in February 1970.

Harrison may have been unable to help his artists make the breakthrough to the mainstream market. But, with every session for those at the margins of The Beatles' circle, the Quiet Beatle was becoming a big noise among his contemporaries. At the same time, he was honing his own musical sensibilities for the solo album taking shape in his mind.

Lennon, meanwhile, made a rare foray back to Abbey Road on 26 November, the day after he handed back his MBE, on an unusual raiding mission. Very few Beatle tracks languished in the can, with the obvious exception being the car crash that was the 'Get Back' tapes. Falling into the same desultory category was 'What's The New Mary Jane', a trippy, acoustic curiosity recorded mainly by Lennon, Harrison and Yoko while sitting cross-legged on the floor of Studio Two in August 1968. It was never going to earn McCartney's approval as a Beatle track but Lennon was not ready to consign it fully to the scrapheap. It was an ideal fit for the Plastic Ono Band template. Late at night, he and Yoko stole into the studio to add overdubs on to the original acetate, augmenting the vocals with whoever happened to be in the studio at the time, mainly EMI staffers and friends. The plan was to rush-release it as a Plastic Ono Band single, with 'You Know My Name (Look Up

The Number)', another discarded oddity, but for whatever reason it never saw the light of day, remaining buried in the vaults until it was eventually dug up for the *Beatles Anthology* project in 1995.

It was Lennon's only appearance at Abbey Road all November, but it belied the fact that he and Yoko had by now released two singles and three albums in 1969. Each one, however, was the sound of Lennon with one hand clapping, stepping further and further away musically from the band that had, up to now, defined his life. Walking beside him, subconsciously or not, were Harrison and Starr as the curtain of the Sixties drew to a close behind them.

Up in Scotland, McCartney was reluctantly starting down the same path. There was no longer any argument. The sum of the parts, once so symbolic, was broken. From now on, for every minute in the studio, for every press conference, for every meeting at Apple, for every decision in the future, it was every Beatle for himself.

George Harrison, the Beatle who most loathed touring, suddenly found himself back on the road as part of the Delaney and Bonnie band that also included Eric Clapton and a cast of stellar musicians. Clapton, Bonnie and Delaney Bramlett and Harrison are pictured here backstage at Birmingham Town Hall on 4 December.

December brought its own winter solstice for The Beatles and the decade they had helped to shape and define. The chilly fog that enveloped the Twickenham 'Get Back' sessions had never fully lifted. By December they were a band officially still on life support but unofficially in extremis. Apple, once a beacon of counterculture optimism, had turned into Bleak House, with its own characters and subplots, and with Allen Klein as the omniscient narrator. Preserving the myth, though, was *Abbey Road*, still imperiously perched atop the album charts on both sides of the Atlantic and across the rest of the world. But for those who had the inside track, there was little point in denying the game was up.

As publisher of *The Beatles Monthly*, a Brian Epstein-sanctioned fanzine dedicated to the band, Sean O'Mahoney had enjoyed unfettered access to the group since the first edition hit the shelves in August 1963. Circulation peaked at 330,000 a month worldwide, thanks to a format that guaranteed slavish devotion to 'the boys', almost like a Beatle version of *Pravda*.

A blind eye was turned when the band dabbled in drugs, and when sexual infidelities had tainted their lovable 'moptop' image, not to mention the whole Johnandyoko soap opera. The Beatles had long outgrown their cute images, but their in-house magazine remained stubbornly entrenched in the past. Eventually, though, not even O'Mahoney could paper over the cracks.

By 1969 sales had slumped, leaving only a rump of hardcore subscribers. And The Beatles now wanted nothing to do with it, forcing its publisher to confront an unavoidable truth. On 1 December, the last issue limped off the presses with a tell-tale front cover from the gloom-laden August photoshoot at Tittenhurst. But O'Mahoney was not about to go quietly. He used the last edition to publish a five-page editorial castigating the band over various things: drugs, their appearances, for being poor role models and for their non-cooperation with the magazine that bore their name. Oh, and the whole thing was no longer fun.

Employing the tone of a finger-wagging, disapproving parent, he wrote: 'The real reason why *The Beatles Monthly* is stopping publication is because it was The Beatles' publication of the Sixties while The Beatles were in their twenties. Now, as The Beatles approach their thirties, I feel – and I believe they do too – that we can't do the job in the Seventies. This is the real crux of the matter.

'The magazine was first published to keep the fans informed about the activities of The Beatles because John, Paul, George and Ringo were very happy to accept the one identity. I don't think this is true anymore. Two of The Beatles have made quite a number of statements about their future intentions. Indeed, if one took them literally, one can only assume that they are rejecting The Beatles' 'image these days.'

Later, he came at them with another stiletto: 'I can't close The Beatles book without mentioning the drug problem. On several occasions, The Beatles have made it very plain that they have experimented with drugs. Many of their close associates have said that they consider mild drugs like pot are okay. I had always hoped that The Beatles would have come out with a straight-forward condemnation of drugs. Although I'm sure at least one will, eventually, personally I believe that to experiment with drugs is utterly stupid. To accept the theory that your own mind is not good enough without taking extra, dangerous chemicals to alter its natural processes seems to display a certain lack of self-respect. The pro-pot brigade will say that pot is no worse than alcohol or smoking and it doesn't lead the user on to more dangerous drugs like heroin. The facts don't bear them out . . . too many girls and boys have died already, starting on pot and going on to something stronger, for there to be any real argument.'

Blissfully unaware of such a character assassination, McCartney remained in rural isolation in Scotland with his new family, wrestling with a nervous system that was now tilting badly and a future that looked utterly forlorn.

Lennon, typically, found himself at the centre of another media storm, though this time not one of his own making. On 2 December he was one of three men nominated as 'Man of the Decade' for an ITV documentary. The other choices were John F. Kennedy, chosen by the British writer and broadcaster Alistair Cooke, and the North Vietnamese President, Ho Chi Min, nominated by American novelist Mary McCarthy. Lennon had been put forward by Desmond Morris, the eminent anthropologist, who spent several hours interviewing him about his musical career and his political activism, now fully revived following the exposure given to 'Give Peace A Chance' in Washington.

He and Yoko were also being shadowed by a BBC film crew for a documentary entitled *The World of John and Yoko*.

To his detractors, a mere pop star like Lennon simply didn't belong in the same rarified atmosphere as a slain, much loved American president. But Morris made a compelling case, citing Lennon's influence on the world's youth through his music and his stated aim to make the planet a safer place despite the nuclear brinkmanship of the Cold War. Endorsing Lennon for his counterculture credentials, and urging viewers to consider his journey from happy-go-lucky moptop to the decade's Pied Piper of Peace, Morris declared: 'For many people, John Lennon's serious statements are completely at odds with the zany, eccentric way he chooses so often to present them to the public. He's frequently, and quite unfairly I think, been written off as a publicity-hungry clown. But you see, this eccentricity of his is more than a mere anti-establishment device, it also represents a plea for fantasy in an unromantic age, a plea for the unofficial and the inconsequential in an age of officialdom over organisation, a plea for unsophisticated fun in an age of sophisticated weapons. Above all – it's a plea for optimism.'

The two men were filmed at Tittenhurst, strolling through the grounds alongside the giant weeping cedars, with Lennon delighted at having been recognised for being the person who had made the biggest impact on the decade. Among his contemporaries in the rock firmament, it put him above Jagger, Dylan and, especially, McCartney, and he took it very seriously. His unbridled optimism for the Seventies as the sun set on the Sixties was infectious, confrontational and contradictory.

Grinning broadly, he told Morris: 'This is only the beginning. The Sixties was just waking up in the morning and we haven't even got to dinnertime yet. And I can't wait, you know, I just can't wait. I'm so glad to be around. And it's just gonna be great and there's gonna be more and more of us. And whatever you're thinking there, Mrs Grundy of Birmingham-on-Toast, you know, you don't stand a chance. A: you're not gonna be there when we're running it, and B: you're gonna like it when you get less frightened of it. And it's gonna be wonderful; and I believe it. Of course we all get depressed and down about it, but when I'm down or John and Yoko is down, somebody else will be up. There's always somebody else carrying the flag or beating the drum, you know. So "they" whoever they are, don't stand a chance because they can't beat love . . . I'm full of optimism because of the contacts I've made personally throughout the world including yourself, whether seeing you on TV or whatever, knowing that there's other people around who I can agree with. And I'm not insane and I'm not alone. That's just on a personal level.

'And of course the Woodstock, Isle of Wight [music festivals] all the mass meetings of the youth is completely positive for me and the fact that now we're all getting to know a way of showing our flags. And when you show your flag you're not alone.' It was a typical Lennon rap – high on idealism, low on reality – but the programme, which would be broadcast on 30 December, kept him firmly front and centre as the spokesman for disaffected youth the world over.

It was a Lennon party political broadcast for peace, though he admitted he was the last person to know how to fix the world's problems. 'The bully, that's the establishment, they know how to beat people up, they know how to gas them and they have the arms and the equipment.' he declared. 'The mistake was made that the kids ended up playing their game of violence, you know, and they couldn't be violent because they've been running it on violence for two thousand years or a million or whatever it is. And nobody can tell me that violence is the way after all that time, there must be another way, but a lot of people fell for it and it's understandable in a way when the bully's right there, it's pretty hard to say, "Turn the other cheek, baby."'

Only a few days later, Lennon's overtures for young people to come together in peace seemed like a hollow sermon.

Saturday, 6 December, should have been the grand finale to the Rolling Stones' first American tour in three years, but a group of Hells Angels turned the venue, a speedway track in Altamont, California, into Satan's playground. Hired as 'security', they enforced their credentials by lashing out with whatever weapons came to hand at anyone who gave them a withering second glance. Eighteen-year-old Meredith Hunter was just one who caught their eye and soon a scuffle broke out as Mick Jagger, just feet away, sang 'Under My Thumb'. The Angels were convinced that the African American had a gun and was ready to invade the stage and shoot Jagger. Minutes later, his life was ebbing away after being stabbed by one of the Angels.

Hunter's shocking death drew a red-stained veil over the peace and love decade. It stunned Lennon, the era's biggest advocate for non-violence, but it didn't deter him from pitching his latest idea – a free festival in the name of peace to be staged in Toronto the following summer. In an attempt to put Altamont into perspective, he said: 'If you create a peaceful scene you stand a better chance.'

Good intentions, though, were occasionally cancelled out by hippie naïveté. He and Yoko had been persuaded to use their fame to shine a light on one of the most heinous crimes of the decade. In 1962 James Hanratty, a petty thief, was found guilty of murdering scientist Michael Gregsten (36) and shooting his lover Valerie Storie (22) in a case that became known as the A6 Murder. It was alleged that, after surprising the pair in a cornfield in Dorney Reach, Berkshire, Hanratty forced them to drive to Deadman's Hill, south of Bedford, where Storie, a laboratory assistant, was repeatedly raped and then shot along with Gregsten. She survived despite being shot five times. Hanratty (25) was hanged two months later for the crime but his family had always protested his innocence, in what became one of Britain's longest-running alleged miscarriages of justice.

Lennon and Yoko were put in touch with his parents and immediately agreed to join the campaign which had already garnered support across the political and legal spectrum but which still divided public opinion. On 10 December, the Lennons held a press conference at Apple to announce their backing for the campaign to overturn the conviction. Flanked by Hanratty's parents, John said, 'I am taking up the case in the hope of forcing a public inquiry into this man's hanging . . . the people who executed Hanratty are the same people who are running guns to South Africa and killing blacks in the street . . . we're not down on any side of the guy's innocent or not; we're anti-killing. But the thing that hooked us on this case, apart from the parents trying and trying, just these two people, eight years going through every channel and being given the runaround and the police saying "you're interfering with the cause of justice" all that bit.'

Lennon was sometimes a pushover for causes célèbres like this, an advocate for any devil that crossed his path. As usual, he dived straight in. Two days after his Apple press conference, Lennon and Yoko hijacked the British premiere of *The Magic Christian*, upstaging bandmate Ringo by turning their arrival into a pro-Hanratty protest. Drawing up outside the Odeon Theatre in Kensington, they emerged from John's white Rolls-Royce brandishing posters declaring 'Britain Murdered Hanratty'. Their car was festooned with similar bumper stickers. Deliberately provocative to ensure maximum publicity, the stunt was also perfectly timed. The Lennons emerged almost at the same time as Princess Margaret and her husband, Lord Snowdon, thus provoking a mad rush by the local cops anxious to ensure the Lennons didn't come within camera range of the Queen's younger sister.

But this time their overexposure and obsession with column inches worked against them. The country's press barons formed a gentleman's agreement to choke off the oxygen of publicity in all their newspapers. Lennon said, 'All the police were trying to get the crowd to pull it [the poster] off and we also came behind her [Princess Margaret's] car – bang, like that. The press were going berserk, TV and everything and the next day not a peep. Even if they hadn't had the posters, they would have put "Lennon insults Margaret and Tony", but they don't want to know about the hanging case because most of the newspapers are already set on that. All their crime reporters are in with the cops anyway.'

Hanratty, however, was a fleeting diversion from the main event. By December, Lennon was back in full-flowing 'Give Peace A Chance' mode. His office at Apple was turned into a command centre from where they conducted dozens of interviews. One of the most abrasive saw them trade verbal blows with Gloria Emerson, the eminent UK bureau chief of *The New York Times*, who derided their peace protests and dismissed Lennon as a fake who lived in a 'never-never land'. She harangued him over his headline-grabbing decision to return his MBE in protest over Britain's involvement in the Biafran war. His campaign, she insisted, had not 'saved one life'.

In a highly charged, rancorous exchange, Lennon accused Emerson, ironically a liberal anti-war campaigner like himself, of still seeing him as a lovable moptop rather than a mature artist. He told her: 'We did a very big advertising campaign for peace, can't you understand that? You want nice, middle-class gestures for peace and intellectual manifestos, written by a lot of half-witted intellectuals and nobody reads 'em ... that's the trouble with the peace movement.'

Every interview, of course, had the potential to expose all The Beatles to the Big Reveal but Lennon held true to the promise he had made to McCartney and Klein in September. Unlike Paul the previous month, Lennon continued to tiptoe around the ongoing issue over the future of the band, compromising his usual candour. When another interviewer asked how long he could go on as a practising Beatle, he stuck rigidly to the party line: 'It depends how

I feel and how they feel, you know, when it happens, there comes a time when it's time for a Beatle product and we always make that decision whether to make it or not, because sometimes we go through hell recording, and sometimes we don't, you know, and sometimes it's not worth it.

'The problem now is – in the old days, when we needed an album, Paul and I got together and produced an album, or produced enough songs for it. Nowadays there's four of us – three of us writing prolifically, and trying to fit it on one album – and it's not like we're wrestling in the studio trying to get a song on, we all do it the same way, we take it in turns to record a track, but usually George lost out because Paul and I are tougher. But we don't want to fight about it.

'Now,' he continued, 'half the tracks on *Abbey Road* – I'm not on "Something" – half the tracks on the double album, and way back, it depends, we're not always on, sometimes there's only two Beatles on a track. But it got to the situation if we had the name "Beatles" on it, it sells, and when we begin to think like that then there's something wrong, you know. Then you begin to think, "What are we selling?"'

The only thing Lennon was selling now was world pacifism even if it meant pimping out his own celebrity. Man of the Decade or a media prostitute? It didn't matter. What did matter was the message and it was finally getting through, especially in America. Its northern neighbour, Canada, that most pro-Lennon of countries, was also calling him back. And provisionally pencilled in the diary for later in the month was a meeting with the hippest world leader on the planet . . .

*

The sound of tyres scrunching on the gravel was the cue that his ride had arrived. Parked in the driveway of Harrison's day-glo painted bungalow in Esher was a 36-seater, single-decker bus containing a gang of musicians, roadies and liggers, shoehorned in alongside a battery of instruments, amps and endless cables. It was just past 10 a.m. and this motley crew were either still banjaxed from the night before or wide awake from the pure buzz of being a band on the run.

The previous evening, 1 December, Harrison and Starr, together with their wives Pattie and Maureen, and Eric Clapton, had been at the Albert Hall to see the group that had already been dubbed the musicians' musicians. Delaney and Bonnie was a turbo-charged collective of session hotshots from America's Deep South that fused country-soul grooves with rootsy blues-driven gospel music. Chiming with the rustic new wave popularised by the likes of The Band, out of the South they came to seduce the rock-star elite – and their followers already included Clapton. The group was fronted by husband-and-wife team Delaney and Bonnie Bramlett, but it was more of an interchanging musical ensemble and an instrumental tour de force that could include, at any given time, the likes of Duane and Gregg Allman, Bobby Whitlock, Leon Russell, Dave Mason, Carl Radle, Jim Gordon, Jim Price, saxophonist Bobby Keys and backing vocalist Rita Coolidge.

Clapton had fallen under their spell when they were on the bill for the American leg of Blind Faith's ill-fated debut tour a few months earlier. So smitten was he that he instantly disbanded his post-Cream group and started gigging with Delaney and Bonnie. Struck by a musical epiphany, he felt it was his duty to spread the gospel back home – but Harrison had, in fact, been converted to this new brand of southern comfort months earlier.

He had already recommended them to Apple after hearing their debut album, *Accept No Substitute*. Early pressings of the album were manufactured by Apple for release at the end of May, but the deal bombed over a dispute with their previous record company, Elektra. The Albert Hall show, meanwhile, was followed by a post-gig party at the Speakeasy Club, where the band hit the stage again and repeated their performance. Harrison was impressed by the easygoing camaraderie that existed between all the musicians – egos were parked by the roadside to allow the music to soar.

Harrison said, 'I remember two occasions being at the Albert Hall thinking, "That's a great band, I would love to be playing with them." One was The Band when they played with Bob Dylan and the other was the Delaney and Bonnie show with Eric.'

Having Harrison in their midst, and hearing him rhapsodise about his band, prompted Delaney Bramlett to throw out an impromptu offer. 'I just said to him, "So are you coming on the road with us? . . . We'll come by your house and pick you up in the morning."'

To his amazement, Harrison agreed, though he thought it highly unlikely they would make good on the invite when everyone sobered up in the morning. Yet, hours later, eyes squinting in the winter sun, here they were, standing outside his front door. Grabbing his Rosewood Telecaster guitar – the same one he had played on the rooftop at Apple back in January, and a twenty-fifth birthday gift from Fender – he found himself briefly back on the concert carousel for the first time since Candlestick Park.

'I thought, why not? And I just grabbed my guitar and an amplifier and went with them. It was fun,' he said.

It was also an extraordinary turnaround for Harrison, who still carried the mental scars of Beatlemania. He had always been the Beatle most consistently opposed to McCartney's entreaties for them to go back to their roots as a touring band. 'I didn't want to go through all that again with The Beatles,' he said. 'I agreed with John, the expectations would be too high.' But the deal, naïve though it sounded, with Bonnie and Delaney was simple. He would be the invisible guitarist standing at the back, playing second string to Clapton, and there would be no fanfare about the Beatle in their midst.

Pattie came out to wave him off, and spoke briefly to Eric, but Harrison, in his excitement, barely acknowledged her as he boarded the bus – another indication of the faultlines running through his marriage. Right away he sought out the company of Clapton. But he was guilelessly unaware of the feelings that had already begun shaping what would become rock music's most notorious ménage à trois between his closest friend and his wife of four years.

The tour saw the band play two shows a night as it swung through a number of provincial English towns and cities over the next five days before crossing the North Sea for a couple of shows in Scandinavia.

Harrison made his debut at Bristol's Colston Hall, where hardly anyone noticed the rhythm guitarist standing almost sullenly at the back, hidden by the stack of amps, his face a mask of concentration. Those who did recognise him were left open-mouthed at seeing a Beatle on stage again.

That first night was followed by Sheffield City Hall, a homecoming at Liverpool's Empire Theatre, and Croydon's Fairfield Halls on 7 December. The only show he missed was in Newcastle as he bailed on the band to visit his mother, whose illness was now beginning to give serious cause for concern. But he returned to the fold, which now included Billy Preston, for a wonderful show in Copenhagen on 10 December that was filmed and which managed to trap lightning in a bottle.

Harrison played it low-key, happy to tuck into bacon butties with everyone else at motorway service stations. At one stop, in South Yorkshire, he thought he had been rumbled. But when a waitress stopped and stared, it was at Clapton, not him. 'He is famous, isn't he?' she asked George. 'Oh yeah,' Harrison deadpanned. 'That's the world's most famous guitarist, Bert Weedon.'

He was experiencing the kind of musical liberation that he simply couldn't get any more from The Beatles. No one in the band had the kind of hang-ups that Harrison experienced, specifically with John and Paul. Anonymity suited him fine – and everyone else in the band quickly sussed out that he didn't expect or want any special treatment. He struck up an easy affinity with Rita Coolidge, who recalled: 'George was such a

profoundly gentle man and at the same time so charismatic . . .
almost like a religious leader in a sense. He had such a magnetic
kind of energy around him. But he was so soft spoken. To me,
he was like a holy man, just his energy, his aura, everything
about him was more beautiful than probably anybody else I had
ever met. And at that time with his moustache and long beard
he looked a holy man. I always felt like I was in the presence of
greatness when I was around him. He was so very humble and
sweet. Every time I got on the bus he would wait for me and sing
"Lovely Rita" to me. It was so fabulous.'

As well as briefly breaking free from the shackles of his old life,
Harrison was also able to explore the gospel-tinged music that
infused Delaney and Bonnie's repertoire. As the tour bus pinballed
across England, he took every opportunity to soak up their church-
hall influences. Hour after hour, he sat with Delaney Bramlett,
picking his brains, trading licks and throwing out song ideas. One
story suggested Delaney had taught him how to play the slide
guitar that in time became his signature instrument, but the man
himself denied this: 'I didn't teach him anything. George already
knew how to play guitar, he just wanted to know my technique,
what I thought about it and what I did. All I did was teach him my
style of playing.'

But there is no doubt that playing with Delaney and Bonnie
changed Harrison for ever. Of course, it worked both ways. On other
nights, round an imaginary campfire, everyone sat in rapt attention
as Harrison told war stories of being in the eye of the Beatlemania
storm. One night after a show the Fabs' resident mystic pointedly
steered the conversation towards the gospel influences that were the
bedrock of Bonnie and Delaney's output. What followed next was
an informal discussion, the consequences of which would haunt
Harrison for years.

In an interview with Harrison biographer Marc Shapiro, Bramlett
alleged: 'George came up to me one night after a show on that tour
and said, "You write a lot of gospel songs and I'd like to know what
inspires you to do that." And so I gave him my explanation. I told

him that I get things from the Bible, from what a preacher may say or just the feelings I felt toward God. George said, "Well, can you give me a for instance?" He wanted to know how I would start.

'So I grabbed my guitar and started playing The Chiffons' melody from "She's So Fine" and then sang the words, 'My Sweet Lord/Oh My Lord/I just wanna be with you'. George said, "Okay." Then I said, "Then you praise the Lord in your own way".

'As it happened, Rita Coolidge, who was on the tour, and my wife at the time – Bonnie – were sitting there and so I told them that when we got to this one part, they should sing 'Hallelujah'. They did. We ran down the example a few times. George seemed satisfied. He said okay and that was the end of it.'

Except, of course, it wasn't. Whatever the truth of the matter, it wasn't the first time, nor would it be the last, that Harrison would find himself accused of stealing biscuits from another musician's cookie jar. But Delaney also found himself the beneficiary of Harrison's generosity in another way. When the tour ended, Harrison handed the American his prized Telecaster guitar as a sign of his gratitude for being allowed to play with a grown-up band. Bramlett later sold it for half a million dollars, though in time it made its way back to the Harrison family.

The tour wound up on 12 December in Copenhagen, the last of three nights in the city. By now tour posters heralded the group as 'Delaney and Bonnie and Friends with Eric Clapton and George Harrison', who now felt confident enough to take the odd solo and prove his chops alongside the guitar gunslinger known as God to his fans. But before their amps had the chance to cool down, the band found itself answering an SOS from another Beatle.

Lennon and Yoko had agreed to a request to put together a charity show at London's Lyceum Ballroom on 15 December in aid of UNICEF. Sensing the opportunity for another publicity coup, Lennon went all out to try to rekindle the spirit of his peace concert in Toronto. He put a call into Clapton who, in turn, had little difficulty in rallying most of the Delaney and Bonnie band to take part. The big surprise was the appearance of Harrison who, normally, would have shunned any musical event involving the Lennons, especially if it meant enduring Yoko's idiosyncratic performances.

The line-up also included Preston, Keith Moon as well as Plastic Ono Band members Klaus Voormann and Alan White. 'I went down there in my Mini and went on stage at the Lyceum,' recalled White. 'Just prior to The Plastic Ono Band going on, Eric Clapton turns up with the whole Delaney & Bonnie band, so we had to hustle another couple of drum kits. Then, Keith Moon joins me on stage, playing my sixteen-inch tom-toms. It was a thing where somebody would hit one chord and it was a jam.'

Musically, it was a long way from good, despite the stellar ensemble. Playing in front of a massive 'War Is Over' poster – the Lennons' latest peace mantra – they performed just two songs, the Toronto staples 'Cold Turkey' and 'Don't Worry Kyoko'. The rest of the show quickly descended into an ear-splitting and self-indulgent free-for-all where bum notes flew like empty bottles in a bar-room brawl. In time-honoured fashion, Yoko emerged from a sack in the front of the stage, much to Delaney and Bonnie's amusement. 'It was just bizarre,' recalled Bramlett. Harrison rolled his eyes and discreetly took his leave. It had been a rare, awkward moment of musical détente between the two Beatles. But the pictures, showing a sullen-looking Harrison, spoke volumes. It was the last time he would ever appear on stage with John Lennon.

And all he had to do was act naturally. Ringo Starr may not have been the most photogenic Fab, but the movie camera loved him. A natural ham, his dry Scouse wit and comedic spontaneity had long marked him out as the Beatle most at ease on a film set. Outwith The Beatles' own celluloid adventures in *A Hard Day's Night*, *Help!* and the credit-rolling cameo at the end of *Yellow Submarine*, Starr had also enjoyed a fleeting turn as a voyeuristic Mexican gardener, complete with Zapata moustache, in *Candy*, the

1968 film adaptation of Terry Southern's louche novel of the same name. Southern, a buccaneering and unconventional writer, was a pioneer of the gonzo journalism later popularised by the likes of Hunter S. Thompson. The Beatles were big fans, and installed Southern among the all-star cast that adorned the cover of *Sgt. Pepper's Lonely Hearts Club Band*.

The UK premiere of *The Magic Christian* was on 12 December – the same day as a charity album was released featuring The Beatles' 'Across The Universe', and the same night as the last of Harrison's Delaney and Bonnie gigs.

The film's cast included a revolving door of Hollywood hotshots such as Yul Brynner, Roman Polanski and Lawrence Harvey, Sellers' fellow Goon star Spike Milligan, comedienne Hattie Jacques, Graham Chapman and John Cleese (who were asked to carry out extensive, last-minute script rewrites) and Christopher Lee, billed as the ship's vampire in a satirical nod to his Dracula days. Equally bizarre was the sight of a barely clad Raquel Welsh as a whip-wielding galley-slave dominatrix.

On paper, it looked a surefire winner using the formula of Southern + Beatle = box office bonanza. Somewhere along the line, though, there was a miscalculation. *The Magic Christian* sank largely without trace, although Starr's laconic performance was one of its few redeeming elements. His goofy charm spared him the vitriol meted out by many reviewers, who savaged the film's self-indulgent mediocrity.

More memorable was 'Come And Get It', the song gift-wrapped by Paul McCartney to Apple protégés Badfinger back in July that played out during the closing credits.

Encouraged by the reviews, and that his notices were better than Sellers', Starr was convinced he could build on a twin-track career that carefully leavened music and films, especially given the fact that his day job was now officially in limbo. In fact, he touted himself for the part of Samwise Gamjee if anyone ever came up with a film adaptation of *Lord of the Rings*, a project that The Beatles had once seriously mulled over during a night of heavy pot smoking.

But there was never any doubt in Starr's own mind as to which role was the greater priority. 'I am a Beatle,' he said ahead of the film's opening night, maintaining the party line after Lennon called it quits. 'If it comes to a toss between doing a film and making a Beatles album, I'll do the album. But I don't mean the film business is just a hobby to me. I'm deadly serious about it. I hope I'm learning about acting from Peter. I've never studied anything and everything's worked out. I never studied the drums. I think it can harm you to study things because you're only learning about what other people think about it, instead of what you think about it yourself . . . I'll pick up some things, but I'll do them my way, because I am me.'

Joe McGrath, the film's director, had cut his cinematic teeth by working with The Beatles on *A Hard Day's Night* and *Help!* before going on to direct pioneering promo clips for the singles 'Ticket To Ride', 'Help!' and 'Day Tripper'. He said, 'I thought Ringo was the star of the film. He was extremely disciplined, always showed up on time, knew his lines. He was obviously cast to help the box office but he more than held his own against some of the big names.'

Meanwhile, on 16 December, twenty-four hours after what would be The Plastic Ono Band's last British performance with John out front, the Lennons flew to Canada. They both felt a special bond with the nation governed by a young and progressive prime minister in the shape of Pierre Trudeau, whose careful nurturing of the youth vote had been key to him winning the country's 1968 election. The principal aim of the visit was to announce the fine details of an event that, ultimately, would never get off the ground – the proposed Toronto Peace Festival, which Lennon name checked at every media opportunity.

This was their third visit to Canada in ten months. And, as on the two previous occasions, the agenda was driven by global conciliation and by a new soundbite – 'War Is Over If You Want It'. The Lennons spent a small fortune – the tab was picked up by Apple on Klein's instructions – plastering it across giant billboards in twelve of the world's major cities, including Paris, Amsterdam,

London, Berlin, Amsterdam, Helsinki, Tokyo, Hong Kong – and, of course, New York, guaranteeing it would not be missed by America's Nixon administration, the main target of the message.

The FBI file on Lennon now carried heavy-duty observations, fuelled in no small way by J. Edgar Hoover's paranoia about rock stars who were looking, he believed, to tear down the pillars of American democracy. To that end, Uncle Sam's door remained firmly shut to a man who was a convicted drug felon, a threat to the government and probably a secret Communist, according to the US president.

The British press again lined up behind the establishment to target Lennon's activism. 'There is an unfortunate image of hippy earnestness directing liberal causes from the deep upholstery of a Beatle's income,' sniffed *The Times* that month. Canada's more liberal officials, thankfully, took a different view from its neighbours. Over the next seven days, the couple were fêted and fawned over by politicians, TV talk show hosts, Canada's leading newspaper commentators, and the likes of Marshall McLuhan, Canada's pre-eminent media theorist and a confessed supporter of the Lennons' campaigning.

Flattered by the attention, Lennon was aware that the message, now taken very seriously, was at last transcending the medium – and the image. The visit was, perhaps, the high watermark of his peace activities. McLuhan, for one, got right to the heart of the matter. He told Lennon: 'That's the problem, coz the minute you've got long hair and the minute you're popular with the kids, the whole adult on the other side of the gap says, you know, you're a bunch of left-wing communists and that.'

Lennon replied: 'Well, the communist fear is that and the American paranoia mainly, it's not too bad in Europe, it's a joke, you know. I mean, we laugh at America's fear of communists. It's like the Americans aren't going to be overrun by communists. They're gonna fall from within, you know. And that's a point. People say, why have you got long hair or why did, when you gave the MBE back, you know, we . . . I worded it against, I'm returning this MBE

288 ND IN THE END

because of Britain's part, in protest against Britain's participation in the Biafra Nigeria thing, you know, that's the way I speak. I just wrote it as I speak. And Britain's policy supporting US in Vietnam and "Cold Turkey" slipping down the charts.'

He continued: 'A lot of people say, now, if you had only done it straight, it would have been much more effective. And it's the same as if you'd only get your hair cut and wear a straight suit, you'd be more effective. One, I wouldn't be myself. Two, I don't believe people believe politicians, especially the youth. They've had enough of short hair and suits saying this is, as if, you know . . . It's like . . . is every priest a holy man just coz he's got a dog collar on, you know. Nobody believes that any more. And we do this intuitively. But after we've done it for a few times, we always had some irrelevancy or something in the campaign, you know. And Yoko's telling me about this ancient Chinese book that tells you how to conduct a battle. And it says the castle always falls from within. Never from without, you know, hardly ever, like America. And it also says, don't have all the doors closed when you're fighting, you know. Don't have every door shut. Coz the enemy will put all the pressure on and you might crumple. Always leave one door open and the enemy will concentrate their fire there and then you'll know where it's coming. So our door open is long hair, nudism, nudity whatever the word is, mentioning "Cold Turkey" in such a serious thing as Biafra and Vietnam, you know, and let the people point their finger, you know. "Oh, he's . . . they're naked," you know. "They look like freaks." But it doesn't interfere with the campaign, you know. Nobody attacks peace.'

During their stay, the Lennons holed up at a farm in Mississauga belonging to Ronnie Hawkins, the larger-than-life Arkansas-born singer-songwriter who had become a mentor to so many of Canada's artistic elite. Most notably, of course, he was best known for his group, The Hawks, which had slowly morphed into Dylan's stellar touring group as The Band. The stay had been arranged by rock journalist Ritchie Yorke, a friend of both parties. The Lennons found Hawkins an absorbing and genial host. Naturally unfazed by their fame, he was happy to turn his property into the nerve centre for their latest media charm offensive. An extra sixteen phone lines were installed to allow Lennon to conduct interviews almost round the clock.

Later, Hawkins was stiffed for a $9,000 phone bill, but he didn't care. He was happy to indulge the whims of 'the most famous man on the planet'. During the day, when the lines went quiet, they zipped around his farm on snowmobiles, laughing at the absurdity of their lives. At night, Lennon spent hours signing dozens of erotic lithographs he had drawn of him and his wife in flagrante delicto while enjoying the odd acoustic jam with his host. They talked about everything – except the one thing Hawkins, like the rest of the world, wanted to know: were The Beatles finished?

In a 1996 interview with a Beatles fan website, Hawkins recalled the surrealism of briefly being caught in the matrix of John and Yoko's manic existence. He recalled: 'We were sittin' in the TV room and the thing of the history of The Beatles when they were first arrived in the US . . . they had a little special on The Beatles and John had never seen it. John liked it. But they told me don't ask anything about The Beatles. This was before the bust-up was known. But I knew John and Paul and them were not talkin' even then. Everything was through their business managers. John was just nice. Yoko I didn't understand because she was super intelligent. She was above a bar-act, which I was.

'At that particular time, I thought I was doin' them a favour. I didn't know that anybody was that powerful. I thought The Beatles were an English group that got lucky. I didn't know a lot about their music. But John was so powerful. I liked him. He wasn't one of those hotshots, you know, all those other heavy metallers, you know how they act. John was a gentleman. Quiet, humble and polite. He wasn't out of control.'

Indeed, apart from the odd joint, Lennon had straightened himself out for the first time in months, having temporarily purged his system of the heroin that partly contributed to his wild mood swings. Canada was then in the grip of a furious public debate over legalising the non-medical use of cannabis. A commission, spearheaded by a judge called Gerald Le Dain, was already fully engaged with opponents and supporters of the contentious legislation. Lennon, since he was in town, was invited to offer his input.

On 22 December he and Yoko had a confidential session in Montreal with members of the commission arguing the case for Canada to prove its progressive credentials by leading the way in decriminalising pot. Secrecy was essential because even members of the commission feared Lennon being busted by the Royal Canadian Mounted Police, possibly acting on orders from the FBI to get their man and hang him high. Watching from a distance, spooks from the RCMP security service already had Lennon under surveillance following his announcement of a peace festival near Toronto, a fact that was kept secret from the government.

He was braced for a grilling from the country's anti-drug establishment. Instead, he found himself face-to-face with legislators genuinely anxious to hear both sides of the story. Straight off the bat, Lennon said, 'I must say, this commission that you've set up ... I don't know what's going on in the rest of the world, you know, in reality, towards drugs, but this seems to be the only one that is trying to find out what it's about with any kind of sanity.'

The nuts and bolts of the testimony remained buried in government archives for years until patient excavation work undertaken by John Whelan of the Ottawa Beatles website allowed observers to reach their own verdict. In it, Lennon declared he was in favour of governments monitoring a kind of marijuana open market to control the prices and denounced all-too-familiar claims that smoking pot would automatically take kids down the road to narcotic perdition. 'If the governments were as clever about preventing people getting arms for revolution as they are about keeping speed and H [heroin] off the market, and cocaine, then there would be no problem. Because if you can't get it, the drugs go in and out of popularity, and the popularity of the drug goes with how much you can get. There's a cocaine phase if cocaine's loose. If there's a big lot on the market, it lasts for a year or two then they clamp down on cocaine, but something is replaced, you get something else instead, so there's always some hard drug available. You can always get it, but it goes in fashion, people change from one drug to another as they get it . . . but when you say marijuana leads to H, it's like saying beer leads to alcoholism.'

Almost overnight on this trip, Lennon had acquired an unlikely statesman-like aura, shedding the widespread bafflement caused by the bed-ins to become a serious speaker on serious topics. It seemed that Lennon was a rock star who wanted to be a politician.

Conversely, Pierre Trudeau was a politician who wanted to be a rock star. When the two men met two days before Christmas, ostensibly to discuss the peace campaign, it was a gift to both of them, a mutually beneficial photo opportunity. The influential leader of the counterculture and the uber-cool head of state. Trudeau was twenty-one years older than Lennon but spoke the lingo of the Sixties like a baby boomer. The meeting was scheduled to last only a few minutes but went on for just under an hour, a sign of the friendship that had been quickly struck.

Broadly speaking, they agreed to keep the finer points of their discussion between themselves before emerging to a battery of flashbulbs and shouted questions from reporters. Lennon told the assembled hacks, with only a dash of hyperbole: 'We spent about fifty minutes together, which was longer than he had spent with any head of state. If all politicians were like Mr Trudeau there would be world peace.'

He rowed back on the big talk and cut to the chase when he later enlarged on the meeting during his 1970 interview with *Rolling Stone* editor Jann Wenner. 'He was interested in us because he thought we might represent some sort of youth faction. I think he was very nervous, he was more nervous than we were. We just wanted to see what they did, how they worked.'

Among the press pack was the *Evening Standard*'s Ray Connolly, one of Lennon's most trusted media intimates, who had arrived in Toronto a few days earlier to cover the story of the Beatle and the prime minister. Arriving at Hawkins' farm, he was greeted by a

Lennon high on adrenaline, his hair dripping wet from having just stepped out of a shower. He was visibly desperate to get something off his chest. Connolly had seen this impulsive look in Lennon's eyes before but even he was unprepared for the bombshell that followed.

He told me: 'He insisted I follow him and Yoko up to the secrecy of their bedroom. And then he just said, "I've left The Beatles," and carried on drying his hair with a towel. I was speechless. At the time, The Beatles absolutely dominated the world of popular culture. *Abbey Road* was still at Number One in the charts everywhere. Why would anyone in his right mind decide to destroy the most popular entertainment ensemble the world had ever known? It didn't make sense. But I wasn't only astonished. I was devastated, too, because I was as big a Beatles fan as anyone.

'There was, of course, something else. As a journalist, I knew that the break-up of The Beatles would be the biggest story I would ever get in my life. John, however, had something more to say. "Don't tell anybody yet," he said. "I'll let you know when you can put it out. Allen Klein doesn't want me to make it public until after *Let It Be* comes out next year."

'He put me in a terrible position,' Connolly continued. 'He knew I could be trusted but, when I look back on it now, especially with what happened a few months later, I can't help wondering if he wasn't setting me up. I think he expected me to put the story before our friendship, which I would not have done. It was the biggest story of my career – and I never told a living soul. So it was also the biggest mistake of my career.'

Four months later, Connolly would have good cause to choke on his integrity.

*

A few days before Christmas, while Lennon was courting Canadian politicians and burrowing further under the skin of Richard Nixon, Paul McCartney returned from the grave. With Linda, Heather and baby Mary in tow, he slipped quietly back into his London home under the cover of late December darkness. No one at Apple knew of his return. Similarly caught napping were the Apple Scruffs who had long abandoned their posts outside Cavendish Avenue. Around six weeks had elapsed since he had finally decided to turn his back on the only adult existence he had ever really known. There had been intermittent phone conversations with Ringo and George, but only radio silence from Lennon. His erstwhile songwriting partner seemed happy to talk to anyone except the one person who sought his attention most. As far as Lennon was concerned, McCartney right now was a non-person.

It was a grim time for Paul and for Linda, a woman who suddenly found herself with a new baby and a new husband whose mental health was showing every sign of buckling. Try as he might, he couldn't shut out all the dissonant voices in his head . . . John . . . George . . . Ringo . . . Allen Klein . . . Lew Grade . . . Peter Brown . . . Derek Taylor . . . Glyn Johns . . . John Eastman. Each one drowning out the other and weighing heavily on his nervous system. Emotionally uptight, McCartney wasn't the type to pour his worries out to others.

Barry Miles could have provided a sympathetic ear but knew only too well that Linda had usurped a lot of Paul's old circle. He told me: 'When Linda moved in she did the usual thing that all new girlfriends do when confronted by a prince and his courtiers – she replaced them all. I didn't even meet her until years later. All the old friends, including Peter Asher, Alistair Taylor, John Dunbar etc., were all suddenly on the elbow list.'

But it was Linda, not for the last time, who provided the balm of recovery. Fed up with Paul's self-pity, yet standing solidly by her man in the battle of The Beatles, she slowly convinced him to put the cork back in the whisky bottle he was reaching for all too easily these days. Step by step, she applied the bandages to his ravaged ego, pointing out – in a mirror image of what Yoko had done with John – the songs he had written, many of them with little or no input from Lennon. He hadn't suddenly stopped being a musician.

And a brilliant one at that. Now, despite being wracked by the insecurity of being unemployed and still bewildered by the turn of events, McCartney faced having to pick up the threads of an old life. And that meant finding recovery in the one thing that had always been his anchor against the storms of life: music.

Lennon and Harrison had already released a number of deliberately non-commercial records but they still counted as solo material. And Starr was raiding his parents' songbook in a bid to prove that he, too, could stand tall. It was only natural that McCartney would allow his thoughts to stray into similar territory.

'I knew I had to get my act together,' he later said. 'I couldn't just let John control the situation and dump us as if we were jilted girlfriends.'

As always, a guitar had stood in the corner of the farmhouse in Scotland. All he had to do was pick it up and let his fingers find the right chords, let his mind settle on a possible melody and let his well-honed instincts do the rest. Within a few days, he had the basic structures worked out for a number of new songs, 'The Lovely Linda', 'That Would Be Something' and the instrumental 'Valentine Day' among them. By the time he arrived back in London, several others were fomenting inside his head. He already had a couple of works in progress, such as 'Every Night' and 'Teddy Boy', a tune that had failed to make the Beatle grade. He said, 'We never got round to doing it well so I just thought, "Well, I'll do it on my own album."'

Hot to trot – a phrase he often employed when inspiration struck – he now carried on recording at home using just 'one mic and nerve' to lay down more tracks. Playing every instrument himself, the recordings were deliberately low-fi and rudimentary, done without a mixing track or VU meters. More important, though, they were his guilty secret.

'We decided we didn't want to tell anyone what we were doing,' he said. 'That way it gets to be like home at the studio. No one knows about it and there is no one in the studio or dropping by.' It felt, he later attested, like a continuation of his Scottish layover, where the only distractions came from the happy sound of children or his wife making food. 'I loved making music and I found that I didn't want to stop . . . I found that I was enjoying working alone as much as I had enjoyed the early days of The Beatles.'

Nostalgic for his cloudless past, McCartney, nevertheless, couldn't fully shut out the darkness that still invaded the present. The power struggle with Klein over Apple and the future of The Beatles still haunted him at night. He remained firmly stuck on the horns of a dilemma. On one hand, his loathing for Klein had only worsened during his time in Scotland; on the other, he was exposed to accusations of sanctimony because he benefited hugely – as they all did – from the benchmark-setting royalties deal the American had struck with EMI and Capitol.

Midway through December it was quietly announced that ATV had officially acquired a ninety-six per cent shareholding in Northern Songs. It had been a bitter and costly saga, the fallout from which would continue to ripple down through future decades. For Klein, it was the biggest humiliation of his career. In the space of nine months, he had lost Nems and now was powerless to prevent those faceless and avaricious stockholders, chewing on fat Cuban cigars, reaping the megabuck benefits of the Lennon and McCartney songbook. Crucially, though, he retained Lennon's backing, a strategically important bulwark in the fast-impending last stand with the Eastmans.

As the year ended, Lennon simply rebuffed any notion that Klein's feet should be held to the fire over fortunes won and lost. Proof lay in his decision to gift Klein his famous white Rolls-Royce, a sign of his personal gratitude for the royalties increase. In an interview with the *NME*, taped in early December before he left for Canada, he again praised his manager for ruthlessly freeing Apple of the financial noose that was slowly choking the life out of The Beatles.

'Paul and I have differences of opinion on how things should be run,' he declared. 'But instead of it being a private argument about how an LP should be done, or a certain track, it's now a larger argument about the organisation of Apple itself. Whether we both want the same thing from Apple in the end is a matter of opinion. But how to achieve it – that's where we digress. Mainly we disagree on the Klein bit. But, you know, I don't really want to discuss Paul without him here. It's just that as far as I can see, Paul was always waiting for this guy to just appear and save us from the mess we were in. And we were in a mess, and only my saying it in the press that time enabled Klein to hear about it and come over.

'I'm a quarter of this building, and it became a question of whether I should pull my money out if I could – which I probably can't. I did say I wanted out at one time. It was just that all my income was going into Apple and being wasted by the joy riding people who were here. I just wanted it to stop. It's no use pretending we can be here all the time when that kind of thing is going on. We needed a businessman. No Beatle can spend his days here checking the accountants.'

He also offered an archetypal Lennon olive branch for the future, couched in non-binding double-speak, while sticking largely to the party line. 'The Beatles split up? It just depends how much we all want to record together. I don't know if I want to record together again. I go off and on it. I really do. The problem is that in the old days, when we needed an album, Paul and I got together and produced enough songs for it. Nowadays there's three of us writing prolifically and trying to fit it all onto one album. Or we have to think of a double album every time, which takes six months. That's the hang-up we have.

'It's not a personal "The Beatles are fighting" thing, so much as an actual physical problem. What do you do? I don't want to spend six months making an album I have two tracks on. And neither do Paul or George probably. That's the problem. If we can overcome that, maybe it'll sort itself out.'

Lennon, though, was already embracing life as an ex-Beatle, the appellation that would cling to them all for the rest of their lives. He and Yoko returned to Britain from Canada early on Christmas Eve and swiftly made their way to Rochester Cathedral in Kent. There, they joined Dick Gregory (a member of the backing chorus for 'Give Peace A Chance' in Montreal in June) in a giant fast and sit-in to highlight world poverty and protest again at American bombing in Vietnam.

But the minute that word spread of the Beatle on their doorstep, hundreds of fans descended on the church grounds, leaving the couple with no choice but to abandon their plans and head home to Ascot.

Jacky Bevan was one of those fans. She recalled: 'I was overcome and had to leave almost immediately or pass out. They went to the Cathedral and a friend of mine was in there and managed to give them a gift, but they were mobbed and didn't stay long.'

Traditionally a time of goodwill to all men, there was scant evidence of that within the Fab Four. The band that had once told us that love is all you need now mainly communicated together through their various proxies.

One reminder of happier times was the traditional Beatles Christmas record, a flexi-disc freebie mailed out to fan club members as a thank-you for another year of unquestioning devotion. Produced by DJ Kenny Everett, all the segments were taped individually, each of them shorn of the collective and Pythonesque esprit de corps that had defined the previous six discs.

By 29 December, the Lennons had looked out their passports again, flying to the small city of Aalborg in Denmark. This time another kind of peace mission was on the agenda: Lennon was seeking to build bridges with Tony Cox, Yoko's second husband, in the hope that he would grant them more access to her daughter Kyoko, then six years old.

Back home, his three bandmates and their wives mingled awkwardly with the other guests at a traditional Hogmanay party hosted by Ringo and Maureen in their newly bought luxury home in London's affluent Highgate. Mostly, they stuck to pleasantries. Circling each other on neutral ground, no one mentioned the War. Or the K word. The nearest they came was a notional plan for the three of them to meet up in the next few days to record a new version of Harrison's 'I Me Mine' for *Let It Be*, a thinly veiled allegory on the band's decline into torpid selfishness throughout the battle-weary months of 1969.

Six miles away, the chimes of Big Ben rang out across London, a funeral bell tolling the end of the Swinging Sixties and the end of The Beatles. A requiem for a sunburst decade that dismantled the old order and, for a time at least, ushered in an era of optimism for a better world. The Sixties provided a small window when a significant chunk of humanity briefly realised its moral potential and flirted with a collective belief that the love you take really is equal to the love you make. But not even The Beatles could fully live up to the unattainable idealism of McCartney's cosmic couplet.

It took Lennon to eventually spell out the harsh reality. Calling 1970 Year One, he issued his own New Year message as the era he had done so much to define retreated into memory. 'We believe that the last decade was the end of the old machine crumbling to pieces. And we think we can get it together with your help. We have great hopes for the new year.'

The Beatles were over, but John, Paul, George and Ringo would go on, separate but bound for ever, shining on until tomorrow and making the world continue to smile with the songs they sang. And, as so often happened, the last word lies with John Lennon . . .

'I met Paul, said, "Do you wanna join me band?", you know, and then George joined and then Ringo joined. We were just a band that made it very, very big, That's all.'

Epilogue

And in the end the only thing left was indeed to let it be. Except, of course, they couldn't. John Lennon's 'divorce' declaration of September 1969 set in motion an unstoppable chain of events. But, as in many break-ups, the finger-jabbing fallout was rancorous, protracted, costly and occasionally vengeful, leaving self-inflicted wounds that didn't fully heal. The Beatles never got back together, their time as a band permanently frozen in the Sixties. Perhaps that's the way it was meant to be.

The tipping point came on 10 April, 1970, when Paul McCartney finally broke ranks with the others and officially announced to the world that The Beatles had split. The disclosure, far from unexpected, came in a DIY press release contained in review copies of his eponymously titled first solo album, guaranteeing it front-page coverage in every corner of the globe.

Millions mourned the death of the band while also weeping for the end of their own innocence. One American commentator bizarrely even likened it to the fall of the British Empire. Lennon screamed betrayal but only because he wished he had done the same thing as McCartney – used the band's demise to sell an album. History then wrongly pigeonholed McCartney as the man who broke up The Beatles. Of course, it was far from true – the real reasons were byzantine, a Gordian knot that proved impossible to unravel.

As the news broke, Ray Connolly cursed his journalistic ethics, knowing he had blown the biggest exclusive of his career after agreeing to Lennon's request to keep quiet. 'Why didn't you write it?' asked Lennon after McCartney had pulled the pin on their mutual non-disclosure pact. 'You told me not to,' replied Connolly sheepishly. 'But you're the bloody journalist,' fired back Lennon.

Allen Klein retained a pudgy grip on Apple, remaining in charge of affairs for Lennon, Harrison and Starr for another three years before agreeing a costly divorce. McCartney, though, would continue to hold Klein to account. His contempt for the American only intensified when Phil Spector was drafted in to turn the *Let It Be* tapes into a coherent album. The American producer, famed for his Wall of Sound approach to records, embellished McCartney's winsome ballad 'The Long And Winding Road' with an orchestra and a female choir without his permission. The song's author sensed sabotage – and pointed the finger of blame squarely at Klein. It was just more petrol tossed on to a raging fire. Within months, he had reached a decision that tore at every fibre of his being: the only way to escape Klein was to end The Beatles' partnership. And that meant suing the three musicians with whom his career would eternally be linked.

By the end of 1970, he would seek a legal dissolution of The Beatles in everything but name. Barry Miles was a partial spectator and one of many who knew that, accidentally, their passing was perfectly timed.

He told me: 'They spanned the decade. They began in black and white and ended in colour. Like European architecture, they went from simplicity and raw energy, Romanesque, through a mature middle period, gothic, then a Mannerist phase, [*Let It Be*] baroque and ended with a return-to-basics, stripped-down early Georgian in *Abbey Road*. The Beatles were always a four-way relationship, like a love affair. They were *the* Sixties band.'

In the weeks and months to come, Lennon would find instant karma on his own while telling everyone he 'didn't believe in Beatles'. Harrison would go in search of his sweet lord while proving that, ultimately, all things must pass; Starr would dolefully admit it don't come easy without a little help from his friends; and McCartney would weep, like the whole world, over the loss of his dear friend, his irreplaceable collaborator, in December 1980. Four sides. One square. A gilded era laid to rest. Yet it was really only a new beginning.

Sources and Acknowledgments

Researching a subject like The Beatles requires you to combine the dexterity of a rock 'n' roll detective with the patience of a jigsaw compiler. It is a layer cake of intrigue, complexities and contradictions – one where stories have become myths, and myths have become legend. And quite frankly, it's a massive undertaking to piece together the overall picture, even for a fan like myself. Memories, once so easy to recall, inevitably get tangled with every constant recalling. Even The Beatles themselves are not immune to this process.

More words have been written about The Beatles than any other band in the world. But the purpose of this book was to examine month by month the various threads that took on a life of their own from the first day of 1969 until the last and then to form them into a cohesive whole, showing how events from one month seriously affected the circumstances of the next. Context became the key that unlocked other doors, especially when examining the Gordian knot of Apple's finances, the labyrinthine trails that formed amid the battle for Northern Songs, and the story of four musicians from Liverpool whose music continues to resonate down the decades. Fact-checking was an absolutely vital and often frustrating fundamental.

In this endeavour I am grateful for the work of others whose efforts helped illuminate the path of investigation. Peter McCabe and Robert D. Schonfeld's 1972 book *Apple to the Core: The Unmaking of The Beatles* remains a benchmark of excellence for anyone wishing to understand how the band's finances spiralled out of control in those dark days of 1969. Similarly, Brian Southall's *Northern Songs: The True Story of The Beatles Song Publishing Empire* provided further substance, while Peter Doggett's forensic fiscal examination, *You Never Give Me Your Money: The Battle for the Soul of The Beatles*, is essential reading for any fan. Other avenues led me to the invaluable biographical works of Philip Norman, Graeme Thomson's *George Harrison: Behind the Locked Door*, Barry Miles's *Paul McCartney: Many Years From Now*, Peter Brown and Steven Gaines' *The Love You Make: An Insider's Story of The Beatles*, the late Geoff Emerick's memoir *Here, There And Everywhere: My Life Recording the Music of The Beatles*, Fred Goodman's *Allen Klein: The Man Who Bailed Out The Beatles, Made the Stones, and Transformed Rock & Roll*, Richie Unterberger's *The Unreleased Beatles: Music and Film*, Alan Clayson's *The Quiet One: A Life of George Harrison*, John C. Winn's *That Magic Feeling: The Beatles' Recorded Legacy*, Anthony Fawcett's *John Lennon: One Day at a Time: A Personal Biography of the Seventies*, *Lennon Remembers* by Jann S. Wenner and Mark Lewisohn's indispensable tomes *The Complete Beatles Chronicle: The Definitive Day-By-Day Guide to The Beatles' Entire Career* and *The Complete Beatles Recording Sessions: The Official Story of the Abbey Road Years 1962–1970*. There is, of course, a massive online resource of information about The Beatles but the sterling work done by Steve Marinucci and The Beatles Bible, in my opinion, raise them above all others.

Writing this book has been the ultimate labour of love infused with a certain sadness. The Beatles were a band to whom the ideals of truth were paramount, so this is a warts-and-all account of their final days. I am extremely grateful to those who cast a judgemental eye over the words, in particular my good friend Russell Leadbetter of the Glasgow *Herald*, whose comprehensive musical knowledge and sense of good prose helped save me from embarrassment on several occasions. Also to Ian Somerville to whom I turned to add another objective viewpoint. And the roll call of appreciation naturally extends to my publishers Polygon and the support and encouragement I received from managing editor Alison Rae and Neville Moir, who head up the 'Without Whom' department.

This has been a long project, one that has seen me stowed away for months in my little Beatles shrine, face bent over a keyboard, peering myopically at thousands of words, hoping – praying – they somehow fit. It would not have been possible without the unstinting support of my family and friends. My beloved wife Susanna and children Jennifer and Christopher have been with me every inch of the way on what really has been a long and winding road. I hope you enjoy it.

Ken McNab
Glasgow, February 2019

Index